Childhood Experience
and Personal Destiny

CHILDHOOD EXPERIENCE AND PERSONAL DESTINY

A PSYCHOANALYTIC THEORY OF NEUROSIS

By WILLIAM V. SILVERBERG, M.D.

Clinical Professor of Psychiatry
New York Medical College

1952

SPRINGER PUBLISHING COMPANY, INC.

NEW YORK

To the memory of
ISABEL BEAUMONT FISHER,
honored colleague and loved friend,
this volume is affectionately dedicated.

Contents

Preface

THE THESIS PRESENTED IN THESE PAGES is that mental illness originates in the adaptations made to traumatic experiences in early life, and that in its details the illness bears the impress of those experiences and the child's reactions to them. The period covered by "early life" is that from birth to the age of six or thereabouts. I do not intend to imply that experiences occurring after this period are not traumatic or are without effect upon the formation of personality. But I believe that the experiences of early life are highly formative, for good or ill, and that they contain most of the qualitative variations of human experience in general. Experience in later life, traumatic or otherwise, mainly reaffirms or contradicts the experiences of earlier life.

However, it is manifestly absurd to suppose that susceptibility to external influence terminates at the age of six years and to maintain that after that time the personality cannot do otherwise than carry out repetitiously and mechanically its already formed patterns of adaptation and behavior. If this were true, how could it be hoped that any process of psychotherapy might be effective in ameliorating mental illness? Or how could it be accounted for that, as sometimes happens, adult life-experience without benefit of psychotherapy produces alterations of personality, both favorable and unfavorable? Experience in the first six years of life generates a complex pattern of adaptive potentialities which are at the disposal of the later personality. Any one

IX

such potentiality or any grouping of them may be more or less utilized or more or less inhibited in meeting or in creating the situations of life in later years. It is in view of this that it seems reasonable to close the books, as it were, in more or less tentative fashion at the age of six years.

While acknowledging that personality may, perhaps even in large part, be determined by inherited constitutional factors, we are constrained to recognize that all attempts hitherto to establish the existence and nature of such factors have met with complete failure and have produced not a shred of convincing evidence. In these circumstances we are bound to emphasize—possibly, overemphasize—the significance of environmental factors in the formation of personality. We can be confident that work along these lines will never be wholly vitiated by the discovery of constitutional factors; the only effect of such discovery would be an altered view of the relative importance of experiential factors. Now they occupy the whole stage; then they might have to share the stage with other performers.

My professional and personal debts in the writing of this volume must now be acknowledged. Every writer of such works as this owes an incalculable debt to Freud, which, in my own case, will be acknowledged *in extenso* in the Introduction and in detail at many points in the text. Of a similar nature, though indeed not so vast, is my debt to Harry Stack Sullivan, whose influence on my thinking will likewise be acknowledged and expounded more fully elsewhere. Clarence P. Oberndorf, Franz Alexander, Sandor Rado, and Clara Thompson, having participated in my psychiatric and psychoanalytic training, all have my deep gratitude and my full awareness of the personal debt I owe them, in addition to the professional one.

In the preparation of this book I have received invaluable assistance from Doctor Lilly Ottenheimer: she showed me that it had to be written, read with enormous patience and fortitude the various chapters as I wrote them, and made numerous suggestions for their improvement. Ruth Steele took over the difficult task of typing from a hand-written script, often almost indecipherable by reason of numerous corrections and after-thoughts, and performed it with utmost skill and devotion. Mr. Harry Ellis, who edited the manuscript, carried out his task with consummate skill and tact, and it is a pleasure thus to record my appreciation of his labors. Many others have contributed to this book. Acknowledgment to some of them is made in footnotes throughout the text. What I have learned from patients, from students—both in and out of class—from acquaintances and from mere passers-by is considerable in amount, but I could not begin to state it in detail and in many instances this would scarcely be desired by them. Many of them will not even know that I intend to include them in this blanket acknowledgment, but all of them, known and unknown, knowing and unknowing, I regard with feelings of warmth and gratefulness.

I wish to acknowledge gratefully various suggestions made by Drs. Bernard Glueck and Frances S. Arkin.

Finally, I want to express deep appreciation of the intelligent cooperation of Mr. Bernhard J. Springer, my publisher, whose help has freed me from much drudgery and whose competent wisdom was always generously at my disposal.

WILLIAM V. SILVERBERG, M.D.

New York, N. Y.
April 1952

Childhood Experience
and Personal Destiny

Introduction

THE NEED FOR A THEORY
OF PERSONALITY

FOR THE PRACTISING PSYCHIATRIST, in so far as he is concerned with psychotherapy, it is a matter of necessity to have some concepts of the nature of the human psyche and its ailments. Such concepts are by no means always systematized and inwardly consistent; they are often not even explicit in the psychiatrist's mind. Many psychotherapists, particularly those who lack training in psychoanalysis, are not even aware that they have a theory of personality and neurosis. But as they treat and advise with their patients, they function in terms of a theory of this kind which is at least implicit.

The kind of problem patients often bring to the psychiatrist nowadays has only within the past half century begun to be thought of as medical. The husband or wife who is unhappy in various phases of the marital relation, the parent with a flighty daughter or a son who promises to become a ne'er-do-well, the person who has difficulty in social living or who feels he has capacities that are somehow missing fulfillment have only recently begun seeking help from the psychiatrist, though all such problems are doubtless, in their individual manifestations, as old as human society. Formerly these people, if they sought outside help at all, have sought it from the minister or from friends or members of their families. Family councils were sometimes held

1

in order to find solutions. Often the family doctor was aware of such difficulties and was even, at times, consulted about them or felt himself privileged to offer gratuitous advice. But it is probably true that, for the most part, people sought and received no outside help in dealing with these intimate and private concerns, and, like Mary in St. Luke's gospel, kept all these things and pondered them in their hearts. Even today most people still deal with their problems in this fashion, but a great many more than used to, now bring their troubles to the psychiatrist.

Confronted with the task of giving his patients help in such matters, as well as in others much more traditionally medical— for example, hysterical manifestationʳ, phobias, compulsions— the psychiatrist bases his efforts upon what he believes human beings are like and what can go wrong with them. Such beliefs, which constitute a theory of personality and neurosis, may be explicit or implicit, but they are always derived from the psychiatrist's own experiences in life—what he has observed extra-professionally about himself and others, what he has read or seen and assimilated, what he has been taught, and what he has learned about human nature from dealing with patients. Experiences of this kind keep occurring continually and are apt to confirm or to call into question generalizations already made; thus the psychiatrist who is alert toward the rich multiplicity of personality and who knows the limitations of his knowledge of personality and his experience with it (including his own) must perforce regard his theory of personality and neurosis as provisional, only partly true, and always subject to revision—always a working hypothesis rather than a completed edifice of theory. Psychiatrists who feel they have nothing more to learn about the human psyche and its ailments and that they have achieved an outlook on these matters which cannot be profitably altered, are ignorant of their own ignorance and of the relative and partial nature of our knowledge about the psychology of human beings, their motivations, their adaptations, and their behavior.

The aim of the present endeavor is to offer an account of the author's views on personality and neurosis based upon his experience *so far* with human beings, both ill and not so ill. This experience has been gained in a psychiatric career of nearly thirty years and a lifetime of more than fifty. Much contact with and observation of suffering people, both neurotic and psychotic, have gone into it, as well as efforts to relieve them of some of their suffering. Living has also contributed its share, for all that is learned from participation in human relationships of all kinds, individually and in groups, all that is learned from the reading of literature of every sort, from seeing plays and films, from studying history, from observing current events, from listening to and making music, from looking at pictures—all this and every other sort of extra-professional experience may be grist for the psychiatrist's mill. For the psychiatrist, perhaps beyond other professional people, the motto holds true: *Nihil humanum mihi alienum.*

Perhaps the single item of greatest import among all these facets of experience is training in psychoanalysis. In 1923 when I began practice, psychoanalytic training in this country was rather hit or miss. Nowadays such training is highly systematized, but at that time it was felt—though by no means demanded—that the prospective psychoanalyst should undergo personal analysis at the hands of someone experienced in the discipline. The day was just past when all that was considered necessary was good will and an assiduous reading of Freud. I began a personal analysis here in 1924, but soon felt the need of a training more systematic and went to Berlin, where a training institute was in operation, which offered lecture courses and seminars and provided supervision of clinical work—the so-called control analysis.

The present debt of every psychotherapist to Freud and his work is immeasurable, whether in the individual case this is acknowledged or not. The influence of Freudian concepts is perceptible wherever psychotherapeutic work is being done. Almost every psychotherapist operates as a matter of course in terms of unconscious psychic functioning, of unconscious conflict, of repression, of unconscious motivations, and of the need for interpretations which involve all these factors. If, in addition, he understands and works with factors of transference and resistance, he may be said to be a psychoanalyst, as Freud saw it. In general it is safe to say that, were it not for Freud's work, we would today be floundering in psychotherapy a great deal more than we are. The fact that our work in this field today has any integration and clear purposiveness is entirely owing to his astute and often accurate intuitions and the hard and careful work that preceded them.

This is not to say, however, that our knowledge of human nature begins and ends with Freud. It does not even begin with him, for many a poet, many a dramatist, many a novelist of former years had intuitively grasped profound and far from obvious truths about human nature, which, however, were of little psychotherapeutic use until they were grasped anew by Freud, formulated by him, and integrated into his growing body of generalizations and hypotheses. It does not end with him either, for he was aware, as he came toward the close of his life, of many questions still untouched and many unsatisfactorily answered, and he knew that an enormous body of truth and knowledge was still to be won. Even if he had not known it, we would know it. Psychology is a young science indeed; its materials are often vague and elusive; and human behavior, despite his great pioneering work, is still largely unpredictable, though somewhat less so than it was in the days before Freud. As psychotherapists we cannot afford to feel that he has said the last word on human nature and its ailments; nor can the human race afford it: it is still too sick and immature and our efforts at therapy still too feeble.

Nor, even granting that the last word is far from said, can we suppose that nevertheless everything written by Freud is infallibly correct. *Et dormitat Homerus.* What has been said above about the fallibility of psychiatrists in general in their theorizings and the necessity for each of us to regard his conclusions about human nature as only partially and *so far* accurate, applies equally to Freud. His work bears the mark of genius, but he too had limitations in the experience, professional and otherwise, upon which his observations and intuitions and their formulations were based.

The present work will be found to show throughout the influence of Freud. Indications will also be seen of influence by the work of Harry Stack Sullivan. Sullivan is the only psychiatrist known to me who might conceivably have made Freud's contributions if Freud had not existed, for he was possessed of great genius and fearless originality and his powers of observation were uncanny. He had psychoanalytic training in the sense that he had undergone personal psychoanalysis, but he always preferred for himself the designation of psychiatrist. He worked in terms of the basic psychoanalytic concepts, but often preferred his own nomenclature for some of these. He used the term *dissociation* rather than *repression,* for example; he regarded transference as an instance of what he called *parataxis* (roughly speaking, mental distortion); resistance for him was a species of *security operation.* Where the psychology of Freud was oriented mainly toward the libido and its vicissitudes, that of Sullivan was oriented toward the ego and the devices it adopted in its attempts at adaptation to external conditions. Sullivan did not speak of the ego; rather he employed the term *self-system,* which he considered to be molded into its individual forms by the agency of the anxiety aroused by parental disapproval and of the feelings of security created by parental love and approval.

He made two important contributions: one is the idea that human personality is essentially a social product, that it does not exist or manifest itself independently of other human beings, as the color of the eyes or the texture of the hair may be said to do, but that it is formed and becomes observable only in the context of relationships with other persons, interpersonal relationships. Thus the psychoanalyst was not the impartial, objective observer of his patient that Freud often seemed to make of him, watching for the appearance of traits and symptoms as they came *from* the patient, in much the same sense as a laboratory worker might watch for changes in the liveliness of a guinea pig or in the glossiness of his coat; rather, in Sullivan's view, the psychoanalyst is a *participant* observer and must take into account that what goes on in the therapeutic interview involves himself and his own behavior, that the patient is not merely demonstrating and manifesting his own personality, but is *reacting* in terms of the analyst's personality and behavior and the situation created for him by these factors. This means that personality is not to be regarded as something fixed, as something always and everywhere the same, regardless of who observes it; it is unlike a simple biologic trait, unlike a chemical reaction, unlike a manifestation of the law of gravitation; rather, personality is flexible, elastic, a grouping of potential adaptations, and therefore highly variable, depending upon the situation offered and the elements of it that are selected as requiring adaptation.

The other important contribution made by Sullivan lies in his insistence that the central, nuclear factor in human psychology is self-esteem. In Freud's psychology the central factor consists in the need to restore psychophysiologic homeostasis (equilibrium) disturbed by libidinal impulses, a matter of domestic economy, so to speak, since he regarded libidinal impulses as arising *within* the individual without necessary reference to external stimulation. Sullivan, too, considered the maintenance and restoration of psychophysiologic homeostasis as the basic function of the human psyche, but he differed with Freud as to the nature of the disturbing factor. This factor, so Sullivan thought, was the lowering of self-esteem, and such a disturbance would obviously arise, not from within the individual regardless of external circumstances, but as a direct result of the attitudes and behavior of other human beings: again, as an outcome of interpersonal relationships. This would be true whether self-esteem is based upon the opinions of others regarding oneself or whether it is based upon *effective aggression*, my term for the ability to achieve what one wishes to achieve, regardless of obstacles. Effective aggression will usually involve, to a greater or less extent, other human beings and their behavior.

It will be a part of my endeavor, though decidedly a minor part, to synthesize and reconcile these apparently antagonistic psychologies. Freud's psychology, as already pointed out, is essentially a libido psychology, and Sullivan's is essentially an ego psychology. But since Freud also worked with the concept of an ego, and since Sullivan also found libidinal factors a basic element in human behavior—he postulated drives for satisfaction and security as indispensable to all organisms—such a reconciliation should not necessarily be impossible.

Freud's work, for seemingly inevitable historical reasons, began with a careful study and formulation of libidinal factors. The instinct theory to which he subscribed at the time—a bipolarity of sex and survival—implied the existence of ego factors as well, but it was not until much later in his work [29] that he began formulating the role played by the ego. The ego was decidedly subordinate to libido in this formulation, for all the energy at its disposal consisted of quanta of libido: it was like a motor set to function if it could receive energy in the proper form, but without this energy, dead and stationary. The functioning of the ego was conceived of as resulting from its libidinization: since libido was regarded as the sole energy, the ego could have no energy of its own, separate and different from libido, and no source other than libido wherefrom to draw energy.

Freud's new instinct theory [34], promulgated in 1920, offered the possibility that Thanatos, which Freud considered to be an instinct arising from energic sources totally different from those giving rise to Eros (roughly equivalent to what he had formerly termed libido), might present a basis for an energy, not libido, which animates the ego. But he continued to regard the ego, as without energy of its own, as a *place* rather than an agency,* a place through which might flow, now Eros, now Thanatos, but without that energy of its own which might give it the power to select either of these in any given circumstances. In speaking of the ego and its functions, particularly its executive functions (whether of initiating muscular action or of initiating inhibition of id-impulses or their repression), Freud seemed always to imply that it possessed an independent energy which gave it power to *select* action (whether destructive or aggressive,

* Freud [35] designated the division of the personality into id, ego, and superego, as a *topography* (τοπος, place; γράφειν, to write; = a description of places).

arising from Thanatos, or constructive, arising from Eros). But
he never supplied the theoretic basis for this implication and left
his co-workers with a theory of instinctual energies insufficient to
account for an ego able to function in truly executive fashion.
For those who have followed him he has left a legacy of confusion and bewilderment in the concept of an ego which must function executively but lacks the wherewithal for this task. Those
who have written on ego psychology attempting to hold this impossible line have obviously been floundering in a quagmire of
unclarity and inconsistency.

A theory of instinctual energies is after all a *Weltanschauung*. Such energies cannot be shown to exist or not to exist. A
theory of instinct describes how things look to its author, and if
one may postulate one type of energy or two, one may also postulate three or four or a hundred, since here all is postulation. The
only value in such *Weltanschauungen* lies in how much of the
phenomena of existence and behavior they explain and how
satisfactorily. In other words, in the evaluation of instinct-theories, the man is deluded who thinks he is dealing with matters
of absolute truth: his real concern is with their utility. Adherence
to one or the other such theory is not a question of loyalty to absolute truth and need not be a question of loyalty to its author.

One adheres to such a theory only so long as the theory is
useful in accounting for that which is empirically observed. In
this respect metapsychology does not differ from metaphysics. If
a metapsychology cannot account for the executive function of
the ego (defined as that part of the personality having, among
others, an executive function), then the metapsychology needs
to be altered in such a way that it can account for it. I propose
to assume that the ego possesses an energy of its own, different
from the libido, and different from Thanatos and from Eros—
an energy whose main characteristic is that it drives toward survival, much like Sullivan's drive for security. What follows in this
volume is predicated upon such an alteration of Freud's metapsychology and upon whatever reformulations may be required
to adjust his metapsychology to this essential modification.

TOWARD A THEORY
OF PERSONALITY AND NEUROSIS

THOSE WHO READ DETAILED ACCOUNTS
of the trials of criminal cases are often puzzled and baffled by the
rule of evidence which restrains a witness from stating conclusions based upon what he has perceived and confines him to reporting his perceptions only. The witness is expected to tell what
he saw and what he heard, but his conclusions as to the mean-
ings of these things or as to the intentions of the persons concerned in his testimony are subject to being ruled out of evidence
either by the objection of opposing counsel or by the trial judge
himself. The layman often finds such procedure difficult to understand, since all of us are forever coming to conclusions as to
another person's intentions when we see him act or hear him
speak. But, nevertheless, there is wisdom in this rule of evidence:
such conclusions are, after all, merely the opinions of those who
make them and in the final analysis only the person who acted
or spoke can say what his intentions were. This reasoning, arrived
at long ago, does not, of course, take unconscious mental functioning into account; but the witness is no more competent to
assay the unconscious motivations of another person than that
person himself, and a psychoanalysis of every person involved
in criminal proceedings whose unconscious intentions are in
question would be cumbersome indeed. Ultimately the jurymen

must decide this matter of intentions, and while their conclusions may be just as unfounded as those of a witness, it is felt that, since somebody must decide, the defendant's interests are better served by leaving such decisions to the unanimous opinion of twelve people, supposedly personally disinterested, than to the perhaps biased opinion of one witness. The point here is that it is a precarious thing to come to a conclusion about what is or was in another person's mind, conscious or unconscious, unless the other person is able to confirm it by his own words.

The foregoing statement has great pertinence when we attempt to say anything at all about what goes on in the mind of a newborn infant or of any child up to the time when he has attained a sufficient proficiency in the use of language. The infant is, in etymological terms, the unspeaking, and he cannot tell us what goes on in his mind. Fond parents, for instance, will often suppose that their two month old infant is showing unmistakable signs of sociability by smiling at them; the pediatrician, on the other hand, tells us that this infant's facial gesture is no smile, but a grimace occasioned by gas pains in the abdomen. I have no way of saying which interpretation of the infant's behavior is right, since only the baby is in a position to know, and he is an "unspeaking," an infant. Whatever is stated about the nature of consciousness in infancy is necessarily the result of conjecture or of reconstruction, reasoning after the fact, and can never be definitively proved.

It is often felt by psychologists that we are on safe ground in supposing that the fetus exists in a state of complete and effortless satisfaction. This supposition is based upon a consideration of the physiologic circumstances of intrauterine life; physiologically speaking, the fetus is living under optimal conditions. It exists enveloped in a warm fluid in which temperature change (if any) has an infinitesimal range: its skin cannot feel too cold or too hot. It needs to engage in no exertion whatsoever; it does not even have to breathe, as all the oxygen it requires is supplied to it by the mother's bloodstream, which flows through the fetus via the placenta and the umbilical cord. It does not need to digest, as the food-substances, already prepared by the mother's physiologic processes for assimilation, come to it by the same means as its oxygen. It does not need to evacuate waste materials, as the same flow of blood carries metabolic products from its body to the mother's, whose physiologic processes dispose of them. It does not need to adjust to changing intensities of light, since the womb is a place of perpetual darkness. All this is true if the mother is in good health and well fed; if she is not, there may be some vicissitudes of fetal life. However, under ordinary conditions, a consideration of these physiologic matters would seem to justify the conclusion that, psychologically speaking, the fetus exists in a state of uninterrupted and effortless satisfaction: in other words, a state of physiologic and psychic homeostasis is maintained up to the beginning of labor.

There arise, however, certain questions in connection with even this apparently simple and justifiable conclusion. We need not, perhaps, question the physiologic facts. But when, at what point in fetal development, may we begin to speak of *psychic* homeostasis? When, if at any time, does or *can* awareness begin in fetal life? Do we have to conclude that in the fetus physiologic homeostasis is identical with psychic homeostasis? If so, does that identity change, once the fetus is born, and when, and how, and why? In cases where the mother is ill and the physiologic homeostasis of the fetus is disturbed, does it have awareness of this? Can it experience anxiety? Does the fetus experience anything psychically when it is headed for intrauterine death? Such questions cannot be answered except by conjecture. The supposition that the fetus in the process of birth experiences anxiety, is merely a supposition and leaves unanswered the question, When does the fetus begin to have the capacity for feeling anxiety?

Another question involves the meaning of fetal movements, which after the fourth month of fetal life can be felt tactilely and can often be seen in their impact upon the mother's abdominal wall. Do the movements signify interruptions of physiologic homeostasis, and are they attempts to restore it? If so, is there any fetal awareness of such interruptions, and how are they felt? This query cannot be answered, but the fact that it can be asked makes us immediately question the absoluteness of the supposed unbroken and effortless satisfaction of fetal life. By asking it, we have implied that even the fetus may upon occasion have a sense of "something is the matter." Perhaps this implication contains a tentative answer to the question, When does the fetal psyche originate? Possibly it begins as soon as the fetus is capable of having a sense of "something is the matter," which comes about ordinarily during the fifth month of its life.

In any case, we are cautioned by this line of thought to regard the concept of unbroken, effortless satisfaction during fetal life as a relative one, and to be skeptical about the contention that the so-called trauma of birth marks the *first* experience of anxiety in the life of the human organism. It has been pointed out by Freud [*36*, pp. 96 ff., and especially p. 101] that the most common somatic manifestations of anxiety—acceleration of the respiratory rate and of the heart beat—have a utility and an expediency in the situation of birth that they do not have in later situations of anxiety: they aid the organism in performing the transition from the placental type of oxygenation and circulatory flow to the autonomous one in which oxygenation depends upon the organism's own respiratory efforts and circulatory flow depends upon the organism's own cardiac action.

Freud [*36*, p. 97] likewise pointed out in the same connection that anxiety is characterized not only by such somatic phenomena but also by a sensation whose "unpleasurable quality seems to have a character of its own." Disturbed physiologic homeostasis in the fetus could perhaps cause the fetus to experience this unpleasurable sensation, which would thus become the most rudimentary manifestation of anxiety, that portion of the psychosomatic complex of anxiety which may be present even in fetal life, and without the presence of which we should be skeptical about a diagnosis of anxiety. Clinically, we often encounter anxiety that has no perceptible somatic manifestations. On the other hand, we are accustomed to diagnose anxiety from the presence of one or more somatic manifestations (sweating of the palms, for instance) even when the unpleasurable subjective sensation is denied. Perhaps we should be more skeptical about this than we are: either the subject of our diagnosis serves a purpose of his own in denying the subjective sensation (for example, maintaining face by denying he is afraid or uncomfortable in the given situation), or, if the subjective sensation is actually absent, the somatic manifestation may have a quite different significance. Again we are confronted with the difficulty of knowing what goes on in the mind of another without verbal confirmation from him. Ultimately such confirmation may be forthcoming, but meanwhile we do well to maintain a question in our own minds. Possibly the fetus feels only *discomfort;* anxiety, as Freud conceived it, perhaps occurs in a full and complete form only after the experience of birth. We may regard the homeostatic state of the fetus as one in which satisfaction is only relatively uninterrupted and effortless—relatively, that is, as compared with postnatal life.

The newborn infant, now literally cut off from his fetal connection with his mother's physiologic processes, is utterly helpless to survive without the care given by the mother or a surrogate for her. His newly acquired respiration and cardiac action fulfill his metabolic needs for tissue oxygenation and for exchange within the tissues of food-substances for metabolic products; his digestive system now begins the lifelong tasks of assimilation of food and elimination of wastes. He is, physiologically speaking, a competent, functioning organism. But there his competence ends. He cannot procure for himself the food which, once it is in his mouth, he is now competent to handle. He cannot keep himself warm, nor protect himself from any of the myriad dangers which beset his intactness and his life. Needs he has and feels, for he cries when he is hungry or cold or when he experiences pain or other discomfort; but fulfill his needs he cannot. If his cry brings no one to divine his need and to satisfy it, he is at the end of his resources.

How the infant *feels* in this situation of relative helplessness—relative because, while the cry is his only resource, it is a resource—is what we should like to know, but can only speculate about. Two workers, Sandor Ferenczi and Trigant Burrow, have engaged in what seem to be useful speculations about this matter. Even though there is evidence that seems to give support to their speculations, it cannot be too strongly emphasized that their hypotheses cannot ever be more than provisionally accepted, since the unspeakingness of the infant will always limit our thinking about the nature of his consciousness to conjecture and reconstruction.

Ferenczi [14] conjectured that the newborn infant, with his intrauterine history of unvarying physiologic homeostasis, regarded himself as omnipotent; that, having never known frustration, the infant supposed this freedom from frustration to be the result of his own powers. Ferenczi based this idea on Freud's findings [24] in cases of obsessional neurosis and his own clinical confirmation of these. The infant's notion of his own omnipotence, according to Ferenczi, becomes modified, as time goes on, in response to two factors: (1) the introduction of more and more frustration, producing more frequent and longer delays between the incidence of a need and its fulfillment, and more frequent and more prolonged disturbances of psychic homeostasis; (2) the emergence, through growth, of new functioning —better muscular coordination and the rudiments of speech.— Thus, while at the start of extrauterine life the infant's subjective omnipotence operates in a hallucinatory manner (he hallucinates fulfillment of his need and it is fulfilled), later on it operates by gestures, and still later by words and by thoughts. Ferenczi appears to have omitted the cry from this series, but Sullivan [72, p. 7] has pointed out that the cry is an instrumentality much used by the infant in his effort to live by the use of power. Infantile omnipotence is ultimately renounced, according to Ferenczi, because increasing frustration, resulting from the gradual withdrawal of the mother or her surrogate from the role of constant watchful helper, demonstrates to the child that he does not possess omnipotence, reconciles him to the need to take into account factors of external reality, and induces in him the endeavor to manipulate them toward his ends. Thus the sense of omnipotence is replaced by the sense of reality [*68*, pp. 387 ff.].

This replacement is never complete; it is made only to the extent that it has a pragmatic value for the child and not because the child perceives any moral value or other virtue in adherence to his newly acquired sense of reality. In so far as functioning in terms of a sense of reality gets him more, in so far as it increases the effectiveness of his activity, he is for it; if it fails him, if this effectiveness is not increased by it or is perchance lowered by it, he will abandon the sense of reality and will attempt to function in terms of a sense of supposed omnipotence. This we see clearly and often in the case of adults, and we may therefore postulate it a fortiori in the case of the child. Furthermore, it should here be remarked that when we speak of omnipotence in the psychic sense, we do not give the word precisely the same meaning as we do when we use it in a metaphysical or in a theological context. In the latter we mean literally *all-power*, power over everything conceivable, as when we speak of God's omnipotence. The omnipotence of the human being, the omnipotence that he sometimes strives for, is more limited in its application: he seeks all-power only over those things which are of direct concern to him. While the child might desire all-power over the movements and activity of the mother or other person significant to him, he would not be interested in power over the Argentinians, for example, or over the Paris subway system. When we use the concept of omnipotence in human psychology, we must confine its application to those factors of the individual's world which are of direct and immediate significance to him.

The speculations of Burrow [*10*] on the nature of the infantile psyche are perhaps implied in Ferenczi's hypotheses, just described, and were certainly assumed by Freud, apparently without the awareness that Burrow had explicitly formulated them. Burrow supposed that psychically the newborn infant exists in a "primary subjective phase" of consciousness. By this he meant that the infant makes no distinction between self and nonself, that he conceives his existence as an unbroken continuum of himself and all the perceived world about him, both persons and things. Thus the mother's nipple in his mouth as he sucks milk and derives a sensory thrill as well as nourishment from it is regarded by him as belonging to his own self, as a part of his own body-image, and not as something nonself, belonging to another person and able to be used and enjoyed only so long as the other person, to whom it belongs, permits. It will be seen that this wide, extended concept of self resembles the "oceanic feeling" mentioned by Freud in *Civilization and Its Discontents* [*38*], where it is related to early states of consciousness.

The increasing frequency and prolongation of disturbances in psychic homeostasis—experiences of intensifying frustration—and the gradual lessening of the mother's or her surrogate's constant and alert attention to the infant's comfort and well-being, teach the infant that his needs or wishes can often not be fulfilled by any efforts of his own; he learns that the satisfaction of his wants requires the mediation of another person, one who is not always available to him and who, even if available, does not always attend to his needs or wishes. Such experience produces a gradual disintegration of the primary subjective phase and results eventually in the awareness that a sharp distinction exists between what is self and what is other, or nonself. Here, too, as in Ferenczi's hypothesis of an infantile sense of omnipotence, experiences of frustration play a dominant part in the transition to a sense of reality in the developing infant. He learns that all the world is not encompassed in his own body, that his oceanic feeling is illusory and untenable, and that he does not possess all-power over all those things which are of significance and concern to his comfort and well-being. These lessons are but tentatively learned.

For the infant the sense of reality has no virtue in itself; the value of the distinctions he learns to make lies in the fact that his disillusionment enables him to adapt himself to the world about him in such a way that he can sometimes manipulate its various factors to achieve wish-fulfillment more readily than he could before he learned the lessons of reality. Bernard S. Robbins

[*60*] has shown that this pragmatic attitude toward the sense of reality exists in adult life.

We must assume, for we see the clearest evidences of it not only in adult human beings but in the behavior of animals as well, that it is inherent in all living organisms to strive toward the fulfillment of needs and wishes which have a biologic provenance and which may or may not have psychic representation. By the latter I mean simply that such needs and wishes may be felt or they may not be felt. The fact that in acculturated human beings and in some animals capable of training, the efforts toward such fulfillment of needs and wishes may be temporarily or "permanently" inhibited does not vitiate the general statement: we suppose that the tendency to fulfillment exists even when behavior fails to give testimony that it is in operation. The man who offers his seat in a crowded bus to a woman would prefer to remain seated but chooses to discommode himself either in the interest of considering himself or of being considered a "gentleman" or in the interest of some other form of altruism. The man who covets his neighbor's wife would try to take her if he could square it with his acculturated set of moral scruples or if he did not fear the humiliation of being rejected by her or the anger of her husband. Inhibiting factors merely complicate the general principle that we set the greatest store by the fulfillment of all that we may wish or need.

We do well to try to maintain this distinction between wish and need, although it is not always easy to distinguish them. A need may be defined as that which is necessary to health and to survival (for instance, the need for sufficient food to maintain health and life). All else desired may be regarded as wish, regardless of the intensity with which it is desired. The fulfillment of sexual desire, while often felt with great intensity, is never necessary to survival, though we often postulate that it is essential to psychic or physiologic health. Many instances could be cited in which sexual abstinence is maintained for long periods without apparent detriment to health. However this may be, whether sexual fulfillment in general is to be considered a need or a wish, it is true that the fulfillment of sexual desire with a specific partner is a wish rather than a need, even though the chooser may insist that it is a need.

It happens often enough that people will make certain conditions, the fulfillment of which is represented as needs, and then bully or otherwise coerce others into fulfilling these conditions. A mother, for example, will get it established that she has an attack of cardiac failure whenever her grown up son disobeys her. Thus her wish to dominate her son is represented as a need. A child who intensely wants a particular toy may attempt to coerce the parents by saying with great feeling, "I *need* it, I NEED it." Subjectively, one often does not take the trouble to distinguish between an intense wish and a need, and often enough one is quite sincere in the feeling or statement of need where merely a strong wish is involved. Under such circumstances, whether that which is desired might be objectively defined as a wish or as a need, the individual puts into operation whatever procedures he is capable of for bringing about its achievement. The degree of success attendant upon these efforts comes under the heading of what I have termed *effective aggression.** In this sense, effective aggression represents the success with which the ego functions in the carrying out of impulses. The impulse may be purely biologic in origin or, arising from biologic sources, may become greatly modified by experiences of acculturation. The impulse to evacuate the rectum when it contains feces is purely biologic (physiologic) in origin. Toilet-training temporarily inhibits this impulse until culturally suitable conditions can be found for its release.

Effective aggression refers to the executive function of the ego. The ego, as Freud saw it, was that part of the psyche in closest contact with the external world. Through it, perceptions

---

* This phrase was introduced in my paper "On the Origin of Neurosis" [65]. The interested reader will there find the formulation of this concept (pp. 116 ff.), as well as remarks on the drawbacks involved in the phrase. In the latter connection it should be noted that the key-word is *effective;* the term *aggression* might be replaced by *action, activity, behavior,* or the like.

of internal and external reality are received and given meaning. The ego also controls the innervations which can produce or inhibit muscular action and therefore motility. An impulse arising from the id, the great reservoir of that energy which Freud called *libido,* can of itself produce no muscular activity, no motility toward its goal, unless the ego acquiesces and sets in operation the necessary muscular innervations. Thus no aggression, effective or otherwise, can occur, unless initiated by the ego. The theoretic difficulty mentioned in the Introduction in connection with Freud's instinct-theories now becomes painfully apparent. In his conception of the ego, Freud set up an executive agency of determining importance: one of its functions is to decide whether or not a given impulse shall receive motor expression or be inhibited. Yet the energy wherewith the ego operates in carrying out this function is not specifically its own: the energy is borrowed from precisely the same source from which the impulse, now submitted to the ego's decision, arises.

We are confronted with a dilemma: either we are dealing with a single, unitary kind of energy, in itself undifferentiated and nonspecific in its aims, upon which any psychic agency, whether impulse or ego, may draw in its attempts to function; or we are dealing with different types of energy, each specific to the type of psychic agency concerned. In a sense, Freud attempted to encompass both horns of this dilemma. In terms of his earlier instinct-theory, libido was a single, unitary type of energy, and yet it had a specifically sexual character: it was uniformly pleasure-seeking. Freud [26, pp. 460 ff.] objected to Jung's attempt [46, pp. 77 ff.] to define libido as nonspecific, as not specifically sexual, and, therefore as a general, undifferentiated energy (somewhat equivalent to Bergson's *élan vital*) upon which any psychic agency might draw. Freud ascribed to the ego no other source of energy but the libido; furthermore in so far as the ego might oppose a libidinal impulse, it had to compete with that impulse for enough energy (libido) to make good its opposition.

Freud's concept of primary narcissism carried the implication that ego and id had originally been one, without differentiation, and that libido was originally at the disposal of this undifferentiated id-ego, or primitive self. Once the differentiation of id and ego occurred, in response to situations threatening the intactness of the whole organism (in psychic terms, this id-ego), id and ego had to compete for quanta of libido. Freud now spoke of ego-libido and object-libido; withdrawal of libido from objects resulted in a proportionate accretion of libido to the ego. But what psychic agency determined the withdrawal of libido from an object, unless it was the ego itself? If libido is to be withdrawn from an object, ego-libido would have to be stronger than id-libido—object-libido can be nothing other than the id's investment of an object with desire for pleasure by means of that object—and the crucial question arises, What factor has produced the ascendancy of ego-libido over id-libido?

The difficulty here is entirely a theoretic one and results from the untenability of the hypothesis of libido as both a single, unitary energy and a specific pleasure-seeking energy. If, whatever their original state, ego and id are seen to be often in opposition one to the other, it is simpler to suppose that their obviously different aims are based upon different types of drive or energy. The fact that ego and id are often enough not in a state of mutual antagonism and that they often operate synergistically does not vitiate this hypothesis of their operating upon the basis of specifically different drives. Just as different people may function, now in antagonism, now in cooperation, so different psychic agencies within the same person may function. Indeed, effective aggression may be seen as an attempt to achieve synergism of id and ego, the goal of total effective aggression or omnipotence being an ideal restoration of the primitive id-ego. If the ego never opposed or modified an id-impulse, or, putting the matter somewhat differently, if every impulse were unquestioningly and successfully put into effect by the ego, something like omnipotence would have been achieved, something resembling the intrauterine state of effortless satisfaction would have been restored, neurosis would no longer exist, and books such as the present one would not be written.

Freud's later instinct-theory does not alter the situation greatly. This theory did introduce a new energic principle, that of Thanatos, thus destroying the conception of libido as a single, unitary energy and requiring it to share the field with another energy having a specifically different *quality*. Freud seemed thereby to resolve the aforementioned dilemma, by abandoning the first horn of it. But he did not adopt the second horn of this dilemma: Thanatos and Eros were equally energies of the id, and the ego was still left to borrow one or the other from the id or to bring about a variety of fusions and defusions of them, by means of what additional energy was not stated. As a matter of fact, neither Thanatos nor Eros, as Freud defined them, was well adapted to become specifically an ego-drive, since survival was given a subordinate role in the theory. Thanatos received the major role; it was the death instinct and drove toward non-survival in its primary position (directed "inward") and toward destructiveness in its secondary position (directed "outward"). Eros was regarded as opposed to the death instinct and drove toward growth, union with others, and what in general one might term constructiveness. To Eros was bequeathed the libido, but, since Freud assigned it the minor role, its operations were seen as mere temporizings, as detours from the highroad of death, as delays and interim arrangements in the major process that had as its goal the decay and disintegration of the living, organic substances of the body into nonliving, chemically inorganic substances. The psyche desired passionately the death of its own soma and the destruction of the soma of others; survival meant little to it in comparison to the peace of biologic nothingness.

This metapsychologic picture seems greatly at odds with human nature—and, in fact, with general organic nature—as it is observed. Freud [*34*, chap. 6] himself attempted to deal critically with it when he first presented it to the world. He raised the questions whether instinctual death is not merely characteristic of the metazoa (many-celled animals) as compared with the protozoa (single-celled animals), and whether instinctual death occurs in the somatic cells of the human body but not in the germ-plasm (the sperm and ova), which consists of single-celled entities like the protozoa. He showed very clearly that death "from natural causes" occurs among the protozoa only when external conditions are unfavorable to life—in stagnant water or in a test tube, where the protozoon is killed by its own unremoved metabolic products; or when amphimixis (nonreproductive, rejuvenating conjugation between protozoa) is prevented from occurring. Freud used these examples to demonstrate his point about instinctual death even among the protozoa, but what he actually showed by the evidence he adduced is that protozoan death occurs only under extraordinary external circumstances—in confined, stagnant water or in the absence of the opportunity for conjugation. This is not death "from natural causes" or endogenous death. It is either accidental death or murder.

Freud must be credited with having presented his new instinct theory with a tentativeness disarmingly frank. He wrote [*34*, p. 76], "I might be asked whether I am myself convinced of the views here set forward, and if so how far. My answer would be that I am neither convinced myself, nor am I seeking to arouse conviction in others. More accurately: I do not know how far I believe in them." Or again [*34*, p. 77], "People unfortunately are seldom impartial where they are concerned with ultimate things. . . . There everyone is under the sway of preferences deeply rooted within, into the hands of which he unwittingly plays as he pursues his speculation." In his later work [*38*] he assumed the validity of his speculation and was never again so critical of it.

I would contend that a metapsychology is useful and valid only in so far as it is able to account for observed phenomena, and that the metapsychology above described fails to account for the drive of all organic life toward survival, which appears empirically to take precedence over all other drives, and for the executive function of the ego. These are serious deficiencies, and Freud's particular "preferences" seem to have relegated the ego to the position of stepchild of psychoanalysis. The historical reasons for this are well known, but whether they were inherent in the material that confronted Freud in his early work and as he went along, or whether they were inherent in his preferences, is a debatable question. There can be little doubt that it is to the advantage of psychology that Freud elected to pursue first the study of libidinal factors and their vicissitudes, as these needed for their elucidation precisely those unique qualities of observation, intuition, and formulation, which he brought to the work. Ego psychology is much more obvious and superficial, and much easier to study and describe. It does not require the genius which was uniquely Freud's. It is perhaps unduly demanding to have expected Freud to do the thorough job with ego factors that he did with libidinal ones. But it seems to me that the legitimate task of his successors is to restore to the ego its full and proper significance and to assign to it its proportionate role in the affairs of the human psyche.

The task demands, I believe, that the ego be given a theoretic basis for its functioning; in other words, to postulate for it a specific kind of drive or energy which has survival of the total organism as its chief goal and which operates by the medium of effective aggression. An advantage of the latter concept is that it permits us to see the ego as concerned with matters not accounted for if we regard it as actuated solely, or even mainly, by motivations of defense. It is an operational concept which accounts for the ego's efforts in the direction of *achievement* as well as of defense.

The psychologists—including Freud, Sullivan (with his anxiety-based self-system), and Horney (with her concept of basic anxiety)—who base the ego's functioning solely or even mainly upon the organism's defensive needs, appear to have overlooked one of the outstanding facts in the observable behavior of the young child: his obvious tendency to *do* something, a something which is neither defense against nor avoidance of danger, but merely wish-fulfilling. Certainly, as we observe the infant and the young child, we see that defense is not his only concern and that his resources for defense are mobilized and utilized only when he senses danger. In the absence of a sense of danger—which is usually the case during the greater part of each twenty-four hours—the child is apt to engage in behavior we would have to describe as *doing* something rather than *avoiding* something. The infant of eight or nine months does not ordinarily spend his waking hours in perceiving dangers and devising means of circumventing them; he sits on the floor or in his play-pen and manipulates in some fashion that appears satisfying to him whatever objects come to his hand: he shakes his rattle, he puts the foot or hand of his rag doll into his mouth, he vocalizes with apparent joy and enthusiasm, and he does such things repeatedly and tirelessly and with obvious pleasure. The somewhat older child who has achieved locomotion has a correspondingly wider repertory of doing. To a vast extent the activity of the young child is not defensive but is simply pleasurable doing, a patent fact not hitherto adequately taken into account in formulating theories of personality and neurosis. Freud was able to show in one instance [*34*, pp. 11 ff.] that a child's game did have defensive significance, but it may be doubted that this is universally, or even most frequently, the case (nor did Freud claim that it was).

It seems reasonable enough to accept Freud's conclusion that for reasons of defense the ego becomes differentiated from the primitive ego-id continuum and that its origin serves a defensive purpose. But it is likewise reasonable to suppose that one of the outcomes of this differentiation—and therefore perhaps one of the considerations motivating it—is that the organism as a whole is thus placed in a better position to achieve fulfillment of its positive needs and wishes. The reasoning here is much like that of Freud in one of his early metapsychologic papers [*28*]: experience teaches one the expediency of denying immediate fulfillment to some of one's wishes, which is counter to the dictates of the pleasure principle; the delay in fulfillment is often dictated by the reality principle in order that the ultimate fulfillment of the wish may be assured. Thus it is seen that the reality principle does not differ essentially from the pleasure principle; the former is merely a modification of the latter and is adopted to make more certain the operation of the pleasure principle in its original form. So the differentiation into ego and id, while undertaken for defensive reasons and while sacrificing the homogeneity, the oneness, of the primitive self, results in a condition superior to the original one—the world and its frustrations being what they are— for the achievement of pleasure-goals.

Indeed, the ego throughout life is characterized by its tendency to compromise and to make sacrifices in order to maintain life and to achieve, even though in delayed and partial and substitutive fashion, goals signalized by id-impulses. The ego's major aim, however, is survival, and in this sense, defense may be said to be its cornerstone. Just as a trapped animal will sacrifice a paw or a leg if this enables it to escape from the trap, so the ego will sacrifice any id-impulse which, if carried out, seems to threaten survival. (Certain "heroic" exceptions to the foregoing statement are discussed in the following chapter.) Survival is thus the main concern of the ego, and its energic force may thus be defined as whatever in the organism drives toward survival. But if survival seems assured or is not threatened, then the ego's other task, the achieving of pleasure-goals, becomes paramount. The drive for survival must be regarded as primarily irrational and as not requiring any rational basis: it merely exists. In so far as this drive might be rationalized, the continued opportunity to achieve pleasure-goals, to *do,* would constitute its rationale. I mention this in order to place these two drives in proper perspective: the drive for survival cannot be reasoned with; when survival is at stake, the ego drops everything else and concentrates its adaptative powers upon it.

Survival is usually striven for even if every potentiality for *doing* is lost. Suicide (or suicidal impulses or thoughts) in such circumstances may seem to contradict the primacy of the drive for survival and thus to give the drive to *do* the major role. This is true only if suicide is taken at its face value and if the fact, clinically demonstrable, is ignored that suicide is essentially an act of vengeance and murder, an act calculated to torture, through a perpetual bad conscience, the someone else (in some instances, perhaps, God) held responsible for one's woes. The act of suicide seems postulated upon a conviction of survival in some form, a contention supported by many of the popular superstitions about death and the dead, particularly, in this instance, the beliefs concerning the possibility of the dead returning and haunting their enemies. Relevant here is the common unconscious conviction that though dead one remains in a sense alive. Frazer [16, chap. 18] deals with such beliefs among primitive peoples.

In any case, the concept of effective aggression can encompass both the defensive function of the ego (its concern with survival) and its function of *doing*, of achieving the pleasure-goals to which the id impels it.

Thus far I have dealt with effective aggression descriptively, endeavoring to define its quality. It is clear, however, that it has also a *quantitative* aspect, which is perhaps the more important one for our purpose. For we have to be concerned not only with the kind of effort made by the ego in its operations, but more importantly with how effective the effort is. To what extent is the ego's effort successful? Does the ego achieve what it attempts to perform in exactly the manner contemplated in its intention at the start of its maneuver? Has it, along the way had to compromise? If so, how much less than its original intention has it had to settle for, or has it had to abandon its original goal entirely? If it has had to compromise or abandon its goal, what are the causes of this change? Has the ego met with obstacles which it may regard as insuperable in the nature of things or merely insuperable to it? Is the compromise or failure due to deficiencies of the particular ego and its capacities, or was the goal to be achieved an impossible one? If the latter alternative obtains, could the difficulty have been foreseen, or was the impossibility not predictable and only discoverable in the course of the attempt? All these questions and many similar ones indicate the quantitative aspects of effective aggression and suggest how these may be linked to self-esteem.

Self-esteem may be regarded as the psychic counterpart to somatic survival. Totally and continuously effective aggression, if such a thing were possible, would result in an indestructible self-esteem. On the other hand, failures in effectiveness of aggression produce a lowering or loss of self-esteem. In the early weeks and months of extrauterine life the relative helplessness of the infant ordinarily evokes in the mother an alert attention to his needs and their fulfillment. But if, in accordance with Burrow's hypothesis, the infant, being in the primary subjective phase, does not distinguish between himself and his mother, this alert behavior of the latter will produce in him the impression that *he* has brought about the desired restoration of homeostasis and that his own *doing* (whether by hallucination, gesture, cry, word, or thought) is responsible for the fulfillment of his need or wish. The difficulty of expressing what *may* go on in the mind of the infant still in the primary subjective phase is well illustrated by the foregoing sentence. The entire structure of language seems predicated upon the distinction between "self" and "other," a distinction which we assume the infant has not yet made. A more accurate version of the sentence referred to would probably be: "This alert behavior on the part of the mother will produce in the infant the impression that the desired restoration of homeostasis *has been brought about* and that a certain action performed (whether hallucination, etc.) is relevant to the outcome (restored homeostasis)."

Thus the infant's doing or aggression is felt by him as effective to the extent to which the mother fulfills his needs. The more alert the mother, the briefer and less frequent will be the periods of disturbed homeostasis, and in accord with his subjective bias, the more effective and powerful the infant will feel himself to be. It would seem that such a sense of adequacy and competence, despite its objective inaccuracy, must be basic to self-esteem and must form the foundation of the healthy ego.

Loretta Bender has pointed out [6] that where such alert care by maternal agencies is inadequate (as in foundling institutions, for example) the outcome in later childhood and adult life is an incurable psychopathy—a marked retardation and flatness, emotionally and intellectually. Such infants are given no basis for the illusion of effective aggression, which the mother's alert attention grants to more fortunate ones, and are therefore unable to establish that degree of self-esteem upon which healthy ego-functioning is based. The work of Bender would suggest that a constitutional factor is here operative, for the very frustrations and delays which, when they occur somewhat later in the infant's life, favor the healthy establishment of a sense of reality, operate with permanently damaging effect when they occur in the earliest weeks and months. It would seem that too much disturbance of homeostasis too soon in life cannot be tolerated by the psychosomatic constitution as it then exists.

One is reminded here of Freud's concept (in *Beyond the Pleasure Principle* [34]) of a *Reizschutz* or protective barrier against excessive stimuli arising both from the external world and from within the organism itself. He likened this to a hard rind developing from the surface membrane of an organism of vesicular shape, as if the originally delicate surface layer had become toughened through continuously repeated contacts with environmental substances and objects. It is as if, in the situation mentioned above, this psychic *Reizschutz* had not yet had time to develop, so that such stimuli, assailing the organism prematurely, break through the surface and do damage to the interior substance. The same stimuli, if they can be held off until after the *Reizschutz* has developed, will be fended off by the latter without damaging effect to inner substance.

This is a perfectly comprehensible concept, but it is difficult to translate it into psychic or somatic or psychosomatic terms. It may be conjectured that this difficulty exists because of our present ignorance of certain factors whose discovery and elucidation may not be too far off. The work of Selye [63] and others upon the physiologic effects of stress and the manner in which the organism meets them and attempts to ward them off or to compensate for them would seem to offer the possibility of giving substance, not too far off in the future, to Freud's conception of a *Reizschutz* and to my attempt to explain the constitutional nature of the damage, clinically described by Bender, which results from too great frustration too early in life.

In the ordinary case, where the incidence of frustration is more gradual and not so drastic, the sense of reality supervenes as an acceptance of a distinction between self and other and as a realization of limits to one's own power. As has already been said, this acceptance and this realization may be unwilling and tentative, but by the end of the first year of life they are established in large degree. This change to a sense of reality would have to be accompanied by some reduction in effectiveness of aggression and some corresponding reduction in self-esteem. These effects are however, counteracted to some extent by the emergence of new capacities—greatly increased muscular coordination (with the concomitant power of locomotion) and the acquisition of the rudiments of language. Such factors not only increase the child's resourcefulness, making him thereby less helpless than he was at birth, but often produce in his parents enthusiastic and affectionate approval. Much of what is lost in self-esteem by the reduction in an illusory type of effective aggression is made up for by these accretions to real effectiveness of aggression and by the pleasing sense of being approved of and having the favor of these important people, the parents. The self-esteem of the one year old is not so absolute or indestructible as it was in infancy; it is more relative and more precarious, but it exists on the more realistic basis of the actual capacities of the child and has the additional support of parental approval.

Throughout life self-esteem has these two sources: an inner source, the degree of effectiveness of one's own aggression; and an external source, the opinions of others about oneself. Both are important, but the former is the steadier and more dependable one; the latter is always more uncertain. Unhappy and insecure is the man who, lacking an adequate inner source for self-esteem, must depend for this almost wholly upon external sources. It is the condition seen by the psychotherapist almost universally among his patients.

In the child, threats to self-esteem are of two kinds: threatened failures of the effectiveness of his aggression and threatened withdrawal of parental (mainly maternal) love and approval. Such threats constitute the psychic counterpart of threats to somatic intactness and survival. In later childhood, threatened loss of parental approval may readily equate, in certain instances, with threats to somatic survival, since parental love and approval may become to the child the guarantee of such survival. The relation of this to self-esteem will be discussed in the following chapter. In the presence of actual danger to such intactness or survival, *fear* is the emotion felt; and the perception of such a danger immediately impending, though not yet present, arouses *anxiety*. Actual injury to self-esteem produces the emotion of *humiliation*, the intensity of which corresponds to the extent of the injury. The perception of an impending blow to self-esteem produces anxiety, as in the case of apprehended somatic danger.

Fear and humiliation produce on-the-spot and usually quite random measures for dealing with the situations that evoke them. One is immediately confronted with a threatening situation and must improvise a defense. Such improvisations may or may not be successful in avoiding the danger or in mitigating its effects; the defense responses may be partially successful, which means also partially unsuccessful.

Anxiety, as differentiated above from both fear and humiliation, produces somewhat different results. Since, in the case of anxiety, the danger is not yet actually present, but only impending or threatening to be present, there may yet be time to plan an effective means of coping with the threat. Forewarned is forearmed, and anxiety has the advantage of a forewarning.

Because the faculty of perception is involved in such foresight of dangerous situations, and because perception is one of the ego's functions, Freud regarded the ego as the seat and point of origin of anxiety. He therefore supposed that measures to avert foreseen danger emanate from the ego. Repression is one such measure: the ego, aware of an impulse arising from the id, perceives from its watchtower overlooking the environment that danger from the outside will attack the total organism if an attempt is made to carry out the impulse. Such a perception arouses anxiety in the ego, and its obvious way of averting the danger is to quell the impulse, if it can. The stronger the impulse—in the ego's own terms, the stronger the temptation to perform the act implied by the impulse—the greater the anxiety, because of the greater likelihood of the ego's initiating the motor actions appropriate to expressing the impulse. The ego's best plan, then, is to quell the impulse by disowning it, by "forgetting" it, by repressing it.

The ego has other devices for dealing with id-impulses that threaten to upset the harmony and safety which the ego has been at pains to establish and maintain in the organism's relations with the outside world. Prominent among these is reaction-formation, in which the ego manifests an impulse precisely opposite to the one actually aroused in the id by the external situation. The impulse manifested in the device of reaction-formation is, as Sullivan once pointed out,* the appropriate id-syntonic impulse with a *not* prefixed to it. If the original impulse is *to kill,* reaction-formation transforms it into *to not-kill,* which may come to mean *to take care of.* It must be added, however, that reaction-formation is not simply a matter of grammar and semantics. If the opposite impulse, the one expressed by the prefixed *not,* does not exist *in its own right* as a psychic potentiality, it cannot be used for purposes of reaction-formation. Suppose that the example given arises in a situation of sibling hostility: the original impulse, then, is to kill the sibling, but owing to the process above described it becomes transformed by reaction-formation into the not-kill, take-care-of impulse. This transformation will the more readily take place if the child has already evolved some tendency to want a baby of his own to take care of, in whatever specific terms he conceives this. In other words, reaction-formation involves of necessity some positive quality in the not-impulse; the negativity of the not-impulse, taken alone, is an insufficient basis for its adoption even as an anxiety-solving device. It seems to me likely that where the appropriate not-impulse lacks positive

* In a lecture in Washington, D. C., in 1935, so far as I know unpublished.

value, the ego will be constrained to choose a different defensive device, such as repression, for example.

Regression, another of the ego's defensive devices, handles the danger-provoking impulse by expressing it in an earlier form, one which has proved in the past to be safe. For example, if one's impulse takes the form of seeking pleasure through exhibiting the penis to the mother in an attempt to seduce her into touching it (as in the case of Little Hans [24, pp. 162, 163, 166]) and the ego senses danger, emanating from mother or father or both, as a likely outcome of such an act, the ego may try to avoid the danger and yet to achieve the pleasure by altering the new impulse into an old version. Thus, sitting on mother's lap and being embraced by her is a way of being pleasurably touched which one has found safe by previous experience, or inducing her to give one a bath requires that she legitimately wash and dry—hence touch—one's genitals.

It is this device of regression which doubtless gave Freud the strong impression that libido is an energy whose manifestations develop in stages or levels, since old manifestations become replaced by new ones and since the tendency toward new manifestations can give place to recurrences of older manifestations when difficulties arise. Certainly he was here correctly observing a general psychic principle to the effect that when new behavior is attempted and for whatever reason fails or seems destined to fail of its purposed goal, it is wise to have recourse to something tried and true. Folk wisdom expresses the conflict in two antithetic proverbs: "If at first you don't succeed, try, try again," and "Let sleeping dogs lie."

A study of the antitheses frequently observed in folk wisdom has still to be made and would probably prove both interesting and profitable. Proverbs, which are the vehicles of folk wisdom, often exist in opposites, such as the pair just mentioned, and indicate the existence of frequent conflict with respect to many proposed modes of behavior. Another antithesis: "Make hay while the sun shines"—do it now; "Don't cross the bridge until you come to it"—put it off until tomorrow. From the viewpoint of common sense, the fact that mutually contradictory proverbs often occur has no very profound meaning beyond the idea that no form of adaptative behavior has universal application and that people have learned to fit their behavior to different situations as they apperceive them. From the viewpoint, however, of unconscious psychic functioning, which often, as we have learned, transcends common sense, these antitheses of folk proverbs may have a significance similar to that of word-pairs which have antithetic meaning but derive from the same etymologic roots [1, 32, 43]. This significance is the existence of profound unconscious conflict with reference to all potential modes of behavior in important matters: it indicates the deep uncertainty with which individuals approach meaningful situations. With reference to the ego's defensive device of regression, the conflict lies between doing something new which may be dangerous and doing something old which is known to be safe. If the uncertainty is resolved by adopting the latter behavior, the ego has altered the impulse by regression.

Whether the general principle which is implied by the antithetic proverbs and word-pairs supports the idea that, because libidinal manifestations show the possibility of regression, they therefore normally "develop" in a series of stages, is quite another matter, depending upon what is postulated concerning the libido and its manifestations.

The devices of the ego thus far mentioned have the common quality of being *autoplastic*. They are *self-molding* devices and attempt to adapt to the environment and its potential dangers by producing alterations in the organism's own impulses. The impulses may be disowned or postponed (repression in varying degrees), or they may be replaced by opposite impulses if such exist in their own right (reaction-formation), or they may be replaced by older and safer forms of the original impulses (regression).

One may also speak of another group of ego-devices which differ from those just enumerated by being *alloplastic*, or *other-molding*. These seek to alter the environment rather than the self and they comprise, doubtless among others, the three maneuvers that I have elsewhere described in detail [66, 67, 68]. I shall here merely name them as the schizoid, the magical, and the transference maneuvers. To classify the two groups of devices as autoplastic and alloplastic is convenient and is accurate in a general sense. But it must be realized that the autoplastic devices are also alloplastic in that their ultimate aim is to change the environment from a dangerous to a safe one, and that the alloplastic devices cannot be engaged in without producing certain alterations in the self.

The autoplastic and alloplastic devices may be further distinguished roughly in that the former are in the main oriented toward defense, while the latter are oriented toward achievement of pleasure-goals. I characterize this as a rough distinction because both types of devices have ultimately a pleasure-goal in view and because the alloplastic devices are often motivated by concern with security and survival, and particularly with self-esteem (which is the psychic version of security and survival). In the most common instances, the autoplastic devices are adopted because the ego senses that the organism is not safe constituted as it is and that inner modifications are essential, whereas the alloplastic devices, which are modes of attempting to alter factors external to the organism itself, may operate with no immediate purpose of producing inner modifications. The former devices might be summed up in the sentence: "I am not safe as I am; I'd better change myself"; while the latter might be expressed: "I am all right as I am; but I have to change him, her, them, or it." Both are adopted in order that aggression may be the more effective and therefore that self-esteem may be maintained at the highest possible level. The ego's own survival (self-esteem) corresponds to the survival of the total organism, when the latter is at stake. When it is not, when somatic survival is not involved in the organism's *doing*, then what is involved is homeostasis, whether described as psychic, somatic, or psychosomatic. When not confronted with emergencies that threaten life, the ego's chief concern is to maintain a high level of competence and thus to avoid illness, whether this takes the form of low self-esteem or a bodily deficiency that impairs competence in *doing*.

Psychic illness, then, implies illness of the ego—low self-esteem primarily occasioned by a diminution in the effectiveness of aggression. All of the ego's defensive devices, which are originally used to promote and improve this effectiveness, indicate that the ego does not feel itself strong enough or safe enough to pursue the organism's aim directly; hence, the devices emerge in an indirection which not only signalizes a relatively weak ego, but which in itself further weakens the ego. The strength of the ego lies in the degree to which it is at one with the remainder of its own organism. Freud [*36*, p. 141] pointed out that the differentiation into ego and id signifies a defect in the human psyche, by which he meant that the human psyche functions poorly in so far as it is at war with itself, and that this differentiation would not have occurred had not the psyche at an early stage of its existence fallen into inner conflict. Since this differentiation never fails to occur even in the healthiest human being, a certain inner psychic disunity seems inevitable in everyone. If the very existence of an ego implies some degree of psychic disunity, the strength of the ego must always be seen as a relative strength: it is *more or less* at one with the remainder of its organism.

Whether an ego may rightly be considered as inherently or constitutionally strong or weak, is a problem about which we are in such profound ignorance that we cannot even propound the question in a form that might evoke responses, nor have we any idea what factors such constitutional strength or weakness might relate to. Our ignorance is here so complete that any statement concerning the constitutional strength or weakness of the ego would be begging the question and would necessarily reflect, not truth, but one's *Weltanschauung*. The very question may in itself be a species of *non sequitur* since, from a strictly biologic point of view, the ego *should* not even exist (if the emergence of the ego is to be regarded as a psychobiologic defect).

It is best to leave untouched this question of a constitutional, inherent quality of the ego. We can only know that, regardless of such a factor, the specific experiences of the organism in its specific environment appear closely related to the ego's necessity to adopt devices of indirection, to the extent to which these are adopted in general, and to the specific nature of these devices in a given case. Likewise related to specific experiences is the matter of whether a given device is temporarily adopted, to be later abandoned, or whether it becomes permanently characteristic of the given ego. We may say, then, that the ego *becomes* weak or strong (perhaps we should say *weaker* or *stronger,* supposing constitutional factors to exist) as a result of what its organism specifically experiences. It grows to be less at one with the remainder of the psyche (more conflicted) or more at one (less conflicted), depending upon its life-situation, which, in early life, is mainly the situation presented by the human environment (the biologic family, in our society).

It is unnecessary to labor here the factor of cultural relativity. It is by now well known from Sullivan's postulates on interpersonal relations, and from the pioneering work of A. Kardiner [47, 48] that different societies (geographically as well as temporally different) evolve markedly varied forms and that each society attempts to mold its denizens to its own specific form. Kardiner's concept of *basic personality* implies that what is "normal" or well-adapted personality in one culture is "pathologic" or maladapted personality in another.

In the consideration of the kind of experience that favors growth or diminution of ego-strength—equivalent, respectively, to psychic health or psychic illness (neurosis)—I shall be concerned solely with our own culture. By "our own culture" I mean specifically the American culture. This may be at times extended to include the contemporary culture of western civilization as a whole, or it may at times be narrowed down to the form of culture extant along the northern Atlantic seaboard of this country. It is not always possible to be aware when one is being excessively general in one's cultural assumptions and when one is being too provincial.

II

THE AREAS
OF EARLY EXPERIENCE

THE LIBIDO THEORY OF FREUD includes the idea that the manifestations of libido may be observed to proceed in an orderly succession of stages from the earliest period of extrauterine life to the period of physiologic sexual maturation (adolescence). The stages as Freud described them are oral, anal, phallic, and genital, with a latency period interpolated between the last two. He did not mean that in any of these stages the manifestations of libido were *exclusively* of the nature indicated by the name of the stage; rather, that they were *predominantly* of the nature characterizing the given phase of development. The implication of the theory was that this genetic account was of universal reference and that it represented a psychobiologic process true of all human organisms in all times at all places; that is, that it paralleled psychobiologically the known facts of embryology. Just as the human fetus progresses through a series of structural and functional developments, regardless of accidental factors of time, place, race, or culture, so the human child was regarded by Freud as inevitably and quite independently of any environmental factors passing through the defined stages. An Abraham might refine the genetic description, subdividing oral and anal phases, but this did not alter the basic concept of a universal psychobiologic process.

Essential to the formulation of this idea were certain facts about the behavior of children, some of which Freud had observed directly, but the majority of which he had culled from the reminiscences of adult patients and from the reconstructions necessitated by his interpretation of their dreams and other psychic productions. These findings constituted the data of infantile sexuality, as Freud termed it, and were recounted in some detail in the second of his *Three Contributions to the Theory of Sexuality* [33].

These data have been confirmed so often, both by other psychoanalysts and by those in a position to make direct observations upon children, that it is impossible to doubt their general validity as facts of observation. Whether such confirmation upholds Freud's use of them as the basis of a psychogenesis or psychoembryology of universal validity is quite another question. The more recent work of cultural anthropologists such as Kardiner [47, 48] indicates that the succession of developmental phases that Freud described is more or less typical of children in western civilization and that children in other cultures undergo developments which vary from this in one or another detail. Cultures may differ radically, one from another, in respect to many of their specific traits, and any culture may be regarded as a more or less fixed entity for any given generation of parents, although cultures actually change as time goes on. Such change is usually slow and gradual, though instances are known of sudden, drastic change. In any case, parents most commonly attempt to train their offspring for adequate participation in the culture as it currently exists. Thus the details of training will vary, depending upon the precise nature of the culture as it is understood by the parents. In a culture, for instance, whose existence depends upon stealing the cattle and agricultural produce of other communities (as among the Comanche [48, p. 74]), the rearing of boys will be in the direction of favoring warlike, aggressive behavior, and positive value will be ascribed to predatory behavior and to skill and enterprise in stealing, in trickery, and the outwitting of others.

Another factor concerns not the actual training in certain directions but the results which inevitably emerge from the specific features of a given culture. A society in which food production is entirely dependent upon the labor of the women (as among the Alor [48, pp. 106, 129 ff.]) will force upon its infants a prolonged separation from their mothers at an extremely early age, while the mothers are laboring in the fields, and will substitute care by somewhat unwilling surrogates (often older sisters) who, in any case, are nonlactating. Prolonged oral frustration is a regular part of the experience of such infants and results in character traits which are not striven for as desirable in that culture, but which are the outcome of specific cultural circumstances.

Whether by conscious or unconscious design or by accident, children are exposed to experiences which are typical for the given culture and which are apt to occur in a certain order or succession, again typical for that culture. What Freud had described in the development of the libido was the result of the succession of experiences which is typical for our western (European and American) culture and did not have the universal and biologic significance he ascribed to it. It is true that biologic factors are inevitably concerned in any typical psychic development in whatever cultural milieu. All human beings are confronted with the following biologic issues (among others): What shall one do about oral needs and wishes? What shall one do about urinating and evacuating the bowels? What shall one do about achieving genital pleasure? Every culture has to be concerned with these questions, because every human organism has to be, but they may be answered very differently by different cultures.

From a biologic point of view there is but one ideal answer to all such questions; however, civilized man has never been able also to be wholly biologic man. The very fact of becoming civilized has always entailed the sacrifice of and compromise with certain goals as defined biologically. This is the meaning of Freud's assertion [38, pp. 91 ff.] that civilized man is inevitably "sick" man.

From the considerations thus far mentioned, it seems to me justified to separate Freud's observations and findings in the matter of infantile sexuality from the theoretic use he made of them. We can accept his data as accurately observed and typical of denizens of our western culture and at the same time reject his genesis of the libido as a universal process, since cultures are already known concerning which this application, if made, would prove false. Thus the universality of libidinal development as Freud described it is obviously an untenable hypothesis; furthermore, it seems highly improbable for similar reasons that any other account of libidinal development laying claim to universality would be any more tenable. The whole approach is clearly wrong and is based upon the false premise that because man is everywhere physiologically the same, he must therefore be everywhere psychologically the same. We might even cast doubt upon the contention that man is everywhere the same physiologically. The man whose physiologic processes are geared to an extremely cold, dry climate or to a low altitude may find himself in great physiologic difficulty if he is moved to the hot, humid jungle or to a peak of the Himalayas. Attempts at adaptation, whether or not they are successful, are typical of living organisms, and this should teach us that we cannot consider the outcome of such attempts, physiologic or psychologic, as universal. In the matter of adaptation there are always two factors in operation: (1) the organism and its range of capacities, and (2) the environing circumstances requiring the adaptation. Since the latter factor is highly variable, we can scarcely expect any specific instance of adaptation to be a universal trait.

We must therefore not seek universal specific traits or universal specific patterns or modes of behavior. Our task should be the less ambitious one of seeking to discover typical behavior patterns in a specifically defined milieu. The problem confronting us can be stated as follows: In a given cultural setting, what is the range of adaptation typical of members of that culture? In terms of psychology, this involves knowing the nature of the experiences which the given culture typically presents to its young and determining the specific adaptive behavior which the psychotherapist accepts as normative when making judgments concerning deviant behavior or psychopathology.

What Freud described as universal phases of development was, I believe, the *areas of experience* and their order of succession as they are usually presented to the children of western civilization by parents performing the task of acculturating their offspring. Freud's description had this much of universality: it would seem inevitable that the first of these areas of experience relates to *oral* factors, regardless of the specific culture. This is true because the human newborn infant, regardless of whatever else may happen to him, has in some manner to be fed. Even in such a culture as the Alorese—with its prolonged separation of the infant from the mother, thus entailing frustrations and delays which mean frequent states of hunger for the child—the infant must somehow receive physiologically adequate nourishment. Certainly there can be no other item of experience which is so important to newborn babies always and everywhere as oral experience. This much we can safely say: the first experiential area through which every human being passes involves oral needs, wishes, frustrations, and gratifications. But here universality is at an end.

In our culture, the second experiential area commonly opens with the parental attempt at starting toilet training and teaching the infant control of the anal and vesical sphincters. This developmental period begins a variety of do's and don't's, introduces the important sequences of rewards and punishments, and marks the ushering in of innumerable disciplinary issues. This is commonly the case in our culture, but not invariably so. Some experts in child training have cast doubt on the wisdom of such early attempts at housebreaking the child, and many mothers have come to the same conclusion, without benefit of expert advice. What seems invariable, however, in our culture is the introduction of disciplinary issues at least as soon as the infant's powers of muscular coordination enable him to move from place to place. With locomotion he is able occasionally for brief periods to escape from the mother's supervision and may thus engage or attempt to engage in some behavior which the mother may see fit to prevent. It is thus possible that the child may first encounter experience with disciplinary matters in this fashion rather than in the area of toilet-training. For this reason, it seems better to term this stage the disciplinary area of experience rather than the anal phase, as Freud called it.

The third of these areas relates to the achieving of genital pleasure in some fashion, ordinarily masturbatory at the outset. This may proceed without interference from the mother or it may be made by her into one of various disciplinary issues. Sooner or later the achievement of genital pleasure comes to involve something other than masturbation; it begins eventually to involve the wish for participation by another person, usually the mother or other caretaker, and usually in the form of the wish to be touched, caressed, or otherwise stimulated genitally. Such a wish may arise from various experiences which give rise to genital stimulation—being washed or dried, being unintentionally touched in the process of being dressed, being stimulated in such leg-riding games as "Go, pretty horsie"; in the boy, being touched while being helped to urinate; or, in the girl, being wiped after urination or defecation.

Increased muscular coordination enables the child to touch his own genitals at will, in a direct, purposeful fashion. The earliest type of masturbation is, as a rule, not manual. It is most commonly performed by the infant by lying face downward and raising and lowering the hips so that the genital region makes rhythmic contact with bed, floor, or table. This performance is dependent upon the infant's being placed in such a position by the mother or other person, or upon his having the muscular coordination necessary to turn himself to such a position. In the earliest weeks and months, manual touching of his own genitals is random and accidental and cannot be repeated at will by the infant.

The genital region is often deliberately stimulated by a mother, nurse, or other person. This is less uncommon than one might think. Mothers of the less "educated" classes are found who regard such stimulation as a standard method of soothing and quieting a restless or otherwise disturbed child. As an interne, I saw a boy of 8 or 9 with abdominal pain whose mother quieted him, during my admission examination, by stroking his penis. An adult male patient once disclosed, with considerable resistance, the deep-seated conviction that a doctor confronted with a gravely suffering patient had, as a last desperate therapeutic measure, to masturbate his patient. This idea was found to be based upon his mother's behavior toward him when he was a child.

However it arises, this notion of participation of another in the achievement of genital pleasure seems to emerge early in life in our culture and is quite generally (though not invariably) discouraged and frustrated. When the child openly expresses such a wish to the mother or other person, punishment of some kind is often given or threatened: in the case of boys, the threat of castration or of some type or degree of loss of the penis or its functioning is frequently made; in the case of girls, where loss of the genital organ cannot be threatened, the punishment sometimes takes the form of disapproval, withdrawal of love, or a beating. The boy, naturally, does not escape the threat of withdrawal of love, whether castration is threatened or not.

The child's bid for genital stimulation and the mother's reaction to it may take the crude forms already discussed or may be expressed in subtler ways. The child's wish to get into bed with Mommy, to sit on Mommy's lap, to have her go to the toilet with him or to go to the toilet with her—these and a variety of similar wishes may contain an idea, more or less vague, of getting into a situation with her in which the desired touching may occur.

Refusal by the mother, whether made crassly or subtly, is seen by the child as arbitrary, since gratification is obviously not a physical impossibility, and may arouse speculation in the child as to the reasons for the arbitrary refusal. The scope for such speculation is wide and ranges from notions of personal undesirability and inadequacy to the notion of a competitor for such favors. The child's speculation frequently embraces the entire range and creates combinations of explanations whose details we shall later investigate.

This experiential area, which corresponds to Freud's phallic phase of libidinal development, is one in which issues of inferiority (comparison in general) and competitiveness become paramount. It is the area marked by what Freud has called the Oedipus complex, which, from the viewpoint of the boy, involves sexual desire for the mother and competitive hostility toward the father. From the viewpoint of the girl, the same factors of sexual desire and competitive hostility are involved, but the objects of these drives are reversed: sexual desire is said to pertain to the father, while hostility is directed toward the mother. In a later chapter we shall have occasion to discuss these matters in considerable detail and to relate them to the experiences in the two preceding areas.

These three types of experience are not presented to the child in completely orderly sequence: they all overlap to some extent, and one must consider a given type of experience as *predominant* rather than exclusive during the period concerned. Masturbatory activity may occur during the predominantly oral phase of experience and, if interfered with by the mother, may thus early in life introduce a disciplinary issue more or less stressed by the mother. Likewise, in the predominantly disciplinary period, factors of oral deprivation may become an issue with the child and may greatly affect the child's attitude toward maternal discipline. Many other examples of this overlapping could be mentioned and will constitute important material in later chapters. Here it is only necessary to make clear that when a given experiential area is referred to, its designation signifies a type of experience merely predominant at that phase. Life in general is not neatly compartmented but forms a continuum whose apparent inconsistencies are often baffling to those who attempt to approach it in strictly logical and rational fashion. Growth and development seem always to involve the partial retention of older and earlier factors along with a simultaneous trying out and testing of newer, unfamiliar ones. An ordered sequence of one, two, three is more typical of the mind in its mathematical operations than it is of the rest of the natural world.

Each of these experiential areas of early life presents its characteristic issues and problems to the growing child: problems of deprivation in the oral area; problems of obedience, conformity, and rebelliousness in the disciplinary one; problems of genital gratification and of comparison and competition in the phallic area. While this much may be stated in general terms, the delineation of these problems as they are presented to the individual child will obviously vary greatly, depending upon particular details such as the specific characters of the parents, their situation (including their relation to each other), the number, age, and character of siblings and other inmates of the household, and on many other factors not easy and, fortunately, not necessary to enumerate exhaustively.

It is clear that each of these experiential areas presents to the child the challenge to find successful solutions of or adaptations to each of the various characteristic difficulties encountered. Success here does not necessarily mean one single thing. The most obvious meaning of success in each instance, from the child's point of view, would involve the immediate and complete gratification of the impulse or impulses concerned: the immediate and unobstructed gratification of oral impulses; the freedom to carry out or not carry out impulses to evacuate bladder and rectum anywhere, at any time, and the opportunity to observe or not observe the other do's and don't's without encountering prohibitive or critical parental behavior or attitudes; the enthusiastic participation of the mother (or other erotically invested person) in the achievement of genital pleasure, in which case issues of comparison and competition would not arise. But it may be that success involves the ultimate achievement of such gratifications after obstacles of various sorts have been surmounted. In still other cases, where the obstacle is the threat of withdrawal of maternal love if the libidinal impulse is persisted in, the successful adaptation may consist in renouncing the gratification of the

impulse and maintaining the mother's approving and affectionate
regard and behavior.

A series of successful adaptations can be described in which
the precise degree of success in impulse-gratification is a steadily
waning factor. Since the mother's task of acculturating her offspring dooms the child to settling for less than complete success
in meeting the various issues presented by the experiential areas,
we have to recognize that his solutions are always relatively successful at best, but that there is a wide range of variations even
among the relatively successful adaptations. Here, obviously,
there is a vast difference between the biologically successful and
the culturally successful. The child whose effective aggression and
self-esteem suffer reduction by reason of his lack of biologic success may regain these and even feel them increase by reason of his
feeling of accomplishment along cultural lines. Such increase
would come about partly because of parental approval of his
accomplishment, but also partly because the accomplishment of
this bit of self-restraint or self-control opens for him new fields of
activity and privilege: the child who can be trusted not to wet or
soil himself can be allowed greater freedom from supervision and
surveillance in other matters, and his pleasurable activity is thus
less apt to be interrupted at frequent intervals and without his
own concurrence.

In general, relative success or relative failure in finding
solutions to the typical problems of the experiential areas determines, at any given moment, the level of effectiveness of the
child's aggression and, correspondingly, of his self-esteem. To this
general statement must be added that the factor of parental
(maternal) love and approval is involved in all the areas of experience and especially in the latter two, in which it is apt to
appear to the child as considerably more dubious and precarious
than in the first of these areas. The effectiveness of his aggression,
then, is concerned with maintaining this approval as well as with
achieving impulse-gratification: the child has a team of horses
to manage instead of just one horse.

The maintenance of self-esteem at a high level will likewise depend upon his relative success in managing this team. We have already said that the strength of the ego varies with the degree of homogeneity of ego and id. To this concept of ego-strength must now be added the idea that the stronger ego is the one that possesses the higher degree of integration within its own organization. The weak ego is not only greatly disunited from the id-factor of its own organism, it has also a degree of disorganization within itself and lacks inner integrity. Such lack of strong inner organization in an ego comes about primarily because of the difficulty of being effective both in achieving impulse-gratification and in maintaining (or achieving) a comfortable degree of maternal love and approval. Here again a constitutional factor may be operative, but we know nothing about it and, in our ignorance, do well to concentrate our attention and thought upon the specific details of environment and experience.

I take it as axiomatic that threats of failure in the effectiveness of aggression, in terms either of impulse-gratification or of maintaining maternal approval, or both, with the corresponding threat to self-esteem (psychic survival), produce anxiety in the ego. The assumption here is that the ego sees and reacts to threats to self-esteem as if they were external dangers threatening the survival of the organism. Both produce anxiety, though perhaps of not quite the same order: if a threat to somatic survival can be obviated by accepting humiliation (loss of self-esteem), the latter is generally chosen as the lesser of two evils. However, the classic hero of tragedy is often the person who chooses the former; he is the culture hero of mythology and is admired by us and given acclaim because his choice is the uncommon, the heroic one; we should all like to have his courage, but ordinarily do not.

But we are not commonly in a position in which this tragic choice is offered to us, unless we are soldiers in time of war, and certainly the child is rarely placed in this position in any objective sense. Transference and episodes of acting out in later life indicate, however, that subjectively the child often feels himself confronted with this tragic choice. When he renounces or delays or otherwise temporizes with impulse-gratification in favor of maintaining parental love or approval, it appears that he has chosen to sacrifice "honor" to safety. Parental love is what often seems to the child his only guarantee of safety. It is sometimes surprising to adults how acutely and vividly a child may visualize being abandoned and cast forth into a cold world by his parents. Our objective awareness that such arbitrary abandoning of a child would be a complete impossibility for the vast majority of parents prevents us from taking the child's fear of abandonment as seriously as it should be taken. The fact that on rare occasions a child is abandoned, should teach us how it may to the child seem not at all impossible and at times even highly probable. Under such circumstances, the tragic choice above mentioned will often have the unheroic (or cowardly) rather than the heroic outcome. Here the heroic choice, the option for self-esteem based on effective aggression, involves utmost efforts to make aggression toward impulse-gratification effective, while jeopardizing parental love; the unheroic choice involves omitting altogether or making merely more or less half-hearted efforts toward impulse-gratification, while sufficiently maintaining parental love to guarantee somatic survival. The fact that the word *cowardly* may be applied to this choice indicates that feelings of humiliation are apt to accompany it.

The tendency in any given child toward making the heroic or the unheroic choice could well involve constitutional (inherited) factors, of whose nature we must again acknowledge ignorance. It is easy enough to see, however, how parental (particularly maternal) attitudes may be such as to favor one or the other choice by the child in specific circumstances. Actual threats of abandonment may be made. Inconsistencies in attitude toward the child, without a rational basis apparent to him, will sometimes raise such doubts of the permanence of parental love as to make the child cautious of behavior that may jeopardize his security as he sees it. Often enough, the child's doubt of parental love or his despair of it will give him courage for the heroic choice. A wide range of possible circumstances is here operative, and adequate understanding of the child's behavior is dependent upon a detailed knowledge of the specific circumstances as perceived by the child.

It may be conjectured that, at the moment of unheroic choice, relief from the anxiety involved in the perception of the near danger of somatic extinction (through parental abandonment) may be so outstanding as to overshadow all other psychic content. Despite the security thus guaranteed by the unheroic choice, later reflection may involve feelings appropriate to failure of effective aggression with respect to the gratification of the particular impulse concerned. These feelings are the usual ones in such instances—inadequacy, incompetence, humiliation; in general, diminution or loss of self-esteem. Excessive concern with survival, to the detriment of impulse-gratification, eventually produces injury to self-esteem, and all events and situations in childhood (or, indeed, in later life) which compel the unheroic choice may be regarded as traumatic in their effects. When such traumatic events or situations occur in childhood, the ego is forced by its anxiety (ultimately about self-esteem) to adopt one or another device, whether autoplastic or alloplastic, as described in the previous chapter. The adoption of these devices, especially when they become "habitual" or characteristic of the given person, tends to weaken the ego, not only by widening the breach between it and its id, but also by disintegrating the ego's own organization. The child who elects to allow the effectiveness of his aggression to diminish with respect to impulse-gratification in order that he may survive by achieving or maintaining maternal approval has introduced a rift in his total capacity for such effectiveness, which no longer trends in a single direction; the child's team of horses, to continue the simile above mentioned, is no longer a team, for now one horse pulls in a direction at variance with that of the other. Such rifts may vary a good deal in extent: the child who merely outwardly conforms while inwardly rebelling has made a relatively narrow rift in his ego-organization, while the child whose inward rebellion becomes unconscious has

made a relatively wider one; a still wider rift occurs in the child
who rebels neither consciously nor unconsciously.

In the following chapters I shall examine in some detail
the nature of the child's experience in the various areas above
described. I shall want also to investigate some of the more typical of the adaptations, both "normal" and pathologic in our
culture, to the difficulties encountered by the child in the areas
of experience. It is to be hoped that out of these investigations
will emerge some clear ideas of the nature of personality and its
pathology as one psychiatrist visualizes these so far.

III

The First Experiential Area:
PROBLEMS OF ORALITY AND DEPRIVATION

THE INFANT'S ILLUSORY SENSE of effective aggression (based, as we have seen, upon the alert attention of the mother*) becomes more and more uncertain during the early months of life, in direct proportion, one would suppose, to the increasing frequency and prolongation of her inattention. This increasing inattention is not apt to involve matters related to the infant's somatic health and survival, such as whether he is warm enough or whether he falls to the floor; it involves, rather, the matter of his hunger and his oral needs and wishes. The mother knows that her child, who is healthy and is growing, is in no immediate danger of illness or death from starvation or dehydration and permits herself, now more and more,

---

* The word *mother* is used throughout this volume to mean *mother or mother-substitute*. The biologic mother is not always the person who gives maternal care to the child, even when she is still alive. To the very young child *the mother* is the person who takes care of him, regardless of her biologic relationship to him. Where this care is divided among two or more persons, complications important for the child's development are apt to occur in our culture, but we shall not consider this uncommon situation. In later childhood, the precise identity of the biologic mother may become an important issue, but in the earlier months the factor of substitution is of no moment. It will be less cumbersome to use the single term *mother*, but the reader should understand that *mother or mother-substitute* is always implied.

whenever her own convenience is at issue, to have the child wait
a little for his feeding; as the child grows older, it seems less and
less essential to her to still the child's hunger the instant he
evinces it or to anticipate it and feed him before he even feels
hungry. So the child is left for longer or shorter whiles with his
oral impulses unsatisfied, and we have seen that, regardless of
the mother's conscious or unconscious intentions in allowing him
to be thus more or less briefly frustrated, it has an "educative"
effect upon him. His illusion of completely or nearly completely
effective aggression and his other illusion of oceanic continuity
with his perceived world become gradually more and more un
tenable: he tends toward a sense of reality, toward a reduction
in his sense of omnipotence, and toward an awareness of distinctions, such as the separateness of self and other.

THE RAGE REFLEX

The changes during the oral phase are not accomplished
without frequent manifestations of rage, which occur whenever
the child is made to wait for gratification of oral impulses beyond his capacity to tolerate the somatic tensions occasioned by
such nongratification—a capacity very low at birth, one would
guess, but gradually increasing during the first year of life. This
rage seems to represent an inborn pattern of potential behavior;
certainly it is not taught to the child and does not have to be
taught. We call it *rage* because it appears to us to be just that; it
manifests itself in scowling facial postures, extreme congestion
of the face, vigorous clonic movements of arms and legs with
tight clenching of fists, and, above all, loud, persistent screaming. We do not, of course, know what the infant engaged in such
behavior is feeling subjectively, but it is perhaps absurd and
overscrupulous objectivism to doubt that *rage* describes it quite
accurately. That such behavior ceases, more or less immediately,
as soon as food is supplied or, in many instances, as soon as the
infant is given some object, not food, to suck on is strong evidence that the manifestations described bear an intimate relationship to the lack of food or other object which may gratify
oral impulses. Rage and the cry of rage are not devices invented

by the ego to deal with frustration and its discomforts, but are ready at hand, a biologic reflex to the stimulus of frustration, and must be regarded as stemming from the id in the same sense as the oral impulses themselves. In later childhood and adult life, the ego handles impulses toward rage and its manifestations and exerts its executive function upon them, as it does with any other impulse which may disturb the relations of organism and environment. The fact that individuals, and indeed whole cultures, handle these rage impulses quite differently does not vitiate the general statement, for we have to reckon with the ego's tendency to take unto itself, to adopt as a part of its repertory, any mode of behavior, whatever its provenance, that (1) promotes effective aggression, (2) does not place itself in danger (loss of or great reduction in self-esteem), and (3) does not place the entire organism in danger (injury or death). The first appearances of rage-manifestations occur without initiation or even decision to acquiesce on the part of the ego; however, the later manifestations or nonmanifestations of rage carry indications of the ego's attempts, more or less successful, to extend its sway over the phenomena of rage as well as the subjective feelings of rage and to utilize them for its own purposes. It is sometimes said that Napoleon (also Hitler) had the faculty of simulating rage which he did not feel and of intimidating others by the verisimilitude of the performance. Whether or not this biographic item is precisely true, it indicates an extreme in that the ego adopts for use in interpersonal relations a mode of behavior which is originally entirely biologic in nature and outside the ego's sphere of influence. Indeed, the capacity for rage and its earliest manifestations would appear to antedate the emergence of the ego from the primitive id-ego unity.

THE NURSING SITUATION

We may suppose that the sense of reality is fairly well established before weaning ordinarily takes place. Weaning signifies a transition in the development of the child, a transition from an earlier, more primitive mode of gratifying oral impulses and hunger to a later, more complex one. Freud made the attempt to distinguish sharply between oral impulses and hunger. He called attention to the fact that the infant appears to enjoy the activity of sucking, whether or not it derives nourishment from the object sucked. He adduced observations of thumb-sucking and sucking on rags and other "pacifiers," as evidence of the distinction. It may be questioned, however, whether the distinction can be legitimately carried to the length to which Freud carried it, omitting from all consideration the matter of extraction of substance out of the object sucked and concentrating solely upon the pleasure derived from the act itself with its accompanying stimulation of the lips, tongue, and interior of the mouth by such an object. May not the child who sucks his thumb or a pacifier be under the impression that the increased saliva produced by the act of sucking is substance derived from the object sucked? Can it not be true, regardless of the preceding consideration, that, while the child would rather suck unprofitably (deriving no substance) than not suck at all, he would prefer the total oral gratification (sucking plus substance) to the partial one and merely accepts the latter by way of compromise?

It is necessary, in any case, to understand that the experience of nursing is not so simple as Freud's distinction would lead one to suppose. It is a matter for great appreciation that Freud made clear to us that pleasure in sucking and pleasurable stimulation and activity of the various parts of the mouth are important elements in the nursing situation and that the significance of this situation is not exhausted by the fact that nourishment is thus obtained and somatic hunger thus satisfied. In our enthusiasm for this valuable addition to our knowledge, we must not forget what we already knew, nor must we ignore other factors in the nursing situation.

Besides the obtaining of nourishment and the pleasure of oral stimulation and activity, the nursing situation involves being held by the mother close to her own body, so that the child experiences tactile sensations of pressure as well as sensations of warmth wherever his body comes into contact with hers. Such closeness will also permit of olfactory sensations, whether of the mother's genuine body odors, artificial odors which she may apply to herself, or a combination of these.

While it is doubtless of some importance whether the child is nursed at the breast or is bottle-fed from birth, the fact that the nursing situation is a composite one, consisting of the several elements above enumerated, would suggest that it may be satisfying to the infant if some of these elements are present, even though not all are. Observation indicates that if the infant is held while he is feeding from the bottle, the procedure is entirely acceptable to him. The only factor of difference between this mode of bottle-feeding and breast-feeding is the nature of the nipple, which is of rubber in the first instance and of flesh in the second. If the other factors of the nursing situation are present, such as those which result from being held close, it appears to matter little to the infant whether what he sucks on is rubber or flesh, particularly if he has been used to the former from birth. The shift from breast-feeding to bottle-feeding usually arouses little or no rage in the infant, provided he is held close by the mother while she is giving him the bottle.

In this composite situation, the obviously indispensable element is the obtaining of hunger-satisfying substance. Instances are known of breast-fed infants, previously avid in their nursing, who at feeding-time, after a brief period of sucking at the nipple, cease nursing and cry, refusing to return to sucking the nipple. Presently such infants may merely cry when offered the breast and refuse even to begin nursing. In such cases investigation will often disclose that the composition of the mother's milk has deteriorated, having become too diluted with water for adequate sustenance. Such evidence would seem to support the statement that the nourishment provided by nursing is the primary factor, though observers with an extreme psychologic orientation might argue otherwise. Such observers would maintain that this deterioration of the mother's milk is a psychosomatic manifestation on the part of the mother, resulting from an ungenerous, hostile attitude toward the baby, and that the infant reacts empathically to the attitude rather than to the wateriness of the milk. A discussion of empathy in general will be found later in these pages, but it may be here adduced that a shift from breast to bottle (with an adequate formula) in such cases generally results in a restoration of the infant's previous oral avidity, even though the bottle is offered by the supposedly ungenerous mother. The fact that infants can be found who continue to suck avidly even insubstantial milk, while steadily losing weight, supports neither contention. While the frustration-rage of the infant may be appeased for a time by providing him with oral pleasure without nourishment or by merely holding him close, the time would not be far off when none of these devices would pacify his rage if he failed to receive nourishment, so long as he still possessed the strength to protest.

Observers of the behavior of infants are well aware of great variations in the oral avidity of different children. The average infant sucks the nipple (rubber or flesh) with eagerness, but instances are known in which this eagerness is excessive and still others in which it is greatly diminished or almost absent. This kind of difference, manifesting itself from birth on, would appear to result from a constitutional factor of some kind, possibly related to variations in a coefficient of general energy produced by tissue metabolism. It would be interesting and possibly instructive to follow into later life a group of children observed at birth and compared for this factor of oral avidity. My impression, based upon much too meager observation, is that the degree of oral avidity evinced in the nursing phase is paralleled in later life by the urgency of the individual's desires and that the later neurotic is recruited from those whose early oral avidity is in excess of the average. Whatever such a person desires, he desires with an urgency beyond average, and all psychic factors are correspondingly stepped up in intensity, including the intensity of anxiety and conflict.

PRELIMINARIES TO WEANING

Despite these variations in oral avidity, the general statement holds true that of the different elements of the nursing situation the indispensable one is the obtaining of nourishment.

In the process of weaning the child from the breast or bottle, this is the one element that is invariably retained, as it obviously must be if the infant is to continue to live and to grow. Too often it happens that this is the *only* element that is retained, and in such cases we see clear evidence that, while the other elements are secondary in importance, they are nevertheless important. Though we may separate it into various elements, the nursing situation as a whole must be a totality, a kind of *Gestalt,* to the infant, and any major change in it is bound to be perceived by him and reacted to. This would imply that in the process of weaning, the more of the secondary elements that are provided for the infant, the less difficult his adaptation will be; the more gradual the mode of weaning utilized by the mother, the less traumatic will be its effect upon the infant.

In this matter of mode of weaning there is a wide range of possible variations; the three factors chiefly involved are (1) the time of the infant's life at which it is begun, (2) the speed, and (3) the thoroughness with which it is completed. Weaning is sometimes taken to mean the shift from breast to bottle, as well as the reduction in the number of daily feedings (increase in the intervals between feedings, as well as omission of night-time feedings). I would regard these as preliminaries to weaning, and in themselves not actually weaning. These changes ordinarily produce little effect upon the infant. It appears, as has already been mentioned, to make little difference to him whether the nipple from which he sucks milk is of rubber or of flesh, provided he is held close in both cases. If, however, at the start of the shift to the bottle, the mother attempts to feed him by holding the bottle and offering it to him as he lies in the crib or carriage, signs of disturbance are apt to appear. Reduction in the number of daily feedings, provided that the infant is getting sufficient nourishment, does not usually produce disturbance, since his alimentary requirements are taken care of by increasing the amount of individual feedings. It sometimes occurs that the infant will wake up at the time for the omitted nighttime feeding and will cry. This must be taken to mean that he misses the accustomed secondary elements of the nursing situation, supposing him to be adequately nourished without the nighttime feeding, and it must therefore be supposed that the omission of this feeding has had a traumatic effect upon him. But the disturbance, if it occurs, is not usually of long duration, particularly if the infant is picked up and held by the mother, or is given a "pacifier," or both, even though he receives no actual feeding.

We may ask why some infants show signs of disturbance in these preliminaries to actual weaning, while others do not. A variety of answers could be offered, including a constitutional one, but many psychologists prefer the explanation based upon empathy. As Sullivan described it, *empathy* designates the subjective emotion of the child based upon what the mother happens to be feeling and conveyed to the child in an unmediated fashion; the transmission is direct and immediate, corresponding to so-called telepathic communication. If the mother has affection or tenderness for the infant, he feels this, regardless of her behavior. Likewise, if the mother is hostile or resentful toward him, he senses this. It would be empathic perception of the latter type which might produce disturbance in these preliminaries to weaning.

The answer seems not altogether satisfactory. We do not know whether empathy as defined exists, and the concept appears to be somewhat mystical. If it existed, we should observe evidence, in the case of the hostile mother, of the infant's disturbance via empathy in details of his experience other than in these weaning preliminaries. Why should he suddenly become empathically aware of her hostility—sufficiently so to wake from sleep—during the first night (or second or fifth) of the omitted nighttime feeding? Empathy would not appeal to me as the solution to the problem of variable reactions to the preliminaries of weaning, though it is conceivable to me that maternal attitudes are involved in the disturbed reactions. The concept of empathy, with its mystical overtones, seems very like the concept of intuition when it rests upon a mystical basis. But it has long been understood that an intuition is not what the word implies (an un-taught-ness), but rather that it is decidedly "taught," that it is a conclusion or a generalization arrived at without awareness of the innumerable small and incompletely registered perceptions that are integrated in reaching the conclusion. An intuition only *appears* "untaught"; actually it is as "taught" as any other conclusion, if we take its preconsciously perceptual basis into account. So the infant who "empathizes" his mother's hostility possibly reaches his awareness of this via various perceptions with which we do not credit him. In our ignorance of what goes on in the infant's mind and in our ignorance about the possibility of extrasensory perceptions generally, we cannot say anything conclusive about empathy.

In some given instances of disturbance over omitted night-time feedings or other items in these weaning preliminaries, it can be shown that nourishment has been actually inadequate, and the amelioration of the inadequacy terminates the disturbance. However, in other instances which do not admit of so easy a solution, it is not always possible to demonstrate maternal hostility, and we must acknowledge that we cannot always understand these disturbances. They are, in any case, uncommon rather than common, and so we may perhaps absolve ourselves from the necessity of dealing further with the problem.

WEANING AND ITS TRAUMAS

Weaning itself, as distinguished from these preliminaries, is marked by the change from ingestion by sucking to ingestion by eating and drinking—eating by using fingers, spoon, or other implement, and drinking from spoon, cup, or glass. The child is at first fed by the mother in the introduction of these new techniques, but eventually learns to feed himself in these ways. Another important factor in the process of weaning is the introduction of semisolid or solid food in addition to the erstwhile exclusively liquid diet. New flavors, other than the meager range offered by milk and water (plus, in some instances, orange or other fruit juice, or possibly cod liver oil in some form), are also introduced upon weaning. Perhaps as important as these new factors in oral experience is the new relative remoteness from the mother's body while feeding. While in some cases a mother offers the spoon or the cup while holding the infant on her lap, this is more apt to occur when weaning is begun early in the infant's life and in no case is it kept up long as it is a great deal less convenient for the mother than the use of the high chair.

Two elements of the original nursing situation are absent from the experience of feeding, once weaning is completed. These are the elements of sucking and of being held close to the mother's body. Sucking is obviously a different form of oral activity from that involved in eating and drinking. Sucking involves sensations created by the intense pressure of lips, tongue, and inner surfaces of the cheeks upon the object sucked; the object, if it is relatively solid, produces reciprocal and equal pressure upon these parts of the mouth and (depending on the nature of the object) also exudes substance which may be swallowed. Eating and drinking, on the other hand, involve having substance placed in the mouth (if one is being fed) or conveying substance to the mouth by means of one's hand, whether or not the substance is in some receptacle, or bringing the lips to the substance and mouthing it or some part of it (if one is feeding oneself). Once the substance is in the mouth, if it is liquid, it may be swallowed at once, or if it is solid or semisolid, it may first have to be reduced to a form capable of being swallowed (by disintegration through pressure or, once teeth are present, by chewing, and by admixture with saliva). All of these operations produce characteristic oral sensations, but these are quite different from those involved in sucking and, to the adult, at least, are considerably less intense.

In the adult, intensity of oral sensations in the activity of eating is apt to result more from the *taste* of the substance than from the oral activity involved. The matter of new tastes is doubtless a factor in the child's oral experience after weaning, but it is difficult to make any general statement on this subject. If the new substance is readily swallowed, it may be assumed that the new taste is acceptable to the infant; if, however, he spits out the new substance, it is not easy to determine whether he does this because the new taste is unacceptable to him, or whether he objects to the *form* of the substance (solid or semisolid) or to its *texture,* or whether he is merely satiated. One may conjecture that certain tastes are inherently pleasant and that, as a corollary, other tastes are inherently unpleasant, while still others are more or less neutral. Sweet substances are generally acceptable upon first offering (the composition of mother's milk is such that its taste is sweeter than that of cow's milk, but the sweetness of candy or of ice cream is obviously much more intense than that of milk). In addition, one may suppose that the less traumatic the infant's oral experience has in general been up to this point, the less suspect a new substance and its taste will be to him. In later life, the tendency to refuse to experiment orally with new tastes and substances as well as the tendency avidly to seek such new experiences seems to relate to early trauma in this experiential area.

Trauma in the matter of weaning relates to the three factors mentioned above. If the transition is made too rapidly and too completely at a too early stage of the infant's life, the effect is traumatic and will give rise to alterations in the ego which may be termed pathologic. The ideal weaning—ideal from the infant's point of view, if not from that of the mother's comfort and convenience—is accomplished slowly and gradually and is not completed until a relatively late period.

"Relatively late" and "relatively early" cannot be defined with precision. The "early" date of complete weaning is limited by the infant's progress in muscular coordination which applies to oral musculature as well as to other structures, such as those involved in feeding himself. No date is physiologically too early for the shift from breast to bottle, but this shift may be traumatic in its effect if the experience of being held close to the mother's body is too often withheld from him at the same time. It is almost certain to be traumatic if, when this shift is made, all contact with the mother's body is withheld, not only at feeding time but on other occasions as well. Such a situation would argue lack of tenderness, if not actual hostility, of the mother toward her offspring, and it would be anticipated that this would also take other forms. A relatively too early date for complete weaning may be tentatively set at six months. At this age the infant is ordinarily capable of handling solid and semisolid foods, but is not yet ready to be systematically deprived of sucking activity and of all contact with the mother's body.

The relatively late date of complete weaning is limited physiologically only by the lactating function of the mother, which, in the absence of supervening pregnancy, *may* continue for two or three years, more or less. J. Clark Moloney [53] in his remarkably instructive films of life among the Okinawans has shown that these mothers take it as a matter of course to breast-feed their children up to the age of two or three; in other words, as long as their lactation continues. It is to be supposed that during this period these children are also being fed by the ordinary postweaning modes of eating and drinking, but that the mothers do not regard this as a reason for withholding from their children the nursing situation in its composite entirety. Such a procedure would probably be regarded in our culture as scandalous and immoral, but Moloney's films indicate that Okinawan children do not in later life suffer neurotically from such maternal indulgence in their infancy and early childhood.

A relatively late date for complete weaning could be set tentatively at eighteen months, since the impression exists that our infants are taken off breast or bottle, as the principal mode of feeding, at about nine months and are generally being fed or beginning to feed themselves, more or less, in a high chair, without supplementary bottle-feedings, by the age of one year.

Weaning is less apt to produce traumatic experience for the child if the various changes and deprivations involved in it, particularly the deprivations, are begun late and are not insisted upon too rigorously by the mother. It is in the matter of excessively rigorous maternal insistence that the factors of *too rapid weaning* and *too early complete weaning* become operative. In the case of many mothers the task of weaning their offspring offers a challenge to the effectiveness of their own aggression and to their self-esteem in terms of the authority they exert and their efficiency as acculturators. Such a mother must be somewhat lacking in tenderness toward her child, since she seems willing to sacrifice tenderness at the altar of her own self-esteem. She fears the untamedness of the child as the possible means of demonstrating her own weakness as an authority and as a disciplinarian, and, in her anxiety for her self-esteem, regards the child as an enemy to be conquered by stern, unrelenting opposition. She would like to feel "No child is going to get the better of me," or "When I say jump, this child is going to jump," and she behaves accordingly. Such inner motivations and similar types may often be kept out of the mother's vivid awareness by the support sometimes given to such stringent attitudes by lectures and publications on child-rearing which emphasize strict regularity of feeding schedules and a ritualistic punctuality in introducing the various changes from exclusive breast- or bottle-feeding to eating and drinking in the adult manner. In supervising these changes, much greater elasticity is called for than is implied by such counsel, but instruction of this kind cannot be shouldered with a major share of responsibility. If the mother did not have inner, usually conflictful, motivations in this direction, she would use her own judgment, contrary as it might be to such advice.

Trauma here signifies an event or a situation (most usually the latter) which produces disturbance of somatic or psychic homeostasis, or both, such that the fear, humiliation, or anxiety that is generated requires the adoption of adaptative devices by the ego.

The differentiation of the primitive unit of self (id-ego) into id and ego, termed by Freud a fundamental defect in the human psyche, occurs as a result of such traumatic experience (frustration) in infancy. Precisely when in the life of the infant it occurs or when it becomes more than an *ad hoc* device— when it achieves the character of permanence—is matter for conjecture. We can be certain, however, that it does not occur first as a structural change and at a later date becomes functionally operative: it comes into being already functioning and it begins to operate in the process and at the moment of its emergence.

The precise date at which manifestations of rage, which, as we have seen, are not originally ego-devices, are added to or substituted for by genuine ego-devices cannot be stated. It may be assumed, however, that this change in adaptation occurs at a stage at which rage no longer "works," and at which frustration and disturbed homeostasis are no longer obviated or greatly mitigated by rage.

RESPONSES TO TRAUMATIC ORAL EXPERIENCE

The ego-device first observed as a reaction to oral trauma is that of finding a substitutive gratification, but one cannot be certain that this is in actuality the ego's earliest attempt at adaptation. The device of finding a substitute would seem to require no autoplastic operation, and it may, in general, be supposed that the earliest ego-devices would be alloplastic in character. I assume here that, granting an awareness of distinctions between self and other, where there is a sense of disturbance the primary tendency will be to look for the source of disturbance in the other rather than in the self: other requires to be changed, not self. I find it difficult to imagine the infant either as able to isolate his own impulses in the manner necessary to treating them as responsible for his difficulties, or as inclined to take an attitude of *mea culpa* in his attempts to cope with them. For him, as it seems to me, it would always primarily be a matter of *tua* or *sua culpa*, and consequently the outer world (other) would require manipulation in some form.

It would be in accordance with these assumptions to conjecture that if there exists an ego-device earlier than that of finding a substitute, one which, though it does not observably manifest itself, nevertheless is in operation, it would be the one I have termed the schizoid maneuver. This I have described [68] as "the effort . . . to deal with helplessness by denial of the separate existence of the outside world, or, to put it more accurately, by affirmation of the all-inclusiveness of one's own psyche." The schizoid maneuver operates in the manner of hallucination, fantasy, or dream, and has the tendency to attempt the undoing of the transition already made from Burrow's phase of primary subjectiveness (the "oceanic feeling") to the sense of reality implied in distinctions between self and other. The ego attempts to annihilate the basis upon which it exists as an entity differentiated from the primitive unity of self. Perhaps the infantile ego has a sense that things were once better and makes the attempt, in schizoid manner, to restore that better state. Whether this involves regression, as defined in the previous chapter, is perhaps more a matter of semantics than of psychic reality. The reality here, as it seems to me, is that the psyche has at so early a stage in life not yet developed to the point where it can have the concern about its own impulses implied in any autoplastic operation. It must be acknowledged, however, that this is begging the question, and that, in making such a statement, one is perhaps betrayed by what Freud has referred to as "preferences," that is, by one's *Weltanschauung.* Since the fact here is that ego-devices emerging prior to substitute-finding, if any, are not empirically observable, the whole matter is of less than crucial importance: whether schizoid maneuvers, with or without regression, occur prior to or later than substitute-finding is of no great moment. Certainly they do occur at a later date and, whenever they occur, are important ego-devices.

It is in any case only by a species of retrospective reasoning (reconstruction) that we can demonstrate the likelihood that the ego has at an early stage utilized the schizoid maneuver as an important device.* Where this has been the case and where the device has been successful in restoring and maintaining homeostasis, the schizoid maneuver becomes, even at so early a stage of life, a characterologic feature which plays an important role in determining the type of reaction to the experiences of later

---

* The reader is referred, for an example of such reconstruction from clinical material, to my paper "The Schizoid Maneuver" [*66,* pp. 387 ff.].

areas (disciplinary, phallic) and indeed, in many cases, in determining attitudes and behavior throughout the whole of life.

The attempt to find a substitute as a reaction to trauma in the weaning process is clearly the most prevalent device of the infantile ego, if empirical observation is to be credited. The effort here takes the form of finding a substitute for one single element of the composite nursing situation, that of the pleasurable oral stimulation and activity involved in sucking. As a substitute for the flesh or rubber nipple, the infant's own thumb is most frequently used, but other substitutes quite commonly accepted are some other portion of his own body, a rag, a part of the pillow or other bedclothes, or a part of a rattle, doll, or other toy—in fact, any available object having the proper size, shape, and texture for mouthing and sucking. It was the wide prevalence of this substitutive sucking that impelled Freud to separate out oral pleasure and activity from the total nursing composite and to regard it as the sole libidinal factor of this stage of life. It is indeed the most the infant can do, by his own resources, in reproducing and restoring the nursing composite, since he is not capable of finding another object from which he can extract milk or other nourishment, nor can he by his own efforts achieve contact with another body. It is faulty reasoning, however, to suppose that, because the only part of the nursing composite he can restore by way of substitution is the element of oral pleasure and activity through sucking, this is all he wants. In so far as he is satisfied by the substitutive sucking, it is a partial satisfaction, as can readily be seen by the frequent persistence, in later childhood and in adult life, of intense yearning for the nursing situation with *all* its elements, as demonstrated clinically by innumerable dreams, transferences, and episodes of acting out.

Infantile masturbation should probably be included among the substitutive devices of the early oral period. While it obviously contains no element that resembles any of the various factors of the nursing composite, it appears to be a means whereby homeostasis can be wholly or partially restored. Its inception and discovery by the infant are accidental. Its method is rarely, if ever, manual, as the infant at the age of which we speak does not as yet possess the muscular coordination required for finding the penis or vaginal cleft manually, much less for manipulating it. The method of masturbation at this period has already been described (page 42). We may suppose that something resembling postpubertal orgasm is achieved in this manner, since the act often leads to quiescence and sleep. For this reason we conjecture that infantile masturbation is instrumental in restoring disturbed homeostasis. Infantile masturbation becomes a *general* method for accomplishing this homeostatic purpose, and only by association and conditioning does it become integrated into the adaptations relating specifically to trauma in the oral area of experience.

In later life, masturbatory activity, now in manual or other forms, may become an invariable sequel to oral frustration and its equivalents. In the infant, psychic attitudes accompanying masturbation may vary greatly, from guilt and self-contempt to triumphant satisfaction, depending in part on the maternal response to infantile masturbation. Most mothers do not notice this behavior, or if they do, do not ascribe a masturbatory significance to it. Such mothers, naturally, do not interfere with the behavior. Other mothers, however, notice it, divine its significance, and adopt stringent measures to prevent it. Such attempts at interference with the infant's effective aggression toward relieving disturbed homeostasis are traumatic in effect and may produce rage or schizoid maneuvers currently, as well as a specific background for the child's later attitudes toward masturbation and genital activity in general.

Once weaning has occurred, the composite nursing situation in the most fortunate cases becomes fractionated in such a manner that its various elements are re-experienced on separate occasions, though never again as a totality; the child receives nourishment, not by sucking, but by eating and drinking, as above described; he receives bodily contact when the mother's tenderness and affection move her to take him in her arms and hold him close, but this no longer occurs simultaneously with his feeding; at still other times he receives oral pleasure through sucking in situations of his own devising, but these opportunities for sucking are no longer provided *for* him by the mechanics of feeding.

This is the case, as I have said, in the fortunate instances. It often happens, however, that the weaned infant gets to be held by the mother little if at all; and it frequently occurs that his own substitutive devices for achieving oral pleasure are blocked and interfered with by the mother. We must take into account the wide range of possible experiences between the extremes of maternal indulgence and maternal deprivation. Most traumatic of all the possibilities would be the latter extreme, the case in which the mother never picks up and cuddles her child after weaning him and is so vigilant and alert in her measures to prevent his substitutive sucking that he rarely, if ever, succeeds in providing this satisfaction for himself. Least traumatic would be the former extreme, in which the mother frequently picks up the child, holds him close, and leaves him free and undisturbed in carrying out whatever substitutive modes of sucking he may be able to find, even perhaps providing him with a rag or other object to suck on. The reader's imagination will supply the vast number of possible variations between the two extremes. The closer any specific variation approaches to the extreme of indulgence, the less traumatic the postweaning situation will be; while the closer the specific instance approaches the extreme of deprivation, the more traumatic will be the experience of the postweaning period.

In the less traumatic situations it would seem that the child does not find it necessary to adopt ego-devices other than that of finding a substitute. The more closely, however, the specific situation approaches the extreme of deprivation, the greater the distress of the ego-in terms of ineffectiveness of its aggression and the greater will become its need to devise measures for promoting effectiveness of aggression, thus salvaging some degree of self-esteem, even if producing no increase or no great increase in gratification.

Here, certainly, the schizoid maneuver is apt to become important, whether or not it has been utilized earlier. It is not easy to say what factors make for success in performing this maneuver and what factors tend to make it less successful. Whether some infants are so constituted (by some manner of inheritance) as to be more readily able than others to derive a degree of satisfaction from make-believe and pretense cannot yet be determined. We see these differences in psychic make-up in older children and adults, but we would be inclined to explain them on the basis of the need to use schizoid maneuvers and the success or failure met with in using them at the precise stage of psychic development with which we are now dealing. It could be conjectured that the variations in degree of satisfaction produced within the nursing situation itself have some bearing here: if satisfaction was never very great, a schizoid maneuver in the weaning or postweaning period is likely to prove relatively satisfactory; whereas if the nursing situation itself has been intensely satisfying to the infant, he is less likely to take kindly to the pseudo-gratification produced by the fantasies and hallucinations of a schizoid maneuver. The better acquainted he is with the real thing, the less gratified he is likely to be with merely imagining it. Whatever the basis, there is no doubt that the schizoid maneuver "works" better for some children in some situations than it does for others in other situations. Where it works well, it will be used often; where it works less well, less frequent recourse will be had to it, though it remains in the psychic repertory, for occasional use.

A type of behavior sometimes seen during the weaning or early postweaning period might be mistaken for another ego device: reaction-formation. The child behaves in such a way as to seem to deny that he has impulses toward re-establishing the nursing situation; he gazes in the direction of the mother's breast only to shake his head and say, "No, no." Clinical material elsewhere described [66, p. 389] contains such an example: while weaning her infant daughter, the mother frequently exhibited her breast, which evoked from the child a pious "No, no," with

shaking of the head. In attempting to evaluate whether such behavior indicates that the child has adopted the ego-device of
reaction-formation, it is necessary to consider the specific circumstances likely to produce this apparent denial of a wish for
the breast. It seems clear that the child's reason for behaving
in this fashion is that she has sensed that such denial is desired
by the mother (who had gone to some pains to *teach* the child
to say "No, no") and, having tried the behavior, the child has
experienced maternal approval for it. Under these circumstances
it could scarcely be supposed that the child herself is convinced
that she no longer wants the breast.

True reaction-formation involves subjective conviction that
the denial of the particular impulse is a *genuine* denial, although
the less stable the reaction-formation in a given instance, the
more wavering and uncertain is this sense of conviction. In so
far as the child is merely going through the motions of denial,
in order to gain maternal approval, while still maintaining
awareness of the impulse apparently denied, we are not dealing
with genuine reaction-formation. A child engaging in such behavior is obviously already highly sensitive to maternal approval,
presumably having been made so by the mother's blow-hot–blow-
cold attitude, and this sensitivity presages later compromise with
impulses when maternal approval is at stake—compromise which
may then take the form of reaction-formation, as one possibility.
However, at the early stage with which we are now dealing, we
cannot, for the reasons given, speak of reaction-formation. We
may say, rather, that a disciplinary issue has been encountered
somewhat prematurely and has been dealt with by the ego-device
of seeming conformity—outward conformity, inner rebellion.
This device, to be discussed in greater detail later on, is not an
outcome of typical experience in the oral area, though it may
occasionally appear at this time and serves as an example of the
overlapping of experiential areas mentioned in the preceding
chapter.

A device sometimes encountered in the period of weaning
is oral rejection or expulsion. The child refuses food which is not

liquid and spits out any food that cannot be swallowed immediately because it requires preparation for swallowing by being broken down by oral pressures and by admixture of saliva. This refusal applies mainly to solid foods, though in some cases semisolid foods are likewise expelled. Where such behavior occurs, we cannot know the precise psychic attitude that initiates and accompanies it. This may be bafflement in that the child does not know what to do with solid food; it may be intransigency, an unwillingness to deal with new situations, an insistence upon the familiar exclusively; or it may be rage and resentment toward the mother who withholds the desired familiar and insists upon the unwelcome unfamiliar. In the last two cases, unduly traumatic experience in the previous life-history may be conjectured. This device of oral rejection, when it occurs, does not usually persist over a long period, though it is apt to recur from time to time. It is important, nevertheless, in the production of later reaction-formations and oral inhibitions, and will sometimes give form to later eating habits and preferences. Some adults prefer semisolid to solid foods and, when given a choice, will always select cream soups, moist hashes, puréed vegetables, and a variety of concoctions which do not require much chewing. The alcoholic, who often will not eat at all during his drinking bouts, might be a case in point.

In sum, the response to trauma in the earlier phases of the oral area of experience—nursing, preweaning, weaning, and early postweaning periods—appears to take three forms: (1) rage and its manifestations, which we consider to be in origin a biologic reflex of disturbed homeostasis; (2) finding a substitute; (3) the schizoid maneuver. Both the last two are regarded as devices of the ego and both are essentially alloplastic. The possibility of regression and reaction-formation as ego-devices of this early period has been considered and in both cases rejected. Repression as a possible ego-device may likewise be rejected for reasons identical with those adduced for rejecting reaction-formation: so long as an impulse remains conscious, it cannot be said that it is repressed, regardless of behavior. *Suppression* (inhibition) sometimes occurs, as in the "No, no" behavior described, but is not typical of this early period and indicates a premature confrontation with disciplinary issues.

THE SEE-TOUCH-SWALLOW SEQUENCE

Before proceeding with the discussion of ego-devices encountered as responses to trauma in the later stages of the area of oral experience, it is necessary to describe a phenomenon first observed in the oral period and of prime importance in later life. This is a behavior pattern which is not seen in its complete form until muscular coordination has developed to the point where locomotion of some sort is possible. It comes into the category of substitute-finding and consists of three or four steps in regular sequence. It is perhaps the most common and ubiquitous behavior observed at the creeping stage.* The child in his creeping about the floor perceives some object such as a piece of paper, a coin, a pin, a crumb of bread, or a piece of string. He creeps toward it, picks it up in his hand, puts it in his mouth and swallows it. This is the complete pattern, and I have called it the see-touch-swallow sequence. In this phrase the mouthing and the swallowing are included in the one word *swallow* (as a less cumbersome alternative), but it should be understood that they are quite separate acts. The seeing, the touching, and the mouthing are all physically necessary preliminaries to the end-act of swallowing—first, perception at a distance (seeing), then closer by (touching), then intimately (mouthing)—but each of these steps may also be regarded as a kind of testing-out of the feasibility and desirability of the act of swallowing with respect to the specific object.

The kind of oral experience made possible by the see-touch-swallow sequence is of a very different order from that which antedates the emergence of this behavior pattern. Prior to this, oral experience has been largely *passive*, so far as object-finding is concerned. The breast or bottle is brought to the child's mouth,

---

* This behavior was described in an earlier writing of the author [65, p. 115], but at that time its importance as a *pattern*, with weighty implications for later psychopathology, was not perceived.

and no necessity exists for the preliminary steps of seeing and touching. The mouthing, sucking, and swallowing have always been *active* experiences for the child, and the only variation in these acts in the later pattern appears in the mouthing (which has now a more marked testing quality as well as the novel quality of preparing the object for swallowing) and in the sucking (which may now be entirely absent). But these variations are produced by the nature of the object and the necessity of adaptation to it. The essential psychically significant change in the child's behavior lies in the fact that he now *initiates* the whole process that leads to swallowing and plays an active or aggressive role throughout. Seeing and touching are the necessary and indispensable preliminaries to an oral experience independent of the mother. This statement may be questioned when it is recalled that weaning and the consequent substitute-finding often, if not usually, antedate the emergence of locomotion. The child does not have either to see or to touch his thumb in order to find it and suck it. Perhaps the same applies to other substitutes, and all such activities do actually constitute independent oral experience.

The behavior pattern of independent, aggressive orality which I have termed the see-touch-swallow sequence has, then, its forerunner in these earlier experiences of thumb-sucking, in which the visual and tactile elements may well be lacking. Once locomotion is possible, however, a wide extension of this type of orality and an enormous increase in the number and kind of possible oral objects ensue, and the addition of visual and tactile sensory factors to the pattern is correlative with this broader range of possibilities.

The sequence is seen with utmost regularity and is the typical behavior of the creeping child, as all mothers can testify. In this stage of life, and often unconsciously in later stages, including adult life, the sequence is intimately associated with all active wishes and deeds of an oral nature, and is an association of enormous importance in determining the particular configuration of many neurotic symptoms and other pathologic manifes-

tations. In terms of this sequence, seeing is the gateway toward
oral gratification. Conflict about the gratification may produce
conflict over one or another step in the sequence.

The standard psychoanalytic interpretation of the self-
inflicted punishment of Oedipus (he blinds himself) is that it
represents a self-castration, the eyeballs being regarded as equivalent to the testes. This has never seemed to me a satisfactory
explanation: castration, in psychoanalytic terms elsewhere, practically always means destruction of the penis rather than the
testes (though the latter would correspond to the more usual
definition of the word, apart from psychoanalytic terminology).
The interpretation emphasizes the *act* of self-blinding rather
than its *consequences*; the fact that Sophocles considered the latter of prime importance is indicated by his *Oedipus at Colonos*,
much of the action of which is predicated upon the blindness of
Oedipus (his helplessness) and upon his self-inflicted exile from
Thebes. Oedipus' act of self-blinding when considered from the
standpoint of the see-touch-swallow sequence leads to a much
more convincing and satisfying interpretation: his conscious
abhorrence of his incestuous behavior with Jocasta, about which
he has now learned for the first time, is expressed by his rendering impossible, by an act of violence, the active quest for pleasure
through the mother's body. The quest for this pleasure, which he
unconsciously locates in its most primitive, oral terms, is thus
declared by him to have been responsible for his incestuous behavior. By cutting off the gateway to orality, he renders non-
functioning his see-touch-swallow sequence at its point of origin,
thus both punishing himself and making certain that he can
never again be actuated by visual perception toward a guilty act
of concupiscence.

Clinical material will sometimes be illuminated by interpretations along similar lines. For example, a male patient in the
middle thirties, during a period of dealing with a strong oral
drive toward his mother, brought the following dream:

"I was seated at a table in a restaurant with my mother
and an older man. He was upbraiding me for something [not

remembered], and I was listening quietly without protest. While scolding me, he gesticulated toward my face and touched my eye. At that I became infuriated, got up from the table, and said, 'You can say what you like, but keep your hands off me!' Mother said approvingly, 'Attaboy, Pete.' And I awoke."

The tirade by the older man, obviously a father-figure, and the patient's reaction to it, are reminiscent of Little Hans's fantasy [24, pp. 179 ff.] of the two giraffes, one of which "called out" at him because he was sitting on (taking possession of) the other. For all the "calling out," Hans continued to sit. But when the father in my patient's dream threatens his eyesight (the gateway to aggressive orality toward the mother), the dreamer reacts sharply and makes the mother, with her "Attaboy, Pete," give support to his oral drive toward her and his means of carrying it out. The restaurant setting gives the clue to the fact that oral issues are concerned.

Inhibitions of the function of seeing, whether in general or in respect to particular objects or situations ("blind spots," some actual scotomata), as well as inhibitions of touching, may derive from their relation to oral pleasure in terms of the see-touch-swallow sequence. Various oral inhibitions may also result from the ego's interference with the completion of the sequence, supposing the first two steps to be permitted complete or partial expression. Where conflict over aggressive orality exists, the ego may block the carrying through of the sequence at any point in this chain of acts, so that the sequence may be clinically observed in a variety of abortive and truncated forms. Much compulsive behavior in adults can be shown to derive from the ego's necessity to take precautionary measures against the tendency to perform the total sequence. Hand-washing compulsions and rituals, for example, may result from the individual's need to interrupt the sequence at the point of linkage at which touching would lead to mouthing and swallowing.

It is understood that seeing and touching, once the predominantly oral area of experience is past, often lead to acts quite other than oral ones. A mechanic repairing a motor, for example, needs to see and to touch in order to diagnose the trouble and to amend it. I do not mean to say that all seeing-touching has invariably an oral goal in mind. In later childhood and in adult life the same sequence of see-touch may often be the preliminary to genital rather than oral behavior, though I shall attempt in a later chapter to show the close relationship between the two and how the former is modeled upon the latter. Here I shall merely mention the almost ubiquitous fact, in our culture, that a man is genitally attracted to a woman by the sight of her breasts (or what may appear to be her breasts) and that "necking" preparatory to genital intercourse commonly involves his touching her breasts; furthermore, many men arrive at judgments of the genital desirability of a woman by noting the shape and size of her breasts, and they may make sharp differentiations on this basis.

However this may be, it should be recognized that in the late childhood area of oral experience, seeing and touching typically lead to goals of oral gratification and are the invariable preliminary acts to such gratification achieved at the child's own initiative. In other words, the see-touch-swallow sequence is the pattern of effective aggression *par excellence,* once locomotion is possible. As has been said, the sequence is a form and means of substitute-finding and is thus to be considered an ego-device, obviously a device of achievement rather than defense. In itself it does not lead to later pathologic outcomes, as other ego-devices, such as the schizoid maneuver, may. It is the later inhibition and interruption of the sequence at some point in the chain that produces psychopathologic effects.

INHIBITION OF THE SEQUENCE

In the genesis of inhibitions of the sequence, an important factor—one that often results in truncations and abortive forms of the sequence—is the introduction, at this stage of beginning acculturation, of disciplinary issues in connection with the child's endeavors to perform the sequence. Here again, the problem of the child's choice between effectiveness of aggression toward impulse-gratification and effectiveness of the effort (also a form of aggression, as I use the word) to maintain maternal approval is provocative of inner conflict, and the choice is often a portentous one. This topic will be more fully discussed in the following chapter; suffice it here to indicate the manner in which uncertainty may arise in the child's mind about the wisdom and safety of performing his see-touch-swallow sequence unmodified, resulting often in attempts to modify it by suppressing and inhibiting one or more of its elements.

In considering the variety of configurations that can be produced in this way, it is necessary to take into account the specific circumstances with which the child is confronted. It must be of rare occurrence that a child is never interfered with by the mother in any of his attempts to perform the sequence. Realistic considerations of the child's health and safety obviously preclude the possibility of complete noninterference by the mother, quite apart from possible tendencies of the mother merely to assert authority, and it would be a negligent mother indeed who did not in many instances try to prevent the child's see-touch-swallow behavior. The circumstances evoking the mother's preventive efforts, the frequency and consistency of the latter (related to her vigilance and alertness), as well as the manner of her efforts, will play a large role in determining the specific details of the child's modification of his sequence. In the case of the more lenient and less threatening and punitive mother, the modification is more apt to occur at a late point in the sequence: while the child does not hesitate to look at and touch an orally desired object, he now usually refrains from putting it in his mouth. Here three variations, at least, are possible: (1) he may, overcoming his initial resentment at frustration (because the mother clearly loves him otherwise), refrain with good humor and relative contentment and cooperativeness; (2) he may, while maintaining a degree of resentment, conform, though remaining aware of his wish; (3) he may, through fear of consequences, repress resentment and wish, and produce his first genuine reaction-formation or his first pathologic inhibition.

It will be noted that a distinction is here implied between

healthy and pathologic inhibition of an impulse. An inhibition may be regarded as compatible with psychic health under the following circumstances: if it is consciously carried out, for a conscious purpose, *and* if it does not too greatly impair effectiveness of aggression and too greatly reduce self-esteem. Where an inhibition involves a thoroughgoing disavowal of an impulse (repression) *or* if it too greatly impairs or reduces effective aggression and self-esteem, it may be regarded as pathologic, whether in terms of itself or of its results.

It will likewise be noted that I imply that repression is indispensable to reaction-formation. It is sometimes questioned whether Freud, in introducing the latter concept, regarded repression as a necessary factor in its production. His original idea about reaction-formation, at an early stage of his work [*33*, pp. 40 ff.], was simply that psychic forces (shame, disgust, moral feelings) coexisted with the impulse, and, gaining the upper hand, crowded out the impulse and became operative in its stead. This might or might not have implied that the impulse had succumbed to repression. As I attempted to establish in the foregoing discussion of the "No, no" behavior, if the impulse remains in awareness, behavior of denial lacks the force of genuine reaction-formation. To me, reaction-formation always implies that the impulse is effectively denied, is no longer in awareness, and its opposite is felt as desired. Clearly, this involves repression of the original impulse.

If reaction-formation is undertaken by the child, what is the negative impulse which must exist in its own right before the ego can have recourse to this device? It must be an impulse of refusal to eat at the mother's wish and bidding which here becomes operative; the existence of such an impulse implies that the child has experienced the mother's chagrin and disturbance when, on a previous occasion, and without rancor or vengefulness, he chanced to fail to eat when expected to. He now utilizes the not-eating impulse (now imbued with spite) to support his reaction-formation, and his repressed resentment can thus be deviously expressed in the very act that denies he has anything to be resentful for.

It may not be easy or even possible to detect which of the three possible modes of modification of the mouthing element of the sequence is being utilized in a given instance, since outwardly it may merely be noted that the child is less inclined than formerly to put random objects in his mouth. However, hints may be offered whereby a diagnosis can be tentatively made. If self-restraint is inconsistent, if he cannot be fully relied upon not to put "illegal" objects in his mouth, this favors the likelihood of his having chosen the second type of modification (outward conformity, inward rebellion), since the rule remains mother's rule and does not have genuine acquiescence from him. Those cases in which self-restraint is more highly consistent might indicate either the first or the third type of modification. Here observation of the child's general mood and temperament, whether of contentment and cheer or of disturbance and sullenness, might offer a means of differential diagnosis.

The three types of modification of the mouthing phase of the sequence present, however, significant differences in terms of later life-history and psychic health. The first two indicate safe passage, so to speak, through this area of experience, the first, perhaps, being of better omen than the second, though the second is doubtless the more common in our culture. The third indicates trouble now and more trouble ahead and allows one to suppose that trauma has occurred in the experiences of the oral era.

Greater trauma—hence greater trouble and poorer prognosis—may be inferred from the appearance of self-restraint in the touching or the seeing phases of the sequence at this stage of life, which begins with locomotion and proceeds through the ensuing year or year and a half. Its limits may be roughly defined as between the ages of one year and two years or two and one-half. Obviously, as has already been apparent, there is apt to be considerable overlapping of the late postweaning area and the disciplinary area, depending upon the child's age when the mother commences her acculturative endeavors.

The three kinds of modification applicable to the act of mouthing are of no significance when applied to the seeing and touching phases, since the nearer to its commencement the sequence is interfered with, the more pathologic is its modification. If we regard one of the modifications of mouthing as pathologic, then a fortiori we must regard any modification of impulses to see and to touch as pathologic. Indeed, we may assume that the trauma which produces the latter results is more severe than that which produces the former result.

With respect to what we may regard as the original impulse—the impulse toward a total nursing situation—we have already implied a variety of vicissitudes. First, I assume that this impulse, however modified, is never abolished and is always, theoretically at least, capable of psychic emergence either in its original conscious terms or in terms more devious. Second, it may become fractionated into the three component parts of the nursing impulse—feeding, sucking, being held close—gratification for which is separately sought. ("Being held close" may be further fractionated into impulses toward pressure sensations, temperature sensations, and olfactory sensations, gratification for any of which may likewise be quested for separately.) Third, gratification of the sucking impulse is likely to be achieved in a substitutive manner, if the infant's efforts in this direction are aided by the mother, are not observed or are not vigilantly observed by her, or, at the least, are not successfully blocked by her. Fourth, failure or infrequent success in such efforts toward gratification has a traumatic effect which is responded to by efforts toward schizoid maneuvers, the effectiveness of which is likely to be determining for later psychopathology. Fifth, the inception of locomotion permits a wide extension of substitute-finding and a decided acceleration (via the see-touch-swallow sequence) in the independent, aggressive quest for oral gratification. Sixth, vigorous interference with the see-touch-swallow behavior may produce the need for the autoplastic ego-devices of repression of the impulse and reaction-formation against it. Seventh, I assume with Freud that the more nearly the original nursing impulse (and/or its components) is permitted, through relative absence of trauma, to remain conscious—that is, the less the impulse needs to be disowned or repressed—and to receive, at least, in the case of the components, a degree of gratification, the less likely is the child to be driven toward seeking indirect, devious (pathologic) modes of gratification. The greater the amount (frequency, intensity) of gratification of the components, or one of them, and the greater the child's freedom independently to achieve this, the less likely is it that in the late oral phase the impulse toward the total nursing situation (involving the mother as a specific person) will emerge sufficiently to influence states of mind and behavior.

SPECULATION IN THE LATE ORAL PHASE

Excessive failure in the performance of the see-touch-swallow sequence appears to generate not only such responses as those already referred to (modifications of the sequence with autoplastic alterations of the ego), but also responses of a different sort. Judging by the reconstructions made from transferences and dreams of adults, the child in this situation engages in a good deal of speculation, partly concerning the reasons for his failure to re-establish the nursing situation, toward which he now has a revivified impulse, and partly concerning ways and means of re-establishing the situation, either in its original terms or in terms closely resembling it. Such speculation as a rule has great variety and richness of content, which varies from hour to hour, day to day, week to week. I am assuming here that the quality of the child's speculation does not differ much from that of the adult preoccupied over a long period with a difficult and complex problem, highly significant to him, for which he is unable to find a really satisfactory solution. He mulls it over, not continuously, but frequently, from time to time, considering it from a variety of angles. His speculation does not proceed in a vacuum, but is often spurred on and altered in subject matter and direction by perceptions coming from the significant and relevant environment, which may seem to confirm, to deny, or to give new meaning to what he has already thought. In the course of such speculation, conviction about this or that may be arrived at, often more or less tentatively, so that some "explanations" of the problematic situation become predominant; or because they appear more feasible (having some likelihood of realization) or more desirable, certain of the "solutions" imaginatively conceived and hoped for may come to have greater appeal than others. The explanations which thus become preeminent are often found, in later life, to constitute the basis for deep-seated unconscious convictions which are guarded by every means resistance can devise from confrontation with reality, and, even when eventually seen in the light of day, are stubbornly maintained as being reality itself. Such convictions frequently lie at the root of mental ailments of every variety. The solutions, memory of which also has the tendency to take deep cover, often influence and determine the configuration shown in later life by numerous of the neurotic behavior patterns. These explanations and solutions must be regarded as ego-devices, since they regularly perform the function of defense against lowered self-esteem or of promoting (at least in terms of hope) effectiveness of aggression.

Speculation having such outcomes may occur at any period of life. It need not occur in the late phase of oral experience unless the appropriate circumstances (namely, trauma resulting from too great failure in the effectiveness of the see-touch-swallow sequence) exist for evoking it. But if the oral experiential area is traversed without the necessity for such speculation, the necessity may nevertheless arise in one of the later areas and with similar results.

Some persons may doubt that a child in the second or third year of life engages in this kind of speculation, and, while granting that older children and certainly adults do speculate in this manner, will not credit the one year old or two year old with such capacities. I find this early speculation far from unbelievable myself, although I can adduce no direct evidence in support of it; certainly I have never heard a two year old speculating aloud in this manner. Memories of adults along these lines, when encountered, are fragmentary and are in any case subject to all the doubts which Freud [30] propounded about the factual authenticity of childhood memories in general. My belief here is based upon the indirect evidence of reconstructions from analytic material and the evidence presented by the therapeutic effect of digging out, after the overcoming of resistance, such long-buried convictions as those above referred to, to which reconstructions give the clue. Personal difficulties, hitherto insurmountable, are sometimes easily and quickly solved as a result of this procedure. The details and subject matter of such previously unconscious convictions will often preclude the possibility that the psychic activity (speculation) that led to them could have occurred at any other than the late oral phase. The line of reasoning which justifies the making of reconstructions from transferences, dreams, and other clinical material is too familiar to require repetition here.* As in paleontologic and archeologic endeavors, reconstructions may be accurate or not, depending on numerous factors. In psychoanalytic work, supposing the reconstructions to be reasonably well and accurately made, the least that can be claimed for them is that they represent an *as if* situation: the patient behaves *as if* such and such had been true at a previous stage of his life. The reader who doubts the likelihood of involved and prolonged speculation on any subject in a child of one or two years will have to be content with my statement that study of the adult mind often indicates that such speculation was engaged in at so early an age.

TYPES OF "EXPLANATIONS" AND "SOLUTIONS"

The details of these late oral speculations, the explanations and the solutions they more or less tentatively produce, the child's line of reasoning in arriving at them, and the considerations which prompt him to adopt them as peculiarly his own are not easy to convey in an orderly and easily comprehensible fashion. The facts which underlie my conclusions have been discovered piecemeal and from a variety of patients, and I do not wish to utilize the often deceptive and misleading device of pre-

* The skeptical reader is referred to Freud's celebrated *saxa loquuntur* passage [18, p. 185] and to his statement [21, p. 370] on the equivalence of transference and memory.

senting a composite picture. The matter now to be discussed will
therefore be somewhat chaotic and not easy to grasp.

The child does not speculate in an orderly manner; he does
not first speculate on the reasons for his difficulties, the explanations, and then, having settled that question, go on to possible
solutions. The speculations exist all as a hodgepodge (perhaps
on the order of Molly Bloom's unpunctuated soliloquy in the
final chapter of *Ulysses*). There are explanations, often mutually
contradictory; objections to the explanations; items of confirmation; solutions; their likelihood if this, their unlikelihood if that;
their advantages or their disadvantages, supposing them to be
possible of achievement—all are intermixed and interwoven in
a way impossible to convey, although the person so engaged seems
able to maintain a modicum of orientation in this labyrinth.

What the child is trying to "explain" to himself in his
speculative efforts is why the nursing situation, which he would
like to re-establish or to have re-established, does not get re-
established. His underlying aim is not idle or even "scientific"
curiosity, but rather, by finding out the cause of his frustration,
to be in a more advantageous position to remedy it, to find a
solution. It cannot be stated in a general way what explanation
the child first hits upon or even where he first seeks it, since this
varies widely from one child to another.

Some of the more common explanations arrived at by the
child are the following:

(1) The mother is "stingy"; she is mean and cruel and
wants to withhold from him the privilege of nursing, because
she derives a certain satisfaction from his state of unsatisfied
longing; or she does not want to give up to him her own precious
substance (the milk).

(2) She prefers to grant this privilege and give this substance to someone else whom she loves better and thus favors over
the child himself. This explanation has numerous variants and
is frequently used by children who are confronted with younger
siblings at the breast during this period of speculation. The recipient of the mother's favor may be seen as a younger sibling

or an older one; it may be "discovered" to be the father; or it may be some other member of the household. (In one case known to me, the recipient was believed to be the patient's maternal grandmother, who was living in the household.) The child may regard her favoritism as voluntary; or he may believe that she is coerced by the recipient (particularly if the recipient is the father), or that she is somehow cajoled or hoodwinked by the recipient; or he may believe that she in some way profits more by granting her favors to the recipient than she would by granting them to the child himself. In the last-mentioned case, the child sometimes invents the "fact" of a mutual nursing situation, in which the mother nurses the recipient in return for his nursing her, and vice versa. Where the explanation involves the idea of mutual nursing with a male, such as the father, further, probably prior, speculation is necessary as to the possible mechanics of this. It must be evident to the child that males have no visible breasts, and he would either have to "invent" invisible breasts for them (a circumstance I have never encountered) or assume that some part of the male body equates with breasts. This would be the penis, and speculation along these lines is as a rule closely bound up with one of the possible solutions, that in which the child hopes to re-establish a nursing situation by sucking on the father's penis. If the recipient in an alleged mutual nursing situation is a female sibling under the age of puberty, the probability is that a penis will be ascribed to her, since she is without perceptible breasts and since such speculation occurs prior to the awareness of the difference in the sexes. I speak of *probability,* because, as it happens, I have never encountered evidence of an explanation involving a mutual nursing of the mother and a female sibling, other than a younger female sibling, although in a few cases such a reconstruction has been required with respect to a male sibling.

(3) Closely related to both of the above explanations is the child's "discovery" that he himself is in some way inadequate and that this accounts for the failure to have the nursing situation re-established. If the mother withholds this boon from him, per-

haps it is because he is unable to force her to do so (by physical strength and skill) or to induce her by "goodness" of conduct or by personal attractiveness or by admiration of his intelligence or by having a *quid pro quo* to offer her. While it is conceivable that he might arrive at such explanations as absolute factors, in which case they would relate to the first class of explanations mentioned, it can be readily seen how they might complement and supplement the second class of explanations. In other words, they are likely to involve comparison with a hypothetic recipient (or a real one in the case of a younger sibling at the breast).

Where the father is seen as the recipient, whether in a unilateral situation (mother nurses father) or a mutual one, a situation is created which is in many ways identical with that described by Freud in connection with issues of genitality and termed by him the Oedipus complex; so much so that this situation perhaps merits the designation of *proto-Oedipus* complex or situation. While subjectively, in emotional terms, very similar to the later Oedipus situation, the critical difference between the two lies in the fact that the nursing situation imagined by the child as participated in by the parents is actually nonexistent (as he conceives it) ; but the parental genital relationship upon which the Oedipus situation is postulated does ordinarily exist. The latter relationship may be known to the Oedipal child, through his witnessing it (so-called *primal scene*), or, as in many cases, he divines it in connection with his awareness of a separate and private parental bedroom or of other features of household arrangements and parental behavior. The factors of parental privacy are as available for the observation of the child in the late oral phase as for the child in the Oedipal phase (three to five years). The only question that need arise is whether the younger child actually comes to conclusions about the parents and their behavior similar to those arrived at by the older child. Reconstructions of clinical material indicate that he may, though certainly not in every case. What I have called the proto-Oedipus situation, while not of universal occurrence in our culture, must nevertheless occur fairly frequently, if one may judge by the frequency with which it is encountered among those with psychic illness.

The proto-Oedipus situation, particularly in its unilateral form, does not necessarily involve the father. It may involve another sibling, older or younger, or any other inmate of the household. One may probably safely say that where the proto-Oedipus situation exists, it arises upon the basis of observation of some sort, since it is not likely to be invented out of whole cloth. This observation, such as it is, justifies the conclusion which, when reached, is likely to evoke all the emotions of bitterness and hostility known to be called forth by the later, full-blown Oedipus situation. The conclusion also produces efforts (which are similar to the responses seen in the later situation) to ameliorate the situation or to adapt to it. As the responses of the Oedipal phase will be dealt with in some detail in connection with the phallic area of experience, I shall not attempt to describe them here.

As to "solutions," it has already been indicated that they relate closely to specific "explanations." Conclusions about the mother's unwillingness, as pure selfishness and ill-will, to restore the nursing situation arouse intense hostility and potential violence. What the mother refuses to grant freely, she shall be forced to grant willy-nilly. I shall not attempt to determine how this solution relates to the kind of treatment the child has received at the mother's hands, or whether, supposing the child never to have been beaten or cowed by the mother, he might "invent" such plans and fantasies of violence. We must here consider that rage is a biologic reflex and therefore violence does not need to be "taught," even by example. Doubtless the mother's violence, where it has been experienced, serves to support the child's natural tendency toward using similar means when circumstances of frustration exist. She shall be physically hurt or intimidated until she submits.

Failing this forced capitulation—and of course it always fails, though some actual attempts and profuse speculation may persist over a long period—the solution thereupon arrived at is apt to be one involving fantasies about and plans for revenge.

Plans for revenge upon the mother may also have their appeal in
terms of the proto-Oedipal explanation and may take a form having profound significance for interpersonal relations in later life.
The revenge involves the feeling or belief that the mother is
responsible, through having at one time nursed the child, for
making him desire so avidly the nursing situation: first she gave
him the breast, "teaching" him to want it, then she took it away
from him, leaving him with intense, unsatisfied desire. He will
somehow do the same to her: somehow, some day, he will first
make himself in some manner indispensable to her, and then he
will reject her, as she has rejected and still rejects him. This will
teach her never again to reject him, since she will now have
learned that she cannot do so with impunity. It is a species of
intimidation in its intent and betrays thereby its intimate relation to the solutions of violence and intimidation already described. In later life, both men and women for whom this
solution has a strong appeal at this early phase, carry out in their
love-life such a pattern again and again. Men unconsciously
motivated by this solution are frequently known as Don Juan
types, but the pattern is seen among women as well.

Other solutions, arrived at in connection with the rivalry
explanation, involve plans to oust the rival by subduing or
intimidating or by outdoing him in whatever field his critical
superiority may be located. In the reactions to and tentative
solutions of the rivalry situation, the object of the child's hostile
feelings is variable, depending upon specific details of the manner
in which the explanation was reached. The object of hostility
may be the mother, the supposed rival, or both, to similar or dis-
similar degree. This variability exists whether the proto-Oedipus
situation takes a unilateral or mutual form. In the course of those
speculations which concern such a situation, the form taken by it
in the child's mind need not be consistently unilateral or mutual.
While one form may be ultimately so greatly preferred to the
other that the latter becomes virtually excluded, there may be
vacillation before this stage is reached. Reconstructions indicate,
however, that there are cases in which the child arrived at no

definitive conclusion, and both types of explanation were tentatively maintained throughout the period.

With respect to the rival, the hostile feelings may involve thoughts, plans, and fantasies of open and more or less murderous aggression toward him, as a solution which seeks to eliminate him from the environment. Such solutions bear a resemblance (in terms of violence) to some of those mentioned above as related to the mother's unwillingness and directed against her.

A frequent solution here is that of reaction-formation. This might originate in the speculative fantasy, "It would be more comfortable and so much safer if, instead of hating him and wanting to hurt or kill him, I could love him, be friends with him, and even take care of him." The further process, whereby this tentative speculation becomes transformed into actual reaction-formation, involves repression (disowning) of the hostile feelings and possibly of the drive toward the total nursing situation with the mother, if not of all its fractionated elements, and involves support of the reaction-formation by an impulse equating with a not-hate, not-kill impulse, which exists in its own right.

The nature of the latter impulse may vary, depending upon whether the rival is conceived to be a sibling or the father. If the rival is a younger sibling, the not-kill impulse takes the form of an impulse to take care of him, somewhat as the mother does. This may correspond to a modified aggression toward the infant sibling, since doing things *for* another is often seen as doing things *to* him, and since taking care of him involves control and dominance over him. Those who have observed children playing with their dolls may have gained the impression, as I often have, that they were as domineering and controlling in their behavior toward the dolls as they were tender. In fact, it has often seemed to me that they could behave tenderly precisely *because* they could be as domineering toward the doll as they liked, without repercussions in terms of any protest, backtalk, or other opposition from the doll. It is even possible, in those instances where the oral drive toward the mother is weakly repressed or not repressed at all, that the child imagines that if *he* gives a maternal type of care to his infant sibling, the mother will lose some of her concern for and interest in the infant and will thus become more available for the child himself. In such cases the not-impulse gains support from the original impulse toward the mother. The not-impulse may also be supported by an impulse on the part of the child toward having a baby of his own, though such an impulse is not encountered, in my experience, nearly as frequently in this late oral stage as it is in the ensuing phases, particularly in the phallic one.

The most common of these impulses ancillary to reaction-formation is the first one mentioned in the preceding paragraph, and since this impulse is so intimately related to the repressed hostility, there is a strong tendency for the latter to escape from repression from time to time, thus rendering the reaction-formation quite unstable.

Where the rival is conceived to be the father, reaction-formation, if undertaken, gains support from impulses involved in the solution which envisages a restoration of the nursing situation with the father (via his penis) rather than with the mother.

It is to be understood that this substitute solution, like many of the other solutions, remains wholly within the realm of fantasy, though imbued with a variety of conative colorings, which, if they were verbalized, would take such forms as, "It would be nice if this happened," or "I hope this will happen," or "I shall try to make this happen." Doubtless it is of the rarest occurrence that a child takes actual steps toward the realization of this fantasy. I was for some time under the impression that this *never* occurred, but recently I encountered a patient who, at the age of three, actually had made such an attempt by touching his father's penis while in the same bed with him. The father's reaction was sharp and punitive, but this did not discourage the patient from making the same attempt upon other adult males at this period of his life. With some of them he was more successful and was often permitted to perform fellatio upon them. We have here an indication of what he would have done with the father, had he been allowed to. The age of the patient at the time makes it difficult to determine whether this is to be regarded as behavior within the oral or the phallic area of experience, but what I wish to point out here is that in one case, at least, the attempt was made to carry this solution beyond the realm of fantasy. Furthermore, such evidence tends to support the contention that such fantasies exist at so early an age and therefore tends to validate reconstructions along these lines made on the basis of clinical material much less direct than this.

The substitutive solution may originally arise in connection with the first of the different types of explanation enumerated above, that involving maternal unwillingness, in which case it is simply another instance of substitute-finding under the egis of the see-touch-swallow sequence. For this reason, the role here ascribed to the father may be taken over by an older male sibling or any other male inmate of the household. One might suppose that an essential condition to this solution is the actual sight of the father's (or other male's) penis. I am not certain that this is invariably the case, though doubtless ample opportunity for such experience during the second year of life exists in most households. Awareness that the father possesses a protruding bodily part which might hopefully be equated with the breast could come about in other ways: the child might perceive a bulge in the clothing in the father's genital region, just as he perceives it in the clothing over the mother's breasts; or he might first sense this tactilely while sitting on the father's lap and later look in this direction and perceive the bulge.

In any case, the fantasy of experiencing something closely resembling the nursing situation with the father rather than with the mother is of frequent occurrence, both in boys and girls. In the former, the fantasy may become the groundwork for future homosexuality, though additional factors, to be discussed in a later chapter, are necessary if a true or neurotic homosexuality is to emerge in later life. In girls, on the other hand, the fantasy is apt to form a basis for heterosexual drives in later life, giving these a distinctly oral coloring and background, also to be later discussed. But it should be recalled that in this late phase of oral experience the child is not ordinarily aware of a difference in the sexes, even where a basis exists for such an awareness; as in the case of the girl with oral impulses toward the father, no great significance is ordinarily ascribed to the difference. The girl here is questing for an oral object similar to the breast and this, rather than any dissimilarity to her own body, is the significance of her discovery, if she makes it at this time, that the father has a penis.

The hopeful substitutive fantasy or solution may emerge in the child's speculations before it has occurred to him that he might have a rival for the mother's nursing favors. No resentment or hostility is felt toward the new oral object, and the greater the child's hope of gratification along these lines, the more his resentment of the mother's "refusal" (and his consequent hostility toward her) is likely to diminish. But nonfulfillment of his new fantasy soon leads him back to his original oral drive toward the mother, with a renewal of resentment toward her and now some hostility toward the disappointing father. It may be in such circumstances that he first evolves his explanation of a nursing situation existing between the parents. If the explanation emerges in this manner, it is likely to take the mutual rather than unilateral form, since it takes coloring from his own oral impulses toward *both* parents.

However, it may happen that the solution of restoring the nursing situation via the father does not occur to the child until he has already conceived of the rivalry explanation. In such cases the solution, at least in the early phases of his speculation about it, may appear to obviate some of the disadvantageous features of rivalry, if the rival is a sibling. It then amounts to withdrawal from the field of combat with all of its many uncertainties and perils, and to entrance into a new field which offers a gratification just or almost as good (in anticipation, at least) and has (as conceived) in the triangular situation involving child, mother, and rival none of the following dangers: (1) the child's hostility toward the mother and toward the rival and the consequences of these, mainly the result of the mother's postulated reactive hostility; (2) the prolonged libidinal frustration and the loss of self-esteem ensuing from the failure to surmount these obstacles to gratification. All these factors may lead to the adoption of reaction-formation or may induce the child to adopt the solution of abandoning the mother to his sibling rival and seeking gratification through the father.

If the solution of oral gratification via the father occurs after the father has been "discovered" as the rival, the basis is set up for a true or neurotic homosexuality in later life. But as I have encountered no such situations in the late oral phase, I will leave for later discussion the factors that might be operative here, if such situations do exist. Of frequent occurrence, however, is the situation in which oral impulses toward the father arise as mere substitute-finding, and rivalry does not enter the picture until there has been some amount of vacillation between the mother and the father as potential oral objects. With the tentative decision, in the course of speculation, that mother after all offers the better possibility of oral gratification, the father is abandoned as an oral object, not without some resentment over the frustration implied. This resentful coloring of feeling toward the father may lead to the idea that the father has been a disappointment because he has his own axe to grind: perhaps he wants—and gets—the same thing from the mother as the child wants. However it may happen, as soon as the father is established in the child's speculations as a rival, hostility toward him becomes greatly increased. The child has now to be concerned over all the dangers mentioned above in connection with sibling rivalry, as well as an additional one.

In the triangular situation involving an infant sibling, nothing has to be feared from the sibling himself: the child wants to eliminate the rival and anticipates that retaliatory behavior will come not from the infant but from the mother thus deprived of her favorite. Where the father is the rival, it can be anticipated that attempts at eliminating him will not only incur the mother's displeasure but will also evoke sharp retaliatory behavior from the father himself. It is here that reaction-formation, if undertaken against hostile impulses toward the father, gains its support from the previously strong oral impulse toward him. *To not-kill* him becomes equated with *to love* him or to seek

gratification from him. At this point, however, his reaction-formation need not be accompanied by a conscious recrudescence
of his oral drive toward the father. His subjective feeling is much
more likely to take the form of friendliness toward him, pleasure
in talk and play with him, feelings of gladness when he returns
home from work, and the like. The reactionary nature of these
feelings may be betrayed by indications of concern for the father's
safety when he is away and frequent questions about when Daddy
is coming home, to which he is impelled by the now unconscious
hostile wishes underlying the reaction-formation combined with
the reaction-formation itself. All this, while it may occur in the
late oral phase, is nevertheless much more typical of the true
Oedipus situation of the phallic phase of experience.

What love means to a child (or to an adult) is not always
easy to know. When the psychiatrist says that the child wants
or needs love, he should understand that the child is not interested in love as an abstraction or even as an attitude. His concern
is always with the concrete behavior toward him which emanates
or may emanate from an attitude of love—bestowal of food and
other gifts on him, contact with him (the more nearly perpetual
the better), playing with him, permitting him to do this and that,
and the like. When the child himself loves, it is always in connection with gratification of one sort or another and in the oral
area of experience it often takes the form of the nursing situation or some fraction of it. Thus the impulse to nurse at the
father's penis would constitute for him a form of love if he were
able to think in such terms, and he would certainly conceive of
it as a friendly situation between them rather than a hostile one.

In connection with the third type of explanation, which
involves inadequacy or inferiority in the child himself, his speculative solutions and plans are likely to be of a much simpler
order than those related to rivalry. For the most part they involve
plans and wishes for self-improvement. The inadequacy may be
sensed as absolute or comparative. Where rivalry has not become
a subject of speculation, the inferiority is felt as absolute, the particular traits or behavior being conceived of as demanded of him
by the mother before she will accede to his wishes; where it has,

the attempt is made to "discover" what in the rival makes him preferable from the mother's viewpoint and, depending on what is thus discovered, to outdo the rival in this respect. It may be discovered that the rival, if a sibling, is better behaved, less troublesome to the mother; the child may then plan how he will be even more docile and conforming than his rival. He may discover that the rival is brighter, more intelligent; then the child will plan to outdo him in swiftness of perception and learning, and in skill of performing those things which seem to gain the rival favor. He may discover that the rival has superior physical attraction—curly hair or straight hair, brown eyes or blue eyes; the child may then cudgel his brains to find out how he can change himself in such respects. (This specific explanation and the almost insurmountable obstacles in the way of its solution may underlie the attempts of many women in our contemporary culture to make radical alterations in their appearance by the use of various cosmetic devices, dyeing of the hair, even surgical operations. Men are also found who to varying degrees attempt the same sort of thing, especially in terms of plastic operations on the nose. For the child, of course, such devices are not available, and, confronted with such a problem, he must derive what comfort he can from hopes of what will happen when he grows up or he must hope that some other feature of his personality or behavior will eventually have superior appeal to the mother.) The rival's favored position may be discovered, particularly in the case of a younger or ailing sibling, to be the result of weakness or illness which evokes the mother's compassion and her assiduous concern and care. Plans are then made to be weak, helpless, or ill, or otherwise in a position to make the mother compassionate toward him. Where the rival is an older sibling or the father, the child may discover the advantage to lie in the rival's strength and the extent to which the mother may benefit by this. Such a discovery may lead to plans to become strong and to fantasies (which are apt to have something in common with speculations concerning a *quid pro quo*) of rescuing the mother from this or that disaster.

Where his explanation takes the form of a *quid pro quo*

which the rival offers to the mother in exchange for her favors, the child examines himself to determine whether he possesses the same thing, whether at all or in greater or lesser degree, or some acceptable equivalent. If his conclusion is a negative one, he is likely to be afflicted with lifelong feelings of inferiority, though the degree of this depends on the definitiveness of his conclusion. The less definitive this is, the more hope he has for improvement in this circumstance as a result of future growth, development, and acquisitions.

The preceding explanation has especial pertinence in those children whose speculations about rivalry tend frequently to be concerned with a mutual nursing situation between mother and rival (usually, in such cases, father). Here the penis is seen as a breast-equivalent, as the child may already have imagined it in connection with his own oral impulses, and he is now constrained to consider whether he possesses any such breast-equivalent that might serve as a competitive *quid pro quo*.

In the case of the girl, lacking both penis and breasts, she is unable to find any breast-equivalent on her own body, and is likely, therefore, either not to favor such explanations as those involving a mutual nursing situation (because she can find no solution that pleases her much) or to set her hopes on the distant future, when she may "grow up" to have breasts or a penis. In fact, reconstructions of the clinical material of female patients rarely indicate speculation along these lines, which are much more commonly reconstructed in the case of male patients. A female patient who speculated about a nursing situation between her mother and grandmother thought of this as unilateral rather than mutual.

The boy who envisages a *quid pro quo* in a mutual nursing situation and thinks of his penis as a means of setting up such a *quid pro quo* with his mother generally compares his own organ with that of the rival, to his own detriment. The relative smallness of his penis and his uncertainty, to say the least, about the value of the substance emitted from it (urine) produce doubts about its comparative acceptability to the mother. Such speculation is apt to end in despair about the efficacy of this solution and in persistent feelings of inferiority on this account.

One may wonder how the child arrives at the notion that the *size* of the penis bears a relation to its desirability as an oral object. In terms of the pleasure of sucking as one of the fractionated elements of the nursing composite it would seem that the large adult penis would offer difficulties, even in anticipation, in terms of its manageability by his oral apparatus; something rather smaller, and therefore more comfortable to be sucked on, would seem more desirable if sucking were the sole consideration. To the child (and, in unconscious fashion, to the adult) it seems self-evident that the larger the penis (or breast), the more *substance* it contains. It is on these grounds that size of the penis has significance. In later life, the attractiveness of large breasts as a genital lure for many men has this basis. For many men the attractive woman's breasts must not only be large but also *firm,* not pendulous. The firm breast likewise carries the promise of being full of substance, while the pendulous breast seems relatively depleted of substance. To many females in later life, size of the sexual partner's penis has the same unconscious meaning, but the full significance of this cannot be appreciated until the female's evolution toward genitality is understood. This will be described in a later chapter.

The child's uncertainty about the value of his urine as the substance to be offered his mother as a nursing *quid pro quo* depends upon more than one factor. The child in the late oral phase has no awareness of the existence of semen. The substance he has hoped for from the father's penis is milk, and he is not troubled in such fantasies by the analogy with his own penis, which emits nothing but urine. If, however, he contemplates the value of his own penis as a nursing *quid pro quo* to be offered to the mother, he compares urine with milk. The greater the disgust he has learned to feel toward urine, the less he will regard this as a desirable substance from the mother's viewpoint.

The despair and the feelings of inferiority which form the sequel to speculation along these lines vary greatly in their intensity from one child to another. To one child, these considerations of size and substance seem absolute and conclusive. To another child, while they make the outlook bleak and unpromising, still the possibility remains that his worst anticipations may not be true and that his *quid pro quo* may prove acceptable, more or less, to the mother after all. To a third child, the despairing conclusion reached will seem valid only for the present and will not deprive him of the hope for a better *quid pro quo* in the future, as he grows up. The determining factor in these outcomes appears to lie in the previous and current attitude of both the parents toward the child. If he feels in general approved, respected, and loved by both of them, the third and healthiest of the three outcomes mentioned is likely to occur. The less consistent and less unanimous such parental attitudes are, the more likely he is to reach the first—unhealthiest—of these.

The second outcome results from parental attitudes lying somewhere between the two extremes. With this outcome the child continues to hope that he has an acceptable *quid pro quo* to offer the mother and is apt, as time goes on, to continue trying out the possibility. This takes the form of exhibiting his penis or of somehow inducing the mother to touch it. What he does here is to project his own see-touch-swallow sequence upon the mother, to suppose that, just as his own oral impulses are aroused by seeing and touching, so hers will be. An important factor for a later exhibitionism comes into being here. In the interpretation of the perversion of exhibitionism, this underlying oral aim is usually overlooked: in unconscious terms, the exhibitionist offers his penis as a lure to his victim's oral impulses, so that in the event the victim is thus seduced, the basis for a *quid pro quo* will be created and the exhibitionist himself will get to suck. Such behavior is of frequent occurrence in homosexual approaches in public places, such as Turkish baths and public toilets, and often results in mutual fellatio. Where exhibitionism does not culminate in an oral act by the exhibitionist, but rather in some form of genital gratification, we may conclude that this pattern, which has its origin in the late oral phase of experience, has been modified by the new impulses and experiences of the phallic phase.

This solution of establishing a *quid pro quo* through an exhibitionistic appeal to another's oral impulses comes into play in the sport of bait-fishing and lure-fishing of all varieties, as well as in some forms of animal-trapping. The provenance of such activities is betrayed by the fact that their end result is the eating of the fish and often of the animal. Where the animal is trapped for its fur and not eaten, nevertheless the achievement of warmth (by wearing the animal's fur) is one of the fractional elements of the nursing composite. The bait-angler who fishes *"pour le sport"* and does not eat his catch (nor give it to anyone else to eat) merely inhibits the end act of the pattern. He nevertheless "keeps his hand in," assures himself of retaining the ability to perform the whole pattern, for he could eat the fish if he wanted to. The fact that such fishing and trapping are often done for commercial purpose does not vitiate the conclusion, for we may assume that all gainful occupations are chosen, in part at least, as a result of such unconscious motivations.

THE BELIEF IN PERPETUAL LACTATION

A striking fact about this entire experiential area and the various speculations induced when the child is more or less traumatized in the attempted pursuit of his see-touch-swallow sequence, is that the child assumes as self-evident that the mother's breast is perpetually lactating. He never questions this assumption, and doubts on this score never play a role in any of the explanations he offers to himself in trying to account for the nonrestoration of the nursing situation.

The child has no way of knowing or divining that lactation is an intermittent function. His age at the usual date of weaning in our culture is one at which his capacity for language is still rudimentary and would be insufficient for grasping such a concept if anyone were inclined to convey it to him. By the time he might be able to understand the complex facts involved in the function, the drive to re-establish the nursing situation has long since ceased to be a conscious issue, and information along those lines would seem to him, as well as to his informant, not relevant to anything at that time happening to him. Moreover, supposing this insuperable language barrier did not exist, it is doubtful whether the child could accept this information as fact. He would prefer to believe that the maternal breast is perpetually full of milk and might well regard such information as just another device for depriving him of it. The acceptance of such information as fact would deprive him of all hope of restoring this situation and would cut out the ground from under all his speculation, all his discoveries and explanations, all his solutions and plans, which have as their ultimate purpose the restoration of nursing. These enable him to maintain some small loophole of hope of which he would be utterly deprived if he knew that lactation is merely intermittent, initiated at childbirth and continuing for a limited time thereafter. To such utter and uncompromising deprivation he would prefer the many and various psychic discomforts involved in his explanations and their solutions. The persistence, in later life, of deeply afflicting feelings of inferiority in the face of all sorts of evidence of actual noninferiority results, often enough, from the unconscious necessity of maintaining just such a loophole of hope (through ultimate self-improvement) in the face of persistent nongratification. It often seems to the therapist that such insistence upon inferiority is merely stubborn, intractable resistance to cure, whereas such insistence actually serves the function of supporting the hope of ultimate success in the unconscious drive toward nursing.

Besides these reasons for ignorance of the intermittent character of lactation, the belief in perpetual lactation may gain support if the child witnesses the nursing of a younger sibling or a succession of these, or sees infants being nursed by other mothers. Such evidence is regarded by the child as proof that a mother can nurse a child whenever she wants to, though he does not really require proof, since he assumes this anyway as a matter of course.

The deeply rooted, unconsciously unquestioned conviction regarding perpetual lactation is sometimes shown in dream material. Dreams are frequently encountered in which the setting is a desert or a beach at the ocean. Such locales generally indicate that the impulses giving rise to the dream are related to the oral area of experience and specifically to traumas occasioned in weaning and in the postweaning period. The desert is a place without moisture, where a man may die of thirst, unless he finds an oasis. If the desert locale includes an oasis somewhere in the course of the dream, the oasis will almost certainly bear the interpretation of the mother's breast or a substitute for it. The beach locale of dreams has in common with desert dreams the element of sand, always significant of dryness, lack of moisture, thirst. The proximity to the ocean in such settings would seem to deny the latter significance until one reflects that the water of the ocean is too salty to drink. Here the situation presented is that of the postweaning period in which one is close to a vast source of moisture, one may see it and thirst for it, but may not drink it. Pertinent here is Coleridge's well-known line, "Water, water, everywhere, nor any drop to drink." The beach at the ocean as a dream-locale would seem to reflect the conviction concerning the mother's perpetual lactation. One is thirsty (on the dry sand), one is close to a limitless source of abundant gratification, *but* one may not partake of it.

IV

The Second Experiential Area:
PROBLEMS OF DISCIPLINE

IT IS NOT POSSIBLE to make a general statement as to the point in the child's life at which he first encounters the factor of parental discipline. The precise point in the case of each child depends entirely upon the personality of the parents (more commonly the mother's) and the judgments and behavior that emanate from it in its interplay with the exigencies, as seen by them, of their task of acculturation. There is no cultural consensus as to the precise age or the precise situation in which disciplinary efforts should be begun, and the choice as to exactly when these should commence is left to the individual mother.

I know of one instance in which experience, perhaps of a disciplinary nature, was introduced in the third week of life. The father of a patient aged 25 informed me that the young man had, as an infant from birth on, been strikingly indifferent toward nursing. He had been breast-fed for a week and had nursed with little vigor and initiative, requiring persuasion to begin and maintain sucking. When after a week he had to be shifted to the bottle, owing to a condition of the mother's breasts, he manifested the same lack of avidity. The father occasionally gave him the bottle at this time, and on one such occasion became exasperated over the infant's lackadaisical nursing and the consequent prolongation of the feeding period, and violently shoved the nipple into the infant's mouth, probably striking the gums painfully with the rim of the bottle. The baby winced, opened wide his eyes (which had been shut), and looked astonished, as the father described it. For a few minutes thereafter he sucked more vigorously, but soon returned to his usual detached, unenthusiastic manner of nursing. It was the father's feeling that in this incident he had disciplined his son prematurely and brutally, and that this bore a causal relationship to the neurotic maladjustment which later developed, in which the nuclear problem was unconscious revolt against authority and discipline. In this judgment the father apparently assumed that the infant, responding to the punishment inflicted, had attempted to conform to the implied demands. Whether anything of this sort actually occurred in the baby's mind is highly questionable, to say the least, but I cite it as an instance of how parents may engage in what they regard as disciplinary behavior very early in the life of the child.

It is not uncommon for disciplinary issues to be introduced in the early stages of the oral area of experience, particularly at the period of weaning or (as in the instance just described) as early as during the weaning preliminaries.

It seems inevitable, as we have seen, that discipline is introduced as soon as the typical behavior of the see-touch-swallow sequence makes its appearance. The mother obviously cannot permit her child the freedom to swallow pins, for instance, and since such behavior ordinarily begins at about the age of one year, we may say that this is the latest probable date for the introduction of disciplinary issues, although this may occur later in some cases where the infant is unusually late in commencing locomotion.

The fact that in expounding the types of experience of the disciplinary area and their outcomes I shall make almost exclusive use of the vicissitudes of toilet-training should not be taken to mean that there are not other and important disciplinary issues at this period. These are so numerous that it would not be possible to describe them exhaustively. They involve matters pertaining to the child's safety, such as playing with knives or matches, or swallowing various objects; matters pertaining to manners—feeding manners, and comments on the appearance or odors of strangers, for example; matters pertaining to morals, such as demands for generosity and unselfishness; and matters pertaining to the mother's specific requirements for freedom from nuisance—boisterous talking, waking at an early hour and being noisy, getting the clothing dirty while at play, and the like.

In this chapter I shall deal in detail with toilet-training rather than with other disciplinary items because some form of toilet-training is *always* attempted, while the other disciplinary issues may vary considerably from case to case, particularly in terms of their specific combinations. Also the various techniques used in toilet-training and the child's responses to these serve as a paradigm for all disciplinary experiences. Approval and disapproval, reward and punishment, discipline through love and through coercion or intimidation—these are the methods used in all disciplinary attempts. To these the child responds either with willing cooperativeness or with feelings of frustration, rage, fear, anxiety, or humiliation which impel him toward docility or toward some form of revolt—one or another of the series of heroic or unheroic adaptations. What will be said with regard to toilet-training applies, *mutatis mutandis,* to the other disciplinary issues as well, and the events which transpire may either confirm and reinforce or discount and offset the various modes of behavior, attitudes, and convictions which emerge as a result of experience with toilet-training.

TECHNIQUES OF TOILET-TRAINING

It happens quite frequently in our culture that mothers begin toilet-training their offspring long before the late phase of oral experience has been reached; that is, before locomotion has emerged. I have known of instances in which this was actually begun during the first months of life, almost immediately upon the cessation of the mother's confinement. Under such circumstances, however, the procedure is not apt at once to take on a strongly disciplinary character, in the sense that the mother is not likely to administer punishment of any kind for the child's early failures to comply with her demands. At this extremely early age, the training generally takes the form of suggestion and temporal conditioning rather than the usual disciplinary pattern of reward and punishment. The mother places the baby on the pot at those times when she anticipates that he is likely to urinate or defecate. If by a fortunate accident he does actually so perform while being held on the pot, she tries by her tone of voice to convey to him her approval of the performance, hoping thus to condition him to repeating it on subsequent occasions. But at this stage she does not, as a rule, penalize him for non-performance or for soiling. A few weeks or months later, however, depending upon how well she can tolerate failure in these attempts, she may begin introducing penalties in the form of a disapproving tone of voice for nonperformance and in the form of vocal expressions of disgust for soiling. By the time the introduction of penalties is begun, the infant may be said to be having disciplinary experience.

Though some authorities on child-rearing recommend early toilet-training it is a good deal more common in our culture for a mother to make a start in this direction at some time after she has undertaken the weaning preliminaries. Here again her discipline is not apt at first to be stringent, and the punitive aspects of it are likely to be either absent or not greatly stressed. Sooner or later, particularly if the child does not respond as she hopes to the method of conditioning by approval, she introduces punitive measures for the child's failures to meet her expectations and wishes. These take the form of disapproval expressed in different ways: head-shaking; tongue-clucking; reproachful, more-in-sorrow-than-in-anger attitudes; disgust; withdrawal; reprimand; and scolding. The punishment may take the form of violent handling of the child in changing the diaper or in sitting him on the pot to show him what he ought to have done; the physical violence is accompanied by expressions of reproach, disgust, or reprimand, all depending upon the degree of the mother's exasperation. It may happen that she slaps the child in her anger, though I would conjecture that this is less common than the other punitive measures.

In our culture, these attempts at toilet-training are not as a rule immediately successful, and the process goes on for periods of varying length. One does hear occasionally of mothers who insist that they had no trouble with this phase of acculturating their offspring, that the child "practically trained himself." My inclination is to be somewhat skeptical of such statements and to wonder whether the mother is remembering entirely accurately. Mothers who report such phenomena generally do so with overtones of pride in accomplishment, although it is difficult to determine whether the pride is in their own accomplishment as successful acculturators or in the accomplishment of their offspring (which reflects credit upon themselves). It may be that the mother's memory is distorted and rendered inaccurate by wish-fulfilling tendencies, whether in terms of maintaining self-esteem or in terms of unconscious feelings of guilt about the overbearing, sometimes callous, handling of the child in toilet-training him. My tentative conclusion upon hearing about children who "practically trained themselves" is always that they have been a good deal intimidated in the process. It is certainly conceivable, and doubtless sometimes happens, that some children feel themselves so loved that they cooperate well in the technique of conditioning by approval and are thus trained quickly in toilet-habits. But the psychotherapist hears reports about no difficulty in toilet-training from precisely those mothers whose children are now being seen by him in consultation or in treatment. He is entitled to wonder, then, why, if toilet-training was so smoothly uneventful, the child is now as a patient presenting problems whose nature is basically disciplinary. It may be that the patient was traumatized in some disciplinary area other than that of toilet-training, but it is generally the case that the mother's character as a disciplinarian does not vary greatly from one disciplinary situation to another. My conclusion is that the therapist does well to have mental reservations about the accuracy of observation or memory (or both) of the mothers of patients in psychotherapy. It can generally be shown in the course of treatment that the patients' toilet-training was not as faultless and smoothly successful as stated by their mothers.

The longer the period of toilet-training and the smaller the mother's success in carrying out this task of acculturation, the more she will attempt to introduce new and different methods of accomplishing it. She is likely also to continue with the old methods, but now with increased stringency: her disgust, her anger, her violence, all become much more vehement as the child grows older and larger and still is not completely toilet-trained. In such circumstances she is obviously being frustrated in terms of her own effective aggression and is being threatened with reduced self-esteem. That a mother confronted with the difficulties of toilet-training her child should become panicky and anxious over the situation and deeply concerned for her self-esteem would seem out of proportion to the realities of the situation and would bespeak pathologic distortion on her part; such states of mind are nevertheless very commonly encountered in our culture.

One novel feature introduced into toilet-training by mothers in this predicament is the technique of anticipating the time when the child is likely to urinate or defecate, particularly the latter,* or of deciding when he *should* urinate or defecate, and placing him on the toilet or potty-chair at certain definite times and leaving him there until he has performed. Leaving him alone and interrupting and postponing his play are apt to have unconscious punitive connotations for the mother. When there is delay about performing, the child may be frequently questioned or examined to see if he has as yet performed and may be nagged and scolded until he does. But often enough he is simply left to himself, immobilized in the potty-chair. When it happens, after a lengthy period in the chair without desired result, that

* Mothers are apt to be considerably more concerned about regulating defecation than urination. This may be partly on practical grounds, since the stool is both more malodorous and harder to clean up than urine, but certainly soiling evokes greater shame and disgrace than wetting, and the mother's own childhood conditioning plays an important role here.

the child later soils himself, the mother is likely to become especially vehement, often slapping the child viciously, especially
if the soiling occurs shortly after she has taken him out of
the chair and dressed him again. The success of this method obviously depends upon the accuracy of the mother's prediction of
the time when the child's bladder or rectum will be full and
ready for emptying, though, as we shall see when we come to
consider the child's attitudes toward all this, quite other factors
may be concerned also. The mother is not always able to predict
these things accurately since the activities of the genitourinary
system and of the gastrointestinal system depend on factors which
she cannot always take into account, some of them being unknown. But she often reacts as if such happenings were the result
of sheer disobedience and spite on the child's part, which is
sometimes the case.

Another feature occasionally added rather late in the
process of toilet-training, often with but sometimes without the
advice of a physician, is the use of the enema. This is often introduced in the course of an illness, but may be introduced in
cases in which the technique of periodic immobilization in the
potty-chair is unsuccessful. The mother (on rarer occasions, the
physician) concludes that the child is constipated, despite the
fact that later in the same day a soiling may occur, to her chagrin.
The remedy she decides upon is sometimes an enema, though she
may administer a laxative, with or without a later enema.

The laxative is apt to confuse the matter of periodicity of
evacuations even more than before and to add fuel to the fire
of the mother's exasperation. I do not wish to be understood as
implying that laxatives should never be given to small children:
there are doubtless instances in which a diagnosis of true constipation is justified. What I am trying to indicate is the unwisdom
of the administration of a laxative as an auxiliary to toilet-training. Of course, this is never done in precisely these terms, but
rather by first concluding that the child is constipated and then
deciding upon a laxative as a remedy. The diagnosis of constipation during the period of toilet-training (and often in later life)

is always subject to some doubt, and especially when the diagnosis is made by the mother, who may have her own purposes to serve. It is often merely the result of her own impatience with the child's recalcitrance in learning to regulate his bowel habits. By making a medical diagnosis the mother (1) absolves herself of "failure" in training the child, and (2) administers what she unconsciously regards as a punishment (medicine) for his obstinacy.

The enema, when decided upon by the mother without medical advice, is in much the same category, from the mother's viewpoint, as the laxative, though she regards it (unconsciously) as much the more coercive and drastic punishment of the two.

The use of the enema or laxative in toilet-training is not commonly found in the general population, though one encounters it not infrequently in the childhood recollections of psychoanalytic patients.

TOILET-HABITS AND PHYSIOLOGY

To the child these attempts of the mother to train him toward civilized toilet-habits present difficulties. His own original preferences and tendencies along these lines are certainly physiologic. It is sometimes maintained that the child whose physiologic mode of urination and defecation is never interfered with eventually toilet-trains himself, the implication being that there is a physiologic development toward such an end-result which will inevitably eventuate. I know of no evidence that supports such a contention. When a child whose toilet-habits have never been subjected to any attempts at modification by the mother "trains himself," it would be reasonable, in my opinion, to conclude that he had somehow perceived that his uncontrolled toilet-habits place him at a disadvantage in the family or with his peers and that he has made a conscious decision to offset the disadvantage by learning to control his acts of elimination. If this ever occurs in our culture, it is a great rarity: even if the mother elects, on theoretic grounds, to allow the child complete autonomy and freedom in these matters, it is difficult to imagine a situation in which all other inmates of the household and all visitors could be taught to maintain a similar unconcern; in other words, it is almost inevitable that the child will encounter more or less vehement disapproval from someone in response to the unrestraint of his toilet-habits. It may even be doubted that this strongminded mother does not, despite her best efforts, somehow convey to the child a response of underlying discomfort (particularly disgust) to which her own childhood training is bound to have conditioned her. Though toilet-training can certainly be a great deal less stringent and traumatic than it ordinarily is in our culture, it may be seriously doubted that the achievement of bowel and bladder control would occur in human beings without some degree of environmental influence.

The argument for natural, physiologic development toward such control often takes support from the fact that domesticated kittens "train themselves." It is true that young pet cats have usually only to be provided with paper, always in the same place on the floor, to learn "cleanliness" in elimination. They do not require the strenuous and often prolonged efforts at housebreaking that young dogs do. But whatever factors may be involved in the facility with which kittens are housebroken, it is clear that these factors cannot be universally valid, as experience with puppies makes abundantly clear. Most wild animals, even when born in a state of captivity, never become "housebroken," even if they live to a great age. It seems a justifiable conclusion that the almost "natural" housebreaking of cats is a special feature of these animals and cannot be adduced in support of a similar supposition about young human beings.

In the newborn child, and, indeed, until efforts are made to modify it, evacuation of bladder and bowel occurs in reflex fashion. The presence of amounts of urine or feces sufficient to produce pressure on or irritation of the walls of bladder or rectum sets in motion reflexes which result in evacuation of these organs. These are not simple reflexes; they consist of more than one action. The operation of the reflexes includes contraction of the wall of the hollow organ (bladder or rectum); relaxation of the circle of musculature (sphincter), whose state of contraction ordinarily serves to keep the hollow organs closed off;* and accessory contractions of abdominal musculature, thus producing external pressure on the hollow organs and aiding in the expulsion of their contents. The abdominal muscular contractions are of greater importance and are more marked in rectal than in vesical evacuation.

The stimulation of the walls of the bladder by urine and of the rectum by feces may be regarded as producing a disturbance in psychophysiologic homeostasis calling for measures to restore it. Restoration of homeostasis can be brought about by immediate urination or defecation as soon as the disturbance—ordinarily termed an urge or a need to urinate or defecate—is felt. It is of automatic occurrence, operating by means of a physiologic reflex, and produces an intermittent spilling over, as it were, of urine and feces, with restoration of homeostasis almost as soon as the disturbance is felt. Obviously, the infant would prefer such a mode of evacuation over another mode which involves prolonging the disturbance of homeostasis; he prefers to urinate or defecate the instant he feels the urge to do so rather than to postpone these acts. His effective aggression demands, if it is to operate ideally, an immediate restoration of disturbed homeostasis, and his physiologic reflex, when it functions unobstructedly, can serve as an example of high effectiveness of aggression. Any interference with the functioning of the reflex tends, therefore, to reduce effectiveness of aggression.

The reflex is not subject to influence by mechanical means, except in so far as it may be *stimulated* by creating pressure or

* Sphincter muscles actually consist of two sets of fibers, the contractions of one set working antagonistically to those of the other set. One set of fibers is of circular form: when they contract, the circle narrows (the hole is tightly closed) ; when they relax, the circle widens (the hole becomes larger in diameter). The other set is of radial form, like the spokes of a wheel: when they contract, the edges of the hole draw back and the circle widens; when they relax, the edges of the hole come into apposition and the circle narrows. Control of the sphincter (in inhibiting a bowel-movement, for example), consists of contracting the circular fibers and simultaneously relaxing the radial ones; opening the sphincter consists of the opposite pair of actions in both sets of fibers.

irritation, on the rectal mucous membrane particularly, as by means of an enema, for instance. But it cannot be *inhibited* by any mechanical means whatsoever. Therefore, if the inhibition of the reflex is to be achieved, no one but the child himself can bring it about: the child has somehow to be induced to inhibit his own reflex, to behave in such a way as to prolong, by his own will, disturbance of homeostasis, and thus by his own effort to reduce the effectiveness of his aggression. How to induce the child to behave in this unbiologic fashion, contrary to his pleasure principle, contrary to ideally effective aggression, is the essence of the mother's problem of acculturation of her offspring.

THE CHILD'S REACTIONS TO TOILET-TRAINING

Taken by itself, the technique of conditioning the child by approval does not constitute an external interference with the operation of the reflex. If the child could be toilet-trained by this means alone, this part of the task of acculturation would hold no potentiality for traumatization: he would have learned to control his sphincters through sheer cooperation with his loved and loving mother. His own reason for inhibiting his eliminative reflexes would then, however, be no preference for "cleanliness" per se; rather, it would be to please his mother, through cooperativeness and good will toward her: for love of her, he sacrifices a degree of his autonomy, suffering for her sake a prolongation of psychophysiologic tension (disturbed homeostasis) and a reduction of effective aggression.

This is highly theoretical, however, since it is open to grave doubt whether training in toilet-habits is ever achieved in this fashion. One occasionally hears reports of such miracles of love and cooperation, but these should, in my opinion, be regarded with the same skepticism which I have attempted to justify in connection with reports of mothers to the effect that their children "practically trained themselves." In any case, it is much the more common experience, in our culture, that conditioning by disapproval is in some manner introduced. In most instances it seems likely that the child's first intimation of what precisely is being demanded of him comes with the mother's earliest manifestations of disapproval of his reflex eliminations. Such manifestations, as we have seen, though they may begin mildly enough, are likely to become more vehement and more unmistakable to the child as time goes on and he continues to be imperfectly toilet-trained. The child who becomes toilet-trained as a result of conditioning by approval for success and disapproval for failures learns to inhibit his reflexes through the combined effects of love and fear of his mother. Such combinations may vary greatly in terms of the precise proportions of the two ingredients: in general, it may be assumed that the greater the effect of love and the smaller the effect of fear (or anxiety) in producing this inhibition, the less traumatic will be the child's experience with this aspect of acculturation; correlatively, the greater the effect of fear (or anxiety) in the specific combination, the more traumatic the child's experience.

The child's first experiences of the mother's disapproval, unanticipated and unforeseen, may well produce fear in the child and random responses to the fear-provoking situation. Through these experiences the child will learn to recognize certain signs which indicate that the mother will presently be manifesting disapproval. Here anxiety rather than fear will be felt, and the child is apt to experiment with the means of averting the danger of which his anxiety warns him. In the course of such experimentation the child may, for the first time in his life, get the notion that something in himself and his own behavior may be responsible for the emergence of the danger. The older the child at this stage and the greater his facility in understanding language, the more likely he is to conceive this notion. His ego-device in this situation is the autoplastic one of inhibiting his eliminative reflex by learning voluntary control of his sphincters.

It must be understood that such voluntary sphincter-control is primarily frustrating, like any prolongation of a disturbance of homeostasis and like any reduction in the effectiveness of aggression. The initial, untaught response to frustration is, as we have seen, rage and its manifestations. Even where love and cooperativeness toward the mother constitute the major ingredient in producing sphincter-control, we may suppose that the frustration inevitably felt will evoke some degree of rage toward the person for whose sake it is undertaken. The rage may not be intense—in some instances it may not be more than a mild resentment—and it cannot be manifested in the act of sphincter-control itself. Empirically, this resentment may be unobserved, because it is mild, because the child has no direct way of manifesting it that makes its relevance clear, and because it may become buried (unrecognizable) beneath manifestations of pleasure in achieving the mother's approval. Even where the major ingredient in sphincter-control is fear or anxiety, the rage appropriate to frustration cannot be directly manifested: while the rage in these circumstances is much greater in degree, it cannot be expressed in clearly relevant fashion and again may be buried under manifestations of relief and pleasure in averting the mother's disapproval and achieving her approval.

The existence of rage of varying degrees consequent upon this self-frustrating inhibition is likely to be manifested in indirect and devious manner. Edith Sterba [71] was, I believe, the first worker to point out that resentment over the enforced self-restraints in sphincter-control often takes the indirect form of the appearance of alterations in eating habits. The child who has previously presented little or no difficulty in eating in the adult manner, having adjusted well to the postweaning situation, now begins to refuse food, spits it out, plays with it, smears it, throws it about, spills it, and the like—anything rather than simply eat it. It is his way of rebelling against the (to him) overdemanding mother. In so far as he is aware, through previous random experience, of his mother's distress when he refuses to eat, such behavior is a means of venting his spite against her and of being revenged for the uncomfortable self-frustration which he is now forced to endure, whether for love or for fear of her. Such vengeful, spiteful behavior has the basic aim, as we have already seen in another connection, of intimidation, of teaching the mother a lesson, so that she will cease doing what-

ever it is that the child objects to—in this case, demanding that
he control his sphincters. It may be supposed, also, that the behavior described in regard to eating constitutes a substitution
and displacement: what he dares not do in matters of elimination he does in matters of eating. He conforms (in toilet-training)
and simultaneously rebels (in eating habits).

It is not necessary to suppose that every frustration, no matter how slight, invariably produces some direct or indirect manifestation of rage. Slight frustrations may generate no response
beyond mild and fleeting feelings of resentment. But the greater
the degree of frustration, the more likely it is that some manifestation of rage, however modified, will be observable. Where
fear of the mother or anxiety concerning her disapproval prompts
the child to learn to control his sphincters, his rage will be the
more intense, and it is probable that he will find some means of
expressing it, such as has just been described. Even if this rage
could be manifested in a manner more direct than this, it is un-
likely that it would be. For the child who fears his mother's
disapproval of his unrestraint in toilet-habits is also likely to fear
the consequences of unrestraint in manifesting rage. This fear (or
anxiety) would in most instances be based upon previous experiences with the mother's responses to his unimpeded expression
of rage.

"HEROIC" AND "UNHEROIC" ADAPTATIONS

The child is here confronted, perhaps for the first time
in his life, with the conflictful situation (discussed in a previous
chapter) in which he must "choose" between doing what he
wants to do (in terms of impulse-gratification) and maintaining
maternal approval, the latter being, in some instances, tanta-
mount to his sole guarantee of somatic survival. The choice is
not necessarily as clear-cut as this implies or as was implied in
the earlier discussion when we described it as either "heroic" or
"unheroic." The truly heroic choice here would be the utter refusal to become toilet-trained, with utter unconcern about the
consequences of this refusal. Such a choice is never made (or,
at least, never maintained), for, while a child may for a time

behave in the heroic manner, it will not be possible for him to do so indefinitely. Sooner or later, the mother will find the means to force him to abandon so uncompromising an attitude, and he is bound to be traumatized in the process.

The unheroic choice would be to conform speedily and completely to the mother's demands, as soon as they are well understood, and to conform without any direct or indirect manifestation of rage, because of the intensity of the child's concern about the mother's disapproval and its consequences to him of bodily harm, of her withdrawal, of her desertion of him, or of her casting him out. It must be supposed that some children feel themselves compelled, because of the generally rejecting attitude and behavior of the mother, to make the unheroic choice in this extreme form.

We occasionally see adult patients who exhibit, both outwardly and inwardly, the extreme docility and spiritlessness implied by a choice of this kind; they are individuals whose spirits have been utterly broken and in whom no small spark of rebelliousness and initiative can still be detected. Such individuals characteristically do not seek treatment themselves; but are brought to the psychotherapist by the mother or some other baffled and disappointed relative. If the therapist attempts to treat such people, he soon finds that their docility is so firmly established as a defensive device of the ego that it forms an insuperable resistance to the psychoanalytic process [73]. What strength they possess is utilized in the determination to behave docilely, no matter what the cost; they accept any interpretation, even forced or wrong ones, but they will never *do* anything beyond ascertaining where authority is and trying to conform to its demands. They are meticulously prompt and reliable about keeping appointments, but they talk little; what talking they do (in response to demands to talk) is extroversive, superficial, and inconsequential; their dreams, if they have any, are fragmentary and of meager content; they are distressed at boring the therapist, and break off treatment (if the therapist has not already dismissed them) because they cannot endure a situation in which they sense that docility to the therapist's demands would require of them a certain indocility.

The use of the adjectives "heroic" and "unheroic" as applied to this matter of choice implies, by connotation, that the former is "good," and the latter "bad." In terms of later consequences, this is more or less what I wish to convey, since the detailed study of the psychic adaptations of adults appears to me to show that, with certain reservations, those adaptations in which the individual is able to achieve a degree of impulse-gratification without too much concern about the disapproval of others are apt to be among the healthier ones. This is of course a value-judgment, as any statement of therapeutic goals is bound to be, and results from "preferences" rather than from anything like objective or "scientific" accuracy in differentiating between "better" and "worse" adaptations.

If no child ultimately makes the heroic choice in its extreme form and if few children are constrained to make the extreme unheroic choice, it must be that there is a choice or a range of choices between the two and that the choice of most children lies between the two extremes. As we have seen, not every child is necessarily confronted with such a choice. The mothers of the most fortunate children are able to make them feel so securely loved and so basically approved of that these children are never placed in a position where such a choice is forced upon them: their sense of frustration is mild, and their security in feeling loved is such that they dare to indulge in some rebelliousness and are given some degree of freedom in this direction. But one gains the impression that, while such healthy situations exist in our culture, they are by no means common, and that the majority of children are confronted with making a choice in the disciplinary area now being discussed.

The choice lies essentially between degrees of disturbance of homeostasis. Disturbance of this kind is already familiar to us in terms of nongratification of impulses, but it is necessary to assume that such disturbance also arises when the child is anxious and foresees the danger of maternal disapproval and its consequences. His choice is therefore not between continued disturbance of homeostasis and complete restoration of it; rather, he must choose between one degree of disturbance and another, and must sense which is the lesser of the two evils. Here there are so many variable factors that a clear account is difficult to give.

One of these factors is the child's frustration-tolerance, the degree of disturbance of homeostasis that he can endure without having to take drastic measures in the attempt to terminate the disturbance. We have already suggested that such tolerance is lower at birth and in the early weeks and months of life than it is toward the end of the first year, and that this variability may relate to factors involved in somatic growth. It has likewise been suggested that infants may have differing constitutional endowments in this respect.

Another factor is the mother's attitude and behavior toward the child, first in the oral area of his experience, and now in the disciplinary area. The more loving, accepting, and tender her attitude toward her child, the greater his tolerance of frustration is likely to become. The child whose mother has been resentful of his existence and the trouble caused her by having to serve his needs and wishes—the unwanted child—is much less likely to develop a high degree of frustration-tolerance. Such mothers may be well aware of their attitudes and may in some manner justify their resentment to themselves; they may be in conscious conflict over their attitudes, so that their behavior toward the child is highly inconsistent; or the conflict may operate unconsciously, resulting in some cases in compulsive, duty-ridden solicitude toward the child, or, in other cases, in sudden, unpredictable hostile impulses toward him, from which the mother recoils in horror. In the last-mentioned case, the mother may be so absorbed in concern about her own attitudes that her actual relation with the child becomes remote and somewhat detached.

Still another factor includes the stage of the child's life at which the mother commences her disciplinary efforts, the specific issues involved, and the specific methods she uses. Where attempts at discipline have been begun during the weaning and the child is thus early introduced to the experience of maternal disapproval, frustration-tolerance is likely to remain at a low level. This applies with especial cogency to those situations in which toilet-training by means of conditioning by disapproval is begun early. The behavior that may evoke maternal disapproval at this stage of life comprises frequent crying-spells; difficulty in falling asleep, wakefulness with crying at night or during daytime naps; feeding difficulties; thumb-sucking or sucking of the bedclothes; or masturbation (which evokes disapproval only if observed and given its correct significance by the mother).

There are mothers who lack the understanding that the readjustments required of the child in weaning already confront him with a difficult task of adaptation and who consequently begin at this time to make stringent efforts to toilet-train him. The deprivations of the nursing situation, the necessity to learn new and unwelcome techniques of feeding, and the simultaneously vehement disapproval of the mother when he fails to control his sphincters cause in him disturbances of homeostasis (frustrations) which are so frequent and so various in origin and in kind that he has little opportunity to learn to tolerate them.

One type of mother functions extremely well maternally so long as the nursing period continues. Mothers of this type love tenderly the infant who is the means of providing them with the great sensory and psychic pleasures which they derive from the nursing situation. Once weaning has been begun, however, those mothers may undergo a sharp change in attitude toward the child. During the nursing period he was the sweet, well-beloved *baby;* now he has become the *child,* her son, her daughter, no longer the "baby"; now he is someone who has to be taught and disciplined; now he may misbehave and has to be made to toe the mark. He has become a challenge to her authority and to her skill and proficiency as an acculturator. Whereas before he was simply the dear little baby at her breast, he is now, so to speak, a *person,* whose behavior may be "naughty" or "good," and she feels that she must speedily transform his naughty behavior into good behavior. It is as if, so long as the child was a source of pleasure to her, she could tolerate any sort of behavior from him, but as soon as the situation becomes unprofitable to her, in terms of pleasure, she views his troublesome behavior with a jaundiced eye. These mothers do seem to intimate demands for a *quid pro quo* from their children, and it is possible that explanations and solutions involving a *quid pro quo* in the speculations of the later oral phase of experience may receive both impetus and support from such maternal attitudes.

The variable factors just described—there are doubtless others as well—as relevant to the degree of frustration-tolerance in a given child can produce a great number of different situations, and specific combinations of these factors will determine the child's specific capacity to tolerate frustration in general. The factors also play a role in determining the *quality* of the frustration tolerated by the child. Where the child has been spared frequent and intense anxiety over maternal disapproval, his tolerance of feelings generated by the latter will be relatively high; perhaps his tolerance of impulse-frustration will be relatively lower in such cases. In the opposite case, his tolerance of the inner disturbance created by maternal disapproval may be lower than his tolerance of impulse-frustration.

These varying capacities for tolerance of frustration, both generally and of different qualities, are of determining significance in the variety of choices between the heroic and unheroic extremes of adaptation in toilet-training.

The possible adaptations will be mentioned in order from the more nearly heroic to the more nearly unheroic; they range in a series from (1) greater tolerance of approval-frustration plus lower tolerance of impulse-frustration to (2) lower tolerance of approval-frustration plus greater tolerance of impulse-frustration. First, the adaptation in which the child has frequent "accidents," frequent failures of sphincter-control. Second, the adaptation in which such failures are more infrequent and yet not sufficiently so that the child can be regarded as completely toilet-trained. These two adaptations may be in part responsible for later bed-wetting, though additional factors are of great significance in the genesis of such behavior. Third, the adaptation in which the child appears to conform to the mother's demands for sphincter-control and yet exhibits resentment and rebelliousness toward the mother and her demands in the indirect fashion already described. Fourth, the adaptation in which conformity is apparent, but the child maintains attitudes of resentment and rebellion which, however, do not achieve direct or indirect expression. The children who make these latter two adaptations will seem to the mother and other observers to be completely toilet-trained; only a very occasional and apparently accidental failure or break in training will betray the inner rebelliousness.

Such adaptations may at times produce curious behavior in later childhood and adult life. This takes the form of defiance by turning conformity to the demands of toilet-training into a *reductio ad absurdum*. One patient related that at the age of twelve, while at a summer camp, he had once maintained control of his anal sphincter so long that he was compelled to defecate in his pants before he could reach a toilet. His shame, he said, was such that he put the soiled underclothing into his trunk, where his mother would be certain to find it when she unpacked it for him (as she was accustomed to do) several weeks later. Another patient, a man in his thirties, was delayed on his way to keep an appointment with me (a trip of forty-five minutes in his car) and, although he felt an urge to urinate, did not stop to do so before leaving his office, lest he be late for the appointment. When five blocks from my office, he was halted by a traffic light, and at this point the urge to urinate became so intense that he took out his penis and urinated on the floor of his car while waiting for the light to change. Disciplinary demands are to be found represented throughout this small episode: sphincter-control; punctuality in keeping appointments; police regulations. The patient tried for a time to obey them all, but his defiant act of urinating on the floor of the car expressed his unconscious wish to make me as a disciplinary figure look ridiculous for making so many, inconsistent demands. He unconsciously read "mother" into all of these: the "remembered" demand for sphincter-control;

my alleged demand for punctuality; the demand of the police that he stop his car at a red light.

It will be seen that a degree of conformity and a degree of defiance or rebellion are ingredients of all of the adaptations in the heroic-unheroic series. The defiance decreases, in the order described, as the conformity increases. The adaptations are all to be regarded as variations of the general adaptation of outward conformity and inward rebellion which in our culture is most commonly seen as the child's response to the attempts to toilet-train him.

The specific adaptation made in this disciplinary area of experience will be highly determining for attitudes and behavior toward authority-figures in later childhood and adult life. The adaptation often gives shape and coloring to later behavior patterns and character traits of a pathologic nature or may, at the least, contribute an important factor in their production. The more nearly a specific adaptation approaches the unheroic choice, the graver the ensuing pathology is likely to be. The unheroic choices involve, to a greater or less extent and in varying combinations, all of the autoplastic ego-devices: repression, reaction-formation, and regression. Repression may operate in the disowning of impulses to defecate and urinate reflexly so that sphincter-control may be more readily maintained; likewise, in the disowning of impulses of rage toward the disciplining mother. Reaction-formation takes the form of impulses to not-defecate, to not-urinate, to not-soil, and to not-wet, and may result in prolonged withholding of stool and urine or in intensive efforts toward cleanliness and neatness, both in matters pertaining to elimination and in other matters only remotely related to defecation and urination. So many authors, notably Freud [20], Jones [44, 45] and Abraham [2], have described the extensive displacements that may be encountered in the child's efforts to negate his innate reflex excremental impulses, that a description will not be repeated here.

The reactionary withholding impulses gain support from the child's spiteful hostility toward the mother and his need to defy and defeat her in their clash of wills. Such defiance could take either the form of withholding the stool which he is aware she desires him to expel ("constipation") or of expelling it in such a way as to make a mess (diarrhea). The impulse toward spiteful withholding is the one which, existing in its own right, may give support to the reactionary constipation. Indeed, in a given instance of constipation it may be difficult to determine whether in the child's subjective attitude there is greater awareness of spiteful feelings than of the feeling that he wishes to conform by not defecating improperly and therefore plays safe by withholding as long as he physiologically can. Of these two possibilities, alternating constipation and diarrhea would suggest the former rather than the latter, and would place the adaptation closer to the heroic choice than is suggested by constipation without diarrhea.

Reaction-formations of cleanliness and neatness gain support from the child's notion of greater somatic comfort when clean than when soiled and wet. But this can be little more than rationalization of his conditioning by the mother's disapproval, and his greater comfort in these circumstances really stems from the fact that by being clean he wards off disapproval. The impulses giving support to this reaction-formation are therefore the same as those which cause him to seek and to maintain her approval in the first place, but are given specific content and coloring by the preferences she evinces. This type of reaction-formation is apt to be more stable—and more troublesome to the child to maintain—than the withholding type, in which the resentment toward the mother is not so well repressed and may at times erupt in the form of the diarrhea which alternates with the constipation. The withholding type of reaction-formation may be more productive of recrudescences of anxiety of low intensity.

The use of regression as an ego-device is here not manifested in clear and unmistakable fashion, and one is entitled to question whether it is justifiable to include it among the ego-devices made use of at this period. As previously defined, regression would involve the return to an older, more familiar version of carrying out a current impulse. With respect to the excremental impulses, this would involve a return from sphincter-control to the intermittent automatic spilling over under the egis of the physiologic reflexes. This is precisely what is ruled out, except as occasional manifestations, in the heroic-unheroic series of adaptations now under discussion. With regard to hostile, resentful impulses toward the disciplining mother who demands inhibition of this reflex, we have already remarked that the child has no direct way of manifesting resentment on this account: he does not evince rage while performing the inhibition. These impulses have in any case to operate indirectly, as we have seen, and take the form of feeding difficulties, insomnia, or constipation. It may be thought that withholding of stools, in so far as this does not result from reaction-formation, is a relatively direct form of resentment against the disciplining mother and that the production of feeding difficulties or sleeping difficulties, being relatively indirect, constitutes a regression to an earlier and safer way of behaving resentfully toward the mother. I would have no great quarrel with such a line of reasoning, except in so far as it implies that such difficulties have existed prior to the mother's attempt to toilet-train the child. But in those cases in which such difficulties appear *after* toilet-training is instituted, they appear for the first time in the child's life. This point is stressed by Edith Sterba [71].

If we consider the matter in more general terms, we are on firmer ground. Regression emerges in the impulses to restore homeostasis disturbed by the mother's new and persistent demandingness. Where effective aggression (and self-esteem) might require heroic insistence upon reflex elimination and unconcern about maternal disapproval, the child may refrain from such behavior and attempt to restore homeostasis by the older means of pleasure-sucking and masturbation. In so far as these do actually restore homeostasis, they reduce the child's tendency to insist upon the older type of elimination and his tendency to resent and defy the disciplining mother. By such regressive means, the child finds a more comfortable way to conform to the mother's demands.

This mode of adaptation, too, has its sequelae in later life. If the regressive behavior is interfered with by an alert and vigilant mother, and disciplinary issues are created around it, feelings of uncertainty and guilt concerning all efforts to achieve pleasure by one's own means alone are apt to arise, their intensity and importance depending upon how sharp a disciplinary issue is established by the mother's attitudes and behavior. Here great variation is possible: the mother's feeling about these activities, her alertness in detecting them, her vigilance in watching for them, the methods she uses for reducing their frequency or preventing them altogether, will be factors in determining to what extent the child is able to make use of them and how much guilt he will feel, then and in later life, about impulses in that direction. The term *guilt* is used here in its psychoanalytic sense. In popular usage guilt generally refers to feelings about some act already committed; in psychoanalytic writings it sometimes has this meaning, but more usually refers to the anxiety felt about an impulse toward an act not yet committed, but regarded as "wrong," either absolutely or in terms of consequences.

If the regressive behavior is not detected or not interfered with by the mother, the consolatory thumb-sucking or masturbation is apt to become a means, in later life, of combating and settling the inner disturbance caused by all manner of frustrations and difficulties occasioned by external reality. Such individuals do not have great trouble in dealing with authority-figures of any kind, and since they have an effective method of dealing with their disappointments and failures in life, they are apt to be more unconcerned with external reality, with its frustrating or its fulfilling potentialities, than other people are. They bear frustrations and disappointments well and often seem enviably well-adjusted to life. However, closer examination of their attitudes and behavior will show that they are much more poorly attuned to reality than others who do not resort to these consolatory devices and that underneath their "philosophical" unconcern with frustrations lies a conviction of omnipotence that borders upon the psychotic. Their conviction is not that they *are* omnipotent, but that they *can be*. The feeling might be thus expressed: "Nothing can ever wholly defeat me. I have always the means for offsetting frustrations and for feeling good. No one can take this away from me, and since I can do it all by myself, independently of anyone or anything else, it enables me to be master of any situation." This is all very well so far as the handling of subjective disturbances is concerned, but the dangerously tenuous relation to external (and inner) reality implied suggests that the device is closely related to the schizoid maneuver. A person would do better to feel worse and remain in closer touch with reality. One wonders whether the drug addictions (including alcoholism) of later life may not in part be derived from such an adaptation, as Rado's work [55, 56] would also suggest. The widespread use, in our own and other cultures, of substances in some manner ingested to make one "feel better" (for example: coffee, tea, tobacco) would suggest that the above-described regressive pattern is a common one and that the distinction between pathologic outcomes (drug addictions) and less pathologic ones (dependence upon coffee and other "stimulants") merely reflects the extent to which the pattern was utilized and the degree of reliance placed upon it in the disciplinary area of childhood experience. The fact that psychoanalytic study of the personality of the addictive drinker demonstrates strong rebellious motivations as well as the more obvious oral ones would suggest that this regressive pattern is an important element in the childhood background of such pathologic developments.

STOOL-HANDLING AS A DISCIPLINARY ISSUE

In all that has been said so far about toilet-training and the adjustments to it, we have considered only the acts of elimination and the issues arising when the acculturating mother begins and continues to demand that the child control these acts by means of his sphincters. However, as first pointed out by Jones [45, p. 671], the issues of this disciplinary area of experience often concern not only acts of elimination, but also the products of these (particularly the stool). The disposal of urine generally presents no problem here, but the disposal of the stool may raise sharp disciplinary issues. Not all children evince a tendency to keep the expelled stool and play with it in some fashion, but certainly a great many do. Such tendencies usually provoke the mother to sharp preventive and disciplinary action, depending somewhat upon the age of the child when he exhibits such tendencies and upon the personality of the mother and her experience with the specific child.

Behavior of this kind cannot occur before the development of muscular coordination (toward the end of the first year) permits the child to do more than accidental, random handling of his stool. But purposive handling of the stool must be of rare occurrence prior to the inception of locomotion, since it would then necessarily require several accidental factors: that the child be left alone and undiapered in the crib, carriage, or play-pen; or, if diapered, that a piece of stool slip out from the diaper. Once the child is able to creep or to walk, he is likely to be left alone for a time sitting on the pot or toilet or in the potty-chair. He is then able to get up (or to squirm out of the potty-chair) and turn around to examine and handle the stool. The handling consists of smearing the stool upon himself or elsewhere, molding it in his hands, mouthing it, or sometimes swallowing it (see-touch-swallow sequence). This behavior, when it occurs, is usually seen during the second, sometimes the third year of the child's life. It may be tentatively conjectured that its first occurrences come about under the egis of the see-touch-swallow sequence and are not based upon any special valuation of the stool because it is his own product. The factor of special valuation is likely, if one may judge by certain reconstructions, to emerge after a disciplinary issue has been made of such behavior rather than before. This statement, however, is rendered dubious as to its universal validity in our culture by the fact that the behavior may not appear until well along in the process of toilet-training, *after* there has been a vigorous clash of wills between child and mother over sphincter-control, and it may then emerge from the child's defiant insistence upon his autonomy over both acts and products of defecation.

It may be that the mother who has hitherto been fairly easy-going and lenient in the task of toilet-training treats this particular "naughtiness" with much greater rigor and vehemence and may thus evoke in the child sharper conflict (in terms of heroic and unheroic choices) than he has hitherto been afflicted with. Where the mother's disciplinary behavior has been vehement and the child's behavior more or less defiant, the handling of the stool may be a device adopted by the child as a further means of defiance. This adaptation, in later life, has all the consequences described by Jones [45] and Abraham [2], which I shall not here repeat. The more docile or intimidated child will not make an issue of this behavior and reacts at once to the mother's strong disapproval with repression of the impulse.

This behavior of handling the stool, when it occurs, rarely persists long, since the majority of mothers in our culture react sharply to it, with vehement disapproval (often bodily chastisement) and with increased vigilance. All of the different adaptations above discussed, in connection with acts of elimination and sphincter-control, are seen in this connection too. In the more heroic (rebellious) adaptations, displacement is likely to be utilized as an ego-device. Ferenczi [15] has described a series of such displacements in which the child gradually and increasingly renounces his stool-handling impulse in favor of impulses to handle other substances and objects, playing first with mud (making mud-pies), then with sand, then with pebbles, and finally with coins, the latter, perhaps, developing into the more abstract interest in financial matters. There is perhaps a suspicious patness about this series, as if Ferenczi had set out to confirm Freud's contention [22] that the stool symbolizes money. While the details of such displacements may vary considerably (depending, in part, upon fortuitous factors determining the child's opportunities), there can be no doubt of the basic fact that substitute-finding is an important ego-device to offset the frustrations encountered in the mother's reactions to stool-handling.

THE ENDEAVOR TO REGULARIZE

Thus far we have considered the child's responses to toilet-training where the mother's methods involve conditioning by approval and conditioning by disapproval of various kinds. We have seen, in some instances, how the child's response is determined or colored by ego-devices already adopted in his attempts to adapt to the deprivations occasioned by weaning. We have postponed until now discussion of the factors involved for the child in other maternal techniques of toilet-training. These would include her attempts at regulating evacuation by introducing punctually scheduled sessions on the pot or other toilet-device, as well as the use of enemas or laxatives for the purpose of regulation. Ordinarily these techniques are introduced rather late in the process of toilet-training (latter half of second year, or third year; in desperate cases, fourth year), though occasional mothers begin to utilize them shortly after the child is able to sit up unaided (end of first year, beginning of second year).

This method of regular sessions on the pot can be particularly baffling and frustrating to the child, the more so the older he is. For the creeping or walking child, able to play with his toys in absorbed fashion, it is frustrating to be interrupted in whatever he is doing by being picked up, placed on the pot, and held prisoner there until the mother decides to set him free again. Rage, manifested by angry screaming, waving the fists, and stamping the feet, is commonly the child's reaction to such interference with the effectiveness of his aggression. Different modes of carrying out this technique will produce varying degrees of rage in the child. The mother may begin by telling the child that the time is at hand and that in a little while he will have to stop playing for a moment and sit on the pot. If the toilet-device is a potty-chair, she may permit him to have some of his toys on the tray of the chair, so that his play is the less interrupted. These devices, while sometimes successful in reducing the child's extreme manifestations of rage, do not always prevent whimpering and whining, and mothers frequently have the experience that permitting the child to go on playing with some of his toys while sitting in the potty-chair distracts his attention from the (to her) main business of defecation. Doubtless, when the mother makes use of such mitigating devices in the regularizing technique, the child, in many cases, does not react with great indignation to the interference with his play and to the mother's insistence upon an evacuation at a particular time. Such children, feeling securely loved by the mother, are likely to become toilettrained by any method whatever through a degree of cooperativeness with the mother's purposes, as soon as they comprehend them. Mothers who use these mitigating devices in the regularizing technique are likely to be of the type who elicit such cooperative responses from their children. Thus, this technique, applied in this gentle, considerate manner, is not necessarily traumatic in its effects. However, it must be said that in many cases the mitigating devices are not used at all, while in others they are more or less abandoned as the mother's impatience and annoyance with the stubbornly untrained child increase.

Although some children do become regulated by this device of scheduled sessions and expel a stool without much delay almost each time they are placed on the pot, it is much commoner that the child resists such regulation, engages in temper tantrums, as above described, or postpones evacuation, sometimes for long periods (an hour or more), until after being removed from the pot, and then soils, or sometimes withholds the stool for a day or more. While the mother may regard such postponing as constipation and may deal with it as a somatic ailment, the child often delays evacuation purposely, thus maintaining a degree of autonomy over this function and defeating the mother's efforts to coerce him toward perpetual sphincter-control. In this he indeed maintains sphincter-control; but on his own terms.

Freud explained such retention of the stool in the rectum as a form of anal erotism, by which he meant that the child engages in this behavior chiefly, or solely, because he finds pleasurable the sensation perceived when the mucous membrane of the rectum is stimulated by contact with the stool. The pleasure so derived may become an additional factor in maintaining the pattern of postponing evacuation, but it may be seriously doubted whether this pattern ever appears unless the mother attempts regulation of bowel-movements in the manner described. In so far as observed data justify this doubt, it is reasonable to assume that the child's pattern of postponement has the primary purpose of defying the mother's demands for expelling the stool. It is in these circumstances that the child may incline to place a high value upon his excremental product and may regard it as a valuable object much desired by the mother; its bestowal, however, lies entirely within his control. Such an attitude might bear important relationship to the *quid pro quo* type of explanation already arrived at in the speculations of the late oral phase, and may be determining for a common outcome of speculation in the disciplinary phase: the pattern of the broken promise.

It can be easily seen that the two reactions described in connection with the mother's attempts to schedule her child's bowel-movements (temper tantrums and constipation) are closer to the heroic than to the unheroic choice. The manner in which in turn the mother responds to these will be of significance in characterologic and symptomatic developments in the child's later life. The mother may be greatly concerned at having evoked so violent a reaction in the child and may be intimidated into breaking off her regularizing efforts. With so convincing a demonstration that rage is effective, the child may adopt temper tantrums as a mode of dealing with all frustrations and may become the highly impulsive adult whose anger is readily aroused and violently expressed. The mother may behave with indifference to the child's tantrums, persisting in spite of them in placing the child day after day upon the pot and leaving him there until he has evacuated or until she concludes he is not going to. Since in these circumstances the child's rage is ineffective, his tendency will be to abandon it (in so far as he is able to control it). The mother may, however, be unable to countenance such defiance of her authority, and may penalize the child for his tantrum, slapping and beating him until he is thoroughly cowed and crying in terror rather than in anger. Such experiences may compel the child from then on to stifle and inhibit all overt manifestations of rage, to disown (repress) impulses toward rage, and even to distort those circumstances in external reality which might impel him toward rage if they were correctly apperceived.

This ego-device with regard to rage may produce, in later life, a variety of pathologic patterns:

(1) It may produce those epilepsies which are not somatic in origin or it may contribute toward those which have a somatic provenance. The epileptic seizure may be regarded psychically as a spasm of violent rage with murderous blows of arms and legs, rendered harmless, however, by being struck at no target. Freud's interpretation of the movements of the hysterical epileptiform seizure is to the effect that these are coital in nature and that the patient is unconsciously performing a violent act of coitus, without a partner, as a result of a sudden emergence from repression of otherwise strongly inhibited genital (or phallic) impulses. While the observation of some epileptic seizures—those in which clonic movements of the extremities are absent or at a minimum —might suggest coital movements, the great majority of such seizures require some distortion of what is observed to be seen as resembling coitus without a partner: the rhythmic, violent flailing of arms and legs—seen in most seizures—has no counterpart in an act of coitus. To my mind, these movements are much more like a murderous outburst of rage, the person striking out and kicking in all directions, at random, regardless of the absence of anyone to be struck or kicked. The investigation of the unconscious motivations and character make-up of the epileptic tends, in my experience, to favor interpretation along the lines of rage and hostility, while attempts to see the seizure as displaced coitus fall flat and fail of confirmation.

(2) It may produce migraine headaches [39] with widely varying symptomatology which seem to have in common the background of a life-situation (familial or occupational) in which the sufferer feels trapped: he resents his situation, wants to get out of it, but feels that his hands are tied with respect to every means of alleviation that occurs to him. This impression was gained by me in the course of interviewing migraine sufferers (more than 50) in consultation work for the Selective Service System during the recent World War. The number is small, and the investigations were brief and superficial. But the

regularity with which "trap" situations emerged in this group was striking and impressive.

(3) It may produce other ailments generally categorized as psychosomatic, such as essential hypertension [5; 12, p. 280].

(4) A frequent characterologic outcome is found in those persons who complain that they cannot get angry even when they know circumstances such as unprovoked verbal attack or insult warrant such a response. Considerable variation is encountered in this group, from sulking (rather than a retaliatory outburst of anger) through rigid self-control (with tense working of facial and other muscles), to blandly ignoring the provocation.

The other ego-device of maintaining self-esteem by heroically defying the mother in postponing evacuation may, in later life, result in various intestinal disturbances: intermittent or fairly continuous functional constipation, which may in its turn set off a train of somatic events leading to other conditions, such as hemorrhoids; mucous colitis (often an outcome of the above-mentioned alternation of postponement and making a mess). It may have characterologic outcomes [2], among which I shall only mention the obvious ones of negativism, obstinacy, and the proneness to make others wait, often disappointing them ultimately.

THE ADMINISTRATION OF ENEMAS AND LAXATIVES

Sometimes, a more immediate effect of the child's rebelliousness by refusing to defecate on schedule is the mother's conclusion that he is "constipated" and her efforts (occasionally aided by a physician) at alleviation. A common treatment for the constipation is the frequent (even daily) administration of enemas. The child reacts initially with rage and terror. Insertion of the enema nozzle (even though lubricated) usually gives rise to pain owing to the reflex tendency to tighten the anal sphincter as soon as the skin around the opening is touched. The more tightly the sphincter is held shut, the greater is the strength required to force the nozzle through the opening and the greater the pain inflicted on the skin around the anus and that portion of the mucous membrane involved in the sphincter action. Pain is a powerful disturber of homeostasis and is regularly reacted to, first with rage, then with terror—terror because the deeply biologic significance of pain is that it warns the organism that some form of damage is either being perpetrated or is about to be. The tendency is somehow to avoid the damaging or potentially damaging agency; in this case, to squirm away from the enema nozzle. Perhaps the child is able briefly for two or three instants to evade the nozzle and learns in these brief moments that his squirming action is capable of achieving the abolition of the unpleasant sensation: his aggression can be effective. But almost at once this aggression is ineffective as the mother persists, succeeds in overcoming the resistance set up by the squirming and the sphincter-action, and gets the nozzle inserted. The child's aggression has failed: he is forced to endure the pain (and the implied damage or threat of damage) despite his best efforts. He experiences then, we may conjecture, rage (crying and random movements of arms, legs, and body) and lowering of self-esteem, since his aggressive efforts to avoid pain and damage have failed completely. Now, with the nozzle inserted, the pain subsides to some extent; but he is still in a position to be further hurt and damaged and, having lost confidence in his ability to avert such consequences, he may well be in a state of terror.*

As water flows into the rectum and, if this is not too blocked with feces, into the colon, these organs begin to contract in response to their overloading with foreign substance (the water), causing abdominal cramps. With this new and different pain, his previous terror, now all too justified, is greatly increased, reach-

* This is an excellent example of how a psychic *Reizschutz* (protective barrier) is broken through by a too powerful external agency. If the parallel with some of Selye's conclusions [63] is valid, the stimulus (external force) would be the equivalent in psychic terms of *stress* in Selye's concept. The reaction would be psychic *shock* and would have the purpose of counteracting, as best the organism may, the psychic damage entailed, and of instigating a process of recuperation. Some of the reactions to the administration of enemas, presently to be discussed, may suggest to the reader the manner in which substance might be given to this concept of psychic parallels to physiologic stress and shock.

ing a climax just before the nozzle is removed and his colonic action expels water, gas, and feces. Some relief of tension and a degree of restoration of homeostasis must ensue upon this expulsive action. But the whole experience has been a shattering and defeating one. Not only has he been compelled to succumb to *force majeure,* having had it clearly demonstrated that he is powerless to avoid pain and damage if a stronger person (the mother) is determined to inflict these upon him, but he has also been forced to acknowledge defeat in his effort to defy the mother's demands by postponing defecation. This is humiliation in its bitterest form and constitutes a severely traumatic event.

In an effort to rehabilitate self-confidence and self-esteem, the child's reaction to his humiliating defeat may be the resolve always to avoid situations in which something is done to him, that is, in which he is—in the precise significance of the word— passive. Such resolves and the effort to maintain them throughout a lifetime may result in those personality structures in which the individual is perpetually and tensely *doing,* is compelled always to try to take the initiative in any situation, and is uneasy and tense when, owing to circumstances, he cannot. He insists rigidly upon taking active roles and cannot enjoy the give and take of intermittent activity and passivity. Such persons always do the kissing, for example, and do not permit themselves to be kissed. They avoid, whenever possible, such passive situations as being medically treated with mechanical devices, being massaged, being anesthetized, being operated upon surgically. When they cannot avoid such things, they approach them with intense and disproportionate anxiety.

Women so afflicted find it difficult to play a passive role in heterosexual situations. Men who do not dare to be passive have a profound horror of and disdain for homosexuality (in so far as they conceive this in essentially passive terms), or if they are, on quite other grounds, neurotically homosexual, as is very occasionally seen, they avoid playing any homosexual role which they consider to be passive and tend to confine themselves to the practices of active pedication (anal intercourse) and active masturbation of the partner. Oral homosexual practices, being highly equivocal as to activity and passivity, are generally avoided by such men.

The details here described should be regarded as examples of a general trend toward avoiding passivity. Each of the examples given, particularly the sexual ones, has additional and much more important roots, and it must not be supposed that every person exhibiting such behavior has necessarily been traumatized in childhood by being given an enema. All of the phenomena adduced can be and usually are derived from quite other experiences in the oral and phallic areas. Nevertheless, whatever can be derived from the early resolve never to be passive has its origin in such experiences as that described. Other passive experiences, having nothing to do with toilet-training, but connected with the typically disciplinary features of the use of force and of attack upon bodily autonomy, may produce identical outcomes.

In the toilet-training situation which employs enemas, the immediate outcome of the child's experience of terror and humiliation may be the abandonment of his defiant constipation and the adoption of behavior more or less in conformity, in so far as his physiology permits, to the mother's demands for a stool on schedule. He may, however, recover from the terrifying and humiliating situation sufficiently to take courage to go on defying the mother with constipation, even at the risk of further enemas. It is not inevitable or invariable that a stool is in the rectum at the same time each day, and many factors contribute to variations in such regularity. Wise mothers know this and behave accordingly toward the child's failures or changes in schedule. Other mothers, however, make a ritual of regularity and torture their children with nagging, punishments, and daily enemas in the effort to have the ritual punctually performed.

The wiser of these unwise mothers who give enemas all too readily will desist at this point and let the child win his victory. But the less wise will replace the ritual of prolonged sessions on the pot with a new ritual of daily enemas. At first each enema will evoke reactions in the child similar to those already described. As the ritual enemas proceed, however, the child makes use of his adaptative capacities and begins to derive a modicum of pleasure from these originally unpleasant experiences. The originally painful stimulation of the anal opening by the nozzle may become pleasant, since stimulation of this zone can give pleasant sensations, provided the sphincter is held relaxed and the stimulation is sufficiently careful (not lacerating or bruising).

It seems to be a general principle of adaptation—human adaptation, at least—that, in so far as it is possible, unpleasant experiences repeatedly forced upon the individual become less so with time and may ultimately be regarded as pleasant. This principle can operate only when the unpleasant experience contains one or more elements which in themselves are or can become pleasant. This principle is responsible, I believe, for the phenomena observed by Freud and formulated by him in the frequently reiterated statement that the symptom, originally causing suffering to the patient and repudiated by his ego, gradually assumes a place in the ego's organization, either losing its subjectively disagreeable quality or becoming a highly, if secretly, valued feature of the total personality. Freud regarded this as the result of the tendency of repressed impulses to return to conscious expression and as a defeat of the ego by the id. However, the role of the ego here may be that of promoting the effectiveness of its aggression (raising self-esteem by learning to enjoy what it cannot prevent). The resultant feelings are more apt to be those of triumph than of defeat.

With frequent repetition of the enemas, the child learns that damage does not occur and no longer feels terror (or anxiety) in the same degree as he originally did. This lessening in terror (or anxiety) may favor that relaxation of the anal sphincter which renders stimulation by the nozzle pleasant rather than painful. The filling of the colon with water continues to produce expulsive efforts and abdominal cramps, but once the certainty of nondamage by this means is established in the child's mind, the pain is no longer felt as so severe. The expulsive act at the close of the enema was, it may be presumed, at no time unpleasant, since it was a familiar occurrence, was an aggressive act, and produced relief of the abdominal cramps, thereby tending to restore homeostasis.

It is in general true that an important factor in the intolerability (severity) of pain is the conviction, promoted by what seems to be a psychophysiologic reflex, that pain means damage, as indeed it ordinarily does. In certain familiar situations (for example, at the dentist's) one can, by a combined intellectual and emotional effort, inhibit the operation of this reflex, thus lessening the pain. With the abolishment of the anticipation of damage, a factor of anxiety is subtracted from the total experience of pain, which, as it seems, is the factor making for high degrees of severity. Obviously this can only be achieved when there is a high certainty of no damage, which involves an intellectual act as well as an emotional act of faith. In a situation such as a leg-amputation without anesthesia, the foregoing considerations would not hold, for the damage (crippling) is actual and there are numerous uncertainties (uncontrollable hemorrhage, for example) in the details of the operation. But the enema situation is one in which the child soon learns that he is not damaged, and the pain of abdominal cramps may therefore become much more tolerable.

This is all very reassuring in terms of transforming an originally traumatic experience into a nontraumatic, even a pleasurable, one. While it may have the excellent effect of convincing the child that he does not need to fear passive experience and his impulses toward passivity, and that he may even enjoy them, in the majority of such cases the recuperative process would go much too far in these directions. The child who has had such daily enemas, now enjoyed by him through a long period, is apt to become devoted to this mode of experiencing pleasure, to the exclusion of other modes more useful than this one in later life. His bowel-function and his anal region become imbued with disproportionate significance, and his emphasis on the value of a passive orientation toward others and toward life in general may tend to impede the emergence of more active and aggressive orientations, which, to say the least, are as important for him in our society as passive ones.

Since enemas, when given, are usually administered by the mother, the child's dependency on her for this daily pleasant experience, in which she physically handles him, may well produce a parasitism from which it may prove difficult to emancipate him and the mother as well. This parasitism becomes especially troublesome and productive of problems in those cases in which there is a background of much speculative activity concerning the restoration of the nursing situation (with its accent on exclusive bodily attention from the mother) and in which the enema-ritual is continued well on into the era of phallic experience, with its decidedly genital coloring. One could scarcely think of a better and more innocent way of producing what is sometimes called a "mother fixation" than by establishing such an enema-ritual at the age of $2\frac{1}{2}$ or 3 and carrying it on for one, two, or three years.

The administration of laxatives by the mother as a means of combating her child's defiant constipation is not frequently seen and, if uncomplicated by the establishment of an enema-ritual, is not likely to have such grave consequences. The undesirable results of this are mainly physiologic, though these may have psychic sequelae. Whatever of natural intestinal periodicity and rhythmicity may have been already established is apt to be disturbed by the inexpert administration of laxatives, and the unscheduled bowel-movements that result may confirm the mother's belief that her child is naughty and mean. This in its turn may impel her to adopt new methods of toilet-training, such as the enema-ritual, if not already instituted, or to increase the stringency of old methods (one or the other form of conditioning by disapproval).

Most of these methods of toilet-training, when rigorously applied by a rancorously determined mother, have the effect of prolonging the period of toilet-training and are likely to generate one or another of the pathologic outcomes already discussed. Less ominous in its potential later results and more likely to be successful is any method that is not begun too early in the child's life, is not too closely linked, in point of time, with weaning, and is not applied with excessive rigidity. The child who shows any tendency to cooperate in the process should be permitted some failures in sphincter-control without being penalized; he should be given some freedom to rebel and should sometimes be allowed to win a victory.

Such counsel is supererogatory to the mother who loves her child and has some sympathy and understanding for the difficulties that acculturation presents to this young and inexperienced creature and has the faith that he has the innate willingness to cooperate with her if given half a chance—that is, if treated with the consideration, kindness, and friendly respect that might be accorded to an adult. This mother will not regard her authority as inviolable and godlike and will place herself much more nearly upon the child's level, as simply an older, wiser, and more experienced person. She will tend gently to guide her child, rather than to coerce him; she will be a good teacher, knowing in advance that her pupil will learn only gradually, making many mistakes in the difficult process of learning, and often rebelling against the self-restraints incidental to the process; but knowing also that he will ultimately learn what she tries to teach him. A mother who loves her child may nevertheless make mistakes in disciplining him. She should be at least as lenient in her attitude toward her own mistakes as she is toward her child's. It is well for her to assume that they are both doing the best they can. If she feels she has dealt unwisely with some specific situation, she should try herself to learn from this unwisdom how she might deal with a similar situation in the future, with this child or perhaps with another. Mothers are people and, like all people, have their limitations, though one sometimes gathers that they ought not have any.

THE PATTERN OF THE BROKEN PROMISE

I have reserved until now discussion of an important psychic pattern which has its origin in the disciplinary area of the child's experience, though certain of its roots are in the late oral phase and in some of the speculations characteristic of that era. This pattern—which I call *the pattern of the broken promise*—can occur only in those children whose frustrations in the postweaning phase have led to a resurgence of impulses to re-establish the total nursing situation and who have consequently engaged in speculation as to why this is not restored and how it may be re-established. From the frequency with which this psychic pattern is seen in the neurotic difficulties of later life, one would conclude that a large number of children have the conviction of a promise made and broken, though it is impossible to suggest how large this number is.

The pattern is seen, however, with utmost regularity as part of the background—currently existing as an unconscious conviction—of those psychoanalytic patients whose weaning, as children, was regarded by their mothers more or less as a signal that now was the time at which to commence toilet-training (plus, perhaps, other disciplinary procedures). It is also seen, but not with the same regularity, among those whose mothers allowed some interval to elapse between weaning and the introduction of acculturative endeavors.

The pattern may be briefly described: the child assumes that the mother has made a tacit bargain with him, promising him that if he accedes to her disciplinary demands (usually toilet-training), she will agree to re-establish the nursing situation. For a time he carries out his part of the alleged tacit bargain, but soon concludes that she has no intention of carrying out her part of it. Thus he believes that she has broken her promise, and this conviction has its consequences, both immediately and in later life.

It will be seen at once that such a line of reasoning and feeling comes into the category of the *quid pro quo* type of explanation of why the nursing situation is not restored (she gets more for her favors from someone else) and appears to the child to offer him an appropriate solution in that it suggests a way of providing the *quid* for this *quo*. While some of the other things he might offer to the mother could occur to him in his earlier speculations, the factors of conformity to her demands for sphincter-control, regularity of bowel-movements, refraining from handling the stool (these details may differ widely from instance to instance) cannot enter his speculations as a possible bargaining point until after the mother has made her first endeavors to toilet-train him.

The child is likely to regard his earlier notions of a *quid pro quo* with great dubiousness and uncertainty: his penis may not be large enough, and his urine may be an unacceptable substitute for milk; he may not be sufficiently intelligent and skillful at this or that to win her admiration, try as he may; he may not be attractive enough to entice her or strong enough to afford her the benefits that strength can give her. But here, in her behavior with regard to toilet-training, she shows him unmistakably that there *is* something she desires of him. She seems to desire it strongly and, best of all, he has it in his power to bestow: to learn to control his sphincters; to produce a stool when she asks it of him; to refrain from keeping and handling his stool—all these things are easily done and at small sacrifice of effective aggression, if in return she will restore to him the deeply desired boon of sucking milk from her breast as she holds him close to her body. He does not know why she wants such things from him, he cannot fathom her reasons; but it is enough that she does want them and is willing to accept them (as he supposes) as a sufficient *quid* for this wonderful *quo*.

So he conforms, making the sacrifices entailed, and awaits the fulfillment of the mother's promise. Perhaps the early stages of nonfulfillment are explained by the child to himself: his conformity is not perfect in every particular; it has not lasted long enough to convince her that he is sincere in his efforts and will never return to his old toilet-habits; and other like explanations. But sooner or later a point is reached at which he must conclude that the promised restoration will not be made. With this conclusion comes a strong surge of feeling: commingled rage and resentment; humiliation at having been gullible, at having been cheated and deceived, and at having naïvely assisted in his own deception; spite, vengefulness, and the determination to teach the mother that she cannot cheat him with impunity. The rage and humiliation are reactions to the realization of the broken promise and indicate the incidence of trauma; they indicate, too, the intensity of the frustration and the depth to which self-esteem has sunk. The vengefulness indicates the effort to offset the frustration by demonstrating effectiveness of aggression and thus raising self-esteem from the low level to which it has dropped; it is the means of "curing" the injured psyche.

Clinical reconstructions of this situation of a broken promise never reveal the slightest tendency on the child's part to question the validity and actuality of his alleged bargain with the mother. Though actually he has only assumed that a bargain was made, it is as real to him as if the mother had made a promise to him in so many words, or, to use a figure which the child at that time is incapable of using, as if she had signed a written contract. Of all the things that may and do occur to his mind in consequence of the broken promise, the one thing that never occurs to him is the question whether the mother really made any promise. *He* made a promise, so genuinely and sincerely that he willingly made sacrifices in living up to it, and this convinces him that she made a promise, too. Furthermore, to question the basis of his very best possibility (as he sees it) of getting the nursing situation restored is to cut out the ground from under his dearest hopes, and for this reason he *prefers* not to question the actuality of the mother's promise. To maintain stoutly that a promise was made, although broken, is to retain the hope, however tenuous, that the nursing situation can and will be restored; perhaps the mother will relent and abandon her chicanery; perhaps the child can force her to live up to her bargain.

We have seen the same ego-device at work in the preference to maintain painful feelings of inferiority. This device is a form of denial of certain external realities; although these realities are not expressly denied, the stubborn and desperate refusal to examine the basis of certain convictions carries the implications of such denial. It is a modified form of the schizoid maneuver combined with a negative form of the see-touch-swallow sequence: one refuses to see what one fears to swallow (to make one's own in the sense of accepting and believing its actuality) and accordingly denies that it is there to be seen.

Attempts to force the mother to keep her promise constitute the immediate and often enduring response to the child's conclusion that he has been hoodwinked. His vengefulness and his coercive efforts combine in the determination to break *his* promise, too. In the immediate situation, the behavior whereby this determination is expressed will vary in detail depending on three different factors: (1) the precise nature of the mother's demands, whether merely for sphincter-control, or for this in addition to a stool on schedule, or for the renunciation of the stool itself, or all of these; (2) the preceding details depend, in their turn, both upon the toilet-training method used by the mother and upon the child's response to this, prior to the bargain; (3) of considerable importance is the degree to which, prior to the bargain, the child has felt intimidated by threats or experiences of the mother's disapproval. The first two will determine which particular elements in toilet-training the child will now refuse to perform, while the latter will determine the manner of his revolt, especially its degree of overtness.

In those cases in which the factor of prior intimidation is minimal, the child simply breaks training: he resumes his babyhood habits of free urination and defecation without regard to place or time; or, if the regularizing technique has already been in use, he renews his tantrums, or perhaps engages in them for the first time, or becomes constipated, either again or for the first time; or he returns to playing with his stool. The mother, who knows nothing of her child's silent reproaches and accusations or their content, is bewildered by this behavior and can only note that her child has unaccountably unlearned everything he had previously learned so well.

The child who has learned to fear his mother's disapproval and has already been intimidated into making one of the less heroic adaptations will not be so open as this in the acts which signify breaking his promise. He will sabotage toilet-training rather than frankly break it: his margin of behavior is narrow, since he is faced with the task of simultaneously breaking training and maintaining a safe degree of maternal approval. This child, while not abandoning sphincter-control altogether, will have frequent accidents of soiling and wetting. If the regularizing technique has been used, or is now instituted as the mother's response to the frequent accidents, he withholds the stool frequently, though not every day, and often couples the withholding with an accident shortly after being removed from the pot and dressed. In such instances, rage which otherwise might take the form of tantrums is attenuated to the much milder form of whining and whimpering. The preserving and handling of the stool, if this had been an issue prior to the bargain, is not resumed in overt form in these cases, though a phenomenon very occasionally seen is picking the stool, if hard and well-formed, out of the pot and hiding it somewhere. In the case of the more or less intimidated child, however, breaking of the contract does not commonly extend to the renewed handling of the stool, partly because his other acts of sabotage tend to generate increased vigilance in the mother, and partly because of the vehement nature of the disapproval that such behavior has previously evoked.

Whatever the child's outward behavior, the broken promise evokes in him attitudes toward the mother of intense hatred and bitterness, and these color his general behavior toward her in other spheres of his life. Quite suddenly the child whose disposition has been sunny and affectionate, particularly of late—during the period of anticipation that the mother's promise is about to be fulfilled—becomes sullen and unfriendly, reproachful and accusatory, unwilling to accede readily to any demands. The details and the intensity of these changes in disposition depend upon how open the child dares to be after previous intimidation.

These attitudes toward the mother, which are likely to persist as basic to the child's total orientation toward her and toward all authority-figures, give a decided coloring to his attitudes in the ensuing phallic area of experience and may become determining factors for his behavior in that area and in later life.

While the psychic pattern of the broken promise can be simply described in general terms, it nevertheless varies so greatly in detail from case to case, that its outcomes in later childhood

and in adult life show a considerable variation in emphasis.
These outcomes are mainly characterologic, rather than symptomatic; the factor they have in common is a deep-seated expectation of being cheated. Types of clinical material which intimate
the existence of this underlying pattern of a broken promise are
many and various. One example will suffice. The patient, a man
in his late thirties, often expected to be cheated in his commercial transactions: when he bought a new car, the dealer agreed,
as an inducement to the purchaser, to install a radio without
extra charge. During a sleepless night the patient worried over the
likelihood that the dealer would palm off on him an old, worthless apparatus that would function badly, if at all. Upon delivery
of the car, he could scarcely wait to examine and test the radio
for confirmation of his suspicions.

Emphasis in the pattern of the broken promise may be
variously placed, however. It may be upon efforts never to be
naïve and gullible, so that a skepticism almost compulsive in its
intensity and ubiquitousness becomes an outstanding trait. It
may be upon never being the first to commit oneself to any line of
action or any interpersonal relationship: such people prefer to
remain aloof from any new project until it is well launched; also,
their chariness of self-commitment may take the form of never
being the first to declare love in a relationship with another person, even if they feel love, though usually they do not feel love, but
remain uncommitted, even in their own consciousness. Emphasis
may be placed upon the avoidance of all promises: such people
feel uneasy about receiving promises or making them, and are apt
to be unduly wary about contracts and agreements of all sorts.
Others who have experienced the broken promise lay great stress
upon maintaining a hawklike vigilance toward all those upon
whom, despite their skepticism, they have come to depend for
anything important to them.

All these attitudes and many related to them are manifested as transferences in clinical and other situations.* The experienced analyst is familiar with the patient who assumes a

* The term *transference* is here used in the sense set forth in my
paper on the subject [67].

sophistication ("You aren't telling me anything new") toward interpretations, owing to a fear of being naïve, or who ridicules interpretations, for fear of being gullible enough to accept them. He is likewise familiar with the patient who does not commit himself to the analytic process, maintaining a constant attitude of "one foot in sea and one on shore" so that he may abandon the analysis at any point. Such patients remain wary of erotic feelings toward the therapist; even if they are aware of such feelings, they prefer to keep them to themselves and to deny them, waiting for the analyst to be the first to declare his erotic feelings toward the patient. Since most analytic patients are aware of the unlikelihood of such a declaration by the analyst, the type of patient under discussion is likely to deny—and therefore not deal with— such feelings for a long period; in many cases, not until the underlying resistance of conviction of the broken promise can be analyzed.

Patients are seen in analysis who keep reiterating in various ways that they do not expect much from the treatment and that they will not blame the analyst if the procedure fails with them. This behavior is often found to stem from an underlying insistence that no promise was made by either analyst or patient. In such cases, the patient's deepest conviction is that a promise *was* made—by the analyst, at least—but the patient attempts to spare himself disappointment by denying what unconsciously he has assumed to be true. The patient who watches every move, facial expression, tone of voice, and gesture of the analyst with utmost vigilance is so familiar as to require no more than mention.

An interesting transference-manifestation sometimes seen in these sufferers from the broken promise is the situation in which a patient will attempt to inveigle the analyst into a promise, usually of cure, or assumes an implied promise of this kind and then does his utmost to compel the analyst to break this promise. This maneuver has the purpose, for the patient, of proving what he thinks he already knows, that all promises made to him are broken, and confirms the conviction achieved in childhood, which he wants to maintain for the reason stated above.

It is very likely to be the case that in the course of a child's life, an actual promise will have been made to him by the mother or other significant person and actually broken, whether for justifiable reasons or out of sheer irresponsibility. It is often supposed by the patient, but sometimes by the therapist, that this occurrence was the traumatic event that produced one or more of the various outcomes we have been discussing.

There are mothers who habitually bribe their children into conformity with their demands, sometimes giving the child the promised reward, but frequently either promising the child something beyond their powers to give or brazenly refusing to grant the reward once the child has conformed. It is obvious that such behavior would serve to confirm, in retrospective manner, a child's now unconscious conviction of a broken promise in the period of toilet-training. "Can't you see how she always behaved?" one patient asked me in this connection.

It is striking, however, that a great many of these later broken promises to which traumatic significance is ascribed were promises broken for justifiable reasons, known to the child, and recognized by him as such at the time of their occurrence. For example, one patient told me that during most of her tenth year she had been promised a bicycle for her next birthday. Meanwhile the family's finances had deteriorated badly, which the patient knew, and the mother explained that she could not afford so expensive a birthday gift and gave the daughter roller-skates instead. This was cited, with great bitterness, as an example of a broken promise. I would maintain that such incidents do not possess traumatic force and serve, as in the case cited, either as a screen-memory for the truly traumatic experience of a broken promise, or, at most, as a reinforcement and confirmation of the early pattern. Children who do not have this pattern as an integral part of their early experience and psychic background, weather later experiences of broken promises, whether justifiably broken or not, without ensuing trauma to the extent described.

THE FATHER AS A FIGURE OF AUTHORITY

The disciplinary issues have been dealt with entirely in terms of child and mother. It may have occurred to some readers that no reference has been made to any disciplinary experience of the child with the father. This omission may seem to them all the more deplorable in view of the fact that, in later life, problems involving attitudes toward and relations with authority-figures so often center about males as such figures. The fact is, however, that at the phase of life under discussion in this chapter the father ordinarily plays a minor and negligible role. It must be a rare case indeed in which toilet-training is initiated and carried through by the father, for I have never encountered such a case, either by direct observation or as a result of reminiscences or reconstructions in adult patients. Other disciplinary issues also are handled more consecutively (with greater continuity) and in more detail by the mother than by the father. The latter may occasionally take a hand in such matters and may, when he does, introduce an element of greater violence than has been used by the mother. When this occurs, the intimidation of the child is likely to be increased and his conviction of the possibility of being hurt, damaged, abandoned, or cast forth may become stronger. This may have the effect either of confirming one of the more unheroic adaptations or of influencing the child to make an adaptation more unheroic than he might otherwise have chosen. Where both parents attempt to play a role in disciplining the child, the child may sense an opportunity to play one disciplinarian off against the other, particularly where the parents differ on some point of discipline.

It must be stressed, however, that the father in our culture usually takes little responsibility for the child's early lessons in acculturation and that his consistent disciplinary endeavors commonly begin at a later phase. When he becomes a factor in disciplinary issues, it is likely that the child's feelings and attitudes toward the disciplining mother will become displaced upon the disciplining father. It often happens in this later phase that the mother's role of disciplinarian is forgotten (repressed) and becomes assimilated to the father's disciplinary role. It is for this reason that, in later life, authority-figures are so often male. But behind such figures lies the now-forgotten disciplinary mother, and all the hatred, hostility, defiance, and rebelliousness, as well as all the conflict over these and ensuing adaptations to authority, originally accrued to the mother in her acculturating role.

As first noted by Rank [57] and later emphasized by Sullivan, the child undergoing stringent discipline at the hands of the mother may make the sharp distinction between this aspect of the mother and the indulgent one experienced in the nursing situation. It is sometimes maintained that the child views this variability of aspect as if it indicated two separate persons: the good mother and the bad mother. Such variability of aspect may long antedate the disciplinary area of experience and may be felt by a child in the processes of weaning. Indeed, the postweaning solution of using the father's penis as a substitute for the breast requires that the child divide his parental environment into a depriving part and an indulgent one. Where the father, in the disciplinary area of experience, plays little or no role in the disciplining, it is possible that he would be regarded by the child as equivalent to the good mother who lets him alone and makes no demands upon him. At the later phase mentioned above, when the father becomes the disciplinarian and the mother's disciplinary role is forgotten, perhaps the father now becomes the bad mother, and the mother returns to her earlier role of good mother.

While some clinical material seems to support the concept of the sharp distinctions here implied, my experience would indicate that they are only exceptionally made and that ordinarily both mother and father continue to be regarded as capable of pleasant and unpleasant behavior toward the child. Patients are seen who, in their initial statements about the parents, will depict one parent as angelic, the other as the devil incarnate. In the majority of such cases it does not require much probing, however, to unearth memory-details which contradict this homogeneity: the angelic parent was occasionally not so angelic, the devilish parent not always so evil.

THE ORIGIN OF THE SUPEREGO

Freud's concept of the superego [35] included the idea that it did not originate until the phallic stage of development and that it arose as a response to the difficulties encountered by the child in the Oedipus situation that characterizes this developmental phase. He regarded it as a species of identification or introjection, whereby ultimately both parents are taken into the psyche and there incorporated both as love-objects and as disciplining agencies. His emphasis, in terms of origin, was upon the former of these, and he accounted for the superego's enduring power as an automatic, unreasoning, and often irrational source of self-discipline by reference to this origin: it is as if the retention of the parents as internalized love-objects depended upon living up to their demands.

The question that I want to raise and to discuss briefly here is similar to that raised by Melanie Klein [50, pp. 28, 179, 194 ff.], namely, whether the superego originates at the relatively late date insisted upon by Freud or whether it originates earlier. This question also involves the reasons for its formation, as well as the manner and date of its origin. In the work above referred to, as well as in subsequent ones, Freud maintained that many of the automatisms of the superego (the specific behavior demanded by the superego under penalty of bad consequences for nonfulfillment) are not derived from individual experience but are phylogenetically determined, having been laid down in the germ-plasm as a result of certain crucial experiences in the history of the race and thus passed on from generation to generation. This is identical with Jung's idea [46] of a "collective unconscious." Discussion of this notion would carry us far afield. I mention it only to ask why, if certain automatisms are present in the psyche from birth (at least) on, they do not begin to show themselves before the fourth or the fifth year of life? The obvious answer to this question is that they might well remain in abeyance until they are stimulated into action by an appropriate constellation of circumstances, such as the Oedipus situation. In accordance with this line of reasoning, Freud's dating of the origin of the superego could be called into question by adducing the existence of situations, earlier than the Oedipal one, which meet this criterion of appropriateness.

Quite apart from considerations of a collective unconscious, the kind of situation in which maternal love (approval) is at stake as a result of certain unacceptable impulses and behavior of the child is already frequently to be observed in this disciplinary area, and we have seen how this kind of situation may arise (prematurely, as we said) as early as the period of weaning. Whether we say that the superego may originate at such times and in response to such situations is perhaps a matter of semantics, but automatisms do arise in this disciplinary area and conflicts there emerge so like those described as emanating from the operation of a superego, that it is of no moment whether the word *superego* is applied to them or not.

The superego is conceived as performing two functions: that of safely maintaining the mother (parents) as a love-object and that of defense against her disapproval and its consequences. In order not to encounter the mother's disapproval and punishment, one begins to demand of oneself the behavior that she demands. This mode of dealing with her disapproval differs sharply from the earlier one in which, if one could prevent her disapproval by avoiding detection, one carried out the impulse, whatever it might be. In the later development, one takes on the mother's own attitude toward the impulse and its resultant behavior and becomes self-critical rather than merely evasive. This is precisely what is implied in some of the more unheroic and docile adaptations to disciplinary issues wherein the forbidden impulse is repressed, rage and resentment toward the mother are repressed, and the child takes the attitude that he wishes to behave as demanded by the mother—all of this in order safely to maintain the mother's loving and approving attitude. One may prefer not to call this superego-formation, but surely it contains most of the elements that go into such formation and would at least merit the designation of a significant forerunner to this process.

V

The Third Experiential Area:

PROBLEMS OF RIVALRY AND GENITALITY

IN THE AREAS OF EXPERIENCE thus far considered, the child's interpersonal relations are relatively simple and consist, for the most part, in the various aspects of his relationship with his mother. We have noted the possibility of interpersonal relations somewhat more complex: the triangular relationships of a proto-Oedipal situation if the child's specific circumstances tend to bring this about; that is, if there is a younger sibling, or if his observations have led him to speculate on the possibilities of a unilateral or mutual nursing situation involving the mother and a rival. But such triangular relationships are far from being universally experienced in the two earlier areas, and it may be stated that the child in the oral and disciplinary areas of experience is principally related to the mother in a one-to-one, or linear, pattern, and that when a third person enters the picture, the child regards him with hostile, competitive feelings. The one not infrequent exception to this is the solution of the late oral phase in which the child may regard the father or older sibling as a potential substitute for the mother in a nursing situation. But this involves merely a displacement of one linear relationship by another.

THE EMERGENCE OF ALLOEROTIC IMPULSES

Thus far the child's play has tended to be either with one of the parents or an older sibling (occasionally with adult visitors to the household) or by himself (with toys). During the first three years of life the child has little opportunity and no great inclination to relate, in his play, with those of his own age. This was strikingly illustrated by observations made in 1924 and 1925 upon a group of children (aged two, three, and four) in the Home for Hebrew Infants. I was endeavoring to construct an intelligence test for such young children by presenting them with a standardized play situation (a group of six toys in a room apart from other children) and noting the items of behavior of children in these three age-groups with the various toys. In the course of this work I attempted to ascertain whether it would be possible to test more than one child at a time and observed that, while the two year olds and three year olds always played with the toys independently of each other, the four year olds would often begin to play cooperatively, though such attempts often ended in quarreling and fighting. This observation is, I believe, the same as that frequently made by child psychologists and is not merely the result of the special conditions obtaining in an institution.

At some time during the child's fourth year, however, his greatly increased skill in language, muscular coordination, locomotion, and looking after himself in general, enable him to enter situations (playing in the yard or playground, playing in the street or going to kindergarten) in which he meets with other children around his own age and joins them in play and other enterprises. Such groups of playmates may be closely supervised by adults, as in kindergartens and some playgrounds, or much more loosely supervised if the locus of activity is in the yard or vacant lot or in a street relatively free of traffic. In the latter situations an older sibling (usually sister) of one of the children is often entrusted with this supervision and carries it out with varying degrees of conscientiousness and consistency, so that there may be in some cases a tyrannical supervision, in others none at all, with a great range of possibilities between the two extremes.

A striking fact observable during this age-period (3½ to 6) is the emergence of genital impulses other than the masturbatory ones already discussed in connection with the two earlier areas. In the experiential area now under discussion, impulses toward achieving genital pleasure *with another person* make their first appearance. The question why these emerge now and not earlier is one that does not admit of a simple answer. Freud accounted for this in his libido theory by the statement that this is the manner in which libido universally develops; in other words, it happens for natural, biologic, or psychobiologic reasons. He suggested that this early genital flowering, to be later replaced by a period of cessation of such impulses and interests, and still later to be renewed by the recrudescent genitality of early adolescence, represents a recapitulation in the individual of the responses of the human species, in the course of its history, to the climatic changes in environment generated by geologic factors; namely, the warm period prior to the Pleistocene ice-age, the ice-age itself, and the ensuing period of recession of the ice, in which we are now living [*35,* p. 46]. This is an ingenious theory, but there are two things wrong with it: (1) the best modern theory of the date of origin of the human species is that this occurred *during* the Pleistocene ice-age itself, not before it, as Freud's reasoning requires; (2) even more damaging to the theory is the lack of universality of the latency period: in many cultures no latency period is observed in the life of the individual, and even in our own culture, it appears lacking in the life-history of many persons. In fact, clinical observation suggests that when such a latency period occurs it results from pathologic adaptations in the period preceding it; in other words, its existence indicates pathologic rather than normal development.

The latency period, as part of the life-history of a person, is much more commonly encountered in our society in those brought up in so-called middle-class homes than it is in those who derive from lower- and upper-class environments. Its existence seems based upon the strong sexual (genital) prohibition which is—or has been, until recently—one of the tenets of middle-class morality. But it is by no means a universal feature in the life-history even of middle-class children.

While a factor of constitutional development cannot be ruled out in the search for reasons why impulses toward genital activity and pleasure with a partner emerge during the fourth or fifth year of life, we do not know its nature and are entitled to doubt that here, as Freud suggested, ontogeny recapitulates phylogeny. In our ignorance of what constitutional factor might produce such a result, we are bound, as in other situations in which we are similarly handicapped, to attempt to find solutions involving environmental factors and interpersonal relations. Such factors are in any case operative, whether in synergism with a constitutional factor or by themselves.

We must consider the greatly widened social scope of the 3½ or 4 year old child, just as, in the oral area of experience, we had to consider the greatly extended scope afforded to the child's activities by the inception of the capacity for locomotion. The four year old's wider range of roving from home, both in space and in time, and his much greater freedom from surveillance and supervision offer him better opportunities than he has had heretofore both for contacts with others and for more untrammeled observation of others and their behavior. As an example of possible effects of this wider ranging upon the emergence of genital impulses, reference may be made to clinical material cited in my paper *The Personal Basis and Social Significance of Passive Male Homosexuality* [*64*, p. 45].

These superior opportunities, occasioned by relative freedom from supervision and wider range of locomotion, would offer occasion for witnessing the sexual behavior of animals and of other human beings, either children or adults. The so-called primal scenes (witnessing or overhearing sexual intercourse of the parents) are apt to occur in this phase of life. These phenomena are variously understood and reacted to by the children who observe them. Most commonly the genital behavior observed is interpreted by the child as a fight between the participants, the male being regarded as the violent aggressor, the female as the conquered, passive victim. The child senses that there is pleasure for the aggressor in such activity and humiliation and pain for the victim.

Freud makes the inference, in the case of Little Hans [24, pp. 183 ff.], that this is the meaning of Hans's fantasies of breaking a window in a railway car and of sneaking under the barrier in the sheep meadow. He supposes that Little Hans knows *instinctively* what he would like to do, genitally, to the mother, for the clinical material presents no primal scene or other observation that might have instructed the child in such matters. One gathers, however, that Freud himself was inclined to postulate the existence of such a scene, though its possibility was emphatically denied by the father, and that he refrained, for reasons of tact, from pressing the point or publishing his suspicions. At many points, the material seems to demand the reconstruction of such a scene, and the father's denial contains (to my ears) emotional overtones of resistance and wish-fulfilling rationalization.

Sometimes the child will sense that there may be pleasure for the victim, too, besides or perhaps rather than, humiliation and pain. The reaction to such experiences is likely to be one of confused and contradictory feelings, the precise emphases in a given instance depending greatly upon the nature of the experiences in the two previous experiential areas and the adaptations thereto. There will be shock and surprise at the unaccustomed violence assumed to be occurring between the parents. There will be identification, envy, and jealousy, but with which and toward which of the parents it would not always be easy to ascertain. There is likely to be anxiety, but the precise nature of the danger warned of by the anxiety would likewise not always be easy to know. Indeed it may be doubted that the child himself, even if he could articulate all the subtle shadings of his feelings, could give a precise and consistent account of his reactions. For the situation he is observing carries numerous potentialities in terms of gratification of various of his own impulses and in terms of various explanations and solutions of matters which heretofore have constituted problems for him.

It is generally assumed that the hitherto "normal" boy reacts by an initial identification with the father in the primal scene: he would like to be doing what the father is doing. Thereupon, since he is *not* doing this and the father is, he feels envy of the father and jealousy of the mother. If both of these emotions are strong, he feels hostility toward both parents and anxiety in so far as he conceives that this hostility might lead him in the direction of hostile manifestations toward both of them. Stronger emphasis upon envy rather than jealousy, or the reverse, would determine the direction and the intensity of the hostility upon one or the other of the parents.

But the reaction may not be as simple and straightforward as this. There may be, depending upon a variety of previous experiences and adjustments, identification with the mother as the victim in the primal scene, a strong sense of her pain and humiliation, an intense hatred of the father as a brute and a bully, and luxuriant fantasies of killing the wicked ogre and rescuing the fair lady from his evil power. But the identification with the mother may, depending upon a different background, occur in terms of a sense of her pleasure in passivity: then she will be envied as the target of the father's activity, and jealousy will be felt toward the father.

The terms *envy* and *jealousy* are often used interchangeably in the language, giving rise to great unclarity. As used throughout this volume, *envy* describes the feeling toward one who possesses what the envier would like to possess, while *jealousy* describes the feeling toward the possession (person or material object) which has either been taken away from one or appears in danger of being taken away. "The Lord thy God is a jealous God" means that the deity holds on tenaciously to his own people; he might be said to envy another deity who had managed to exert a superior attraction upon them. But the semantic confusion of the two words probably signifies the invariable linkage of feelings involving triangular situations containing a person, his possession (human or otherwise) and a rival for this. A situation frequently experienced is one in which another person seems

about to take away something or someone regarded as a possession. It is perhaps in the uncertainty as to whether one's own
possession of the object or person is authentic and the uncertainty as to whether the rival's attempt is going to be successful
that great confusion of emotion arises and that great difficulty is
found in labeling what one feels with any precision. The situation
is an uncomfortable welter which contains potential envy of the
rival (if he succeeds) as well as jealousy of the possession (whether
he succeeds or not), and therefore the whole confused state may
be described by the person experiencing it as envy or jealousy,
without regard to precise definitions.

Another important reaction to the witnessing of primal
scenes deserves brief mention here. This reaction is more apt to
occur if the first witnessing of parental sexuality occurs relatively late in the Oedipal phase, during the period of the child's
attempts to control and renounce his Oedipal impulses. The reaction is one of indignation to the effect that both parents are
hypocrites—perhaps, however, only one: they do not practice
what they preach; what they would penalize him for doing, they
do themselves. The effect is one of disillusionment and tends to
undermine parental authority. It tends also to weaken the cogency of the automatisms now, perhaps, in process of formation
as a superego. This reaction is the more likely to occur in those
cases in which the parents have tended to establish themselves as
strongly punitive, unapproachable, godlike authorities. In so far
as they have succeeded in creating this impression, the child's
disillusionment and ensuing indignation are the greater. Depending upon its intensity, this reaction may in later life have the
outcome of the so-called "constitutional psychopathic inferiority,"
marked by what often seems a total absence of superego automatisms. Less drastic outcomes would be the cynical tendency to
believe that all authority-figures and all seemingly good people
are essentially corrupt and the tendency always to search for the
clay feet of idols. This is frequently acted out in situations with
the analyst. The tendency to regard all restraint on the individual
(by government or by ethically-tinged agencies) as instituted for

the benefit of the authority-figure is another common outcome of
this reaction and results in that moral iconoclasm and bankruptcy
which characterized Hitler and some of his fellow Nazis. (This
viewpoint is affirmed by Maurice Samuel [62]).

I shall not attempt even to enumerate the many other subtle
variations of reaction and combinations of reaction to the primal
scene, much less to indicate the backgrounds of each of these: a
lengthy volume could (and perhaps should) be written on the
subject. My purpose in mentioning primal scenes at this point is
to adduce these as a possible source of the emergence of impulses
toward genital activity and pleasure with a partner at the stage
of life under discussion. Not all children experience such scenes.
They constitute one possible source of such genital impulses in
addition to the others mentioned; but when such experiences are
a source, a distinctive form is given to the emerging impulse: in
the case of *most* boys, the impulse to penetrate the female
(mother's) body with the penis; in the case of *most* girls, the
impulse to have the genital cleft penetrated by the (father's)
penis. Many reservations have here to be made, some of which
will be the subject of later discussion. The impulses, even when
taking the forms described in the text, are likely to be or shortly
to become conflictful. The italicized "most" makes allowance for
those boys whose genital impulses, after witnessing a primal scene,
may take the passive form of wanting to be penetrated, and for
those girls who, in the same situation, conceive the impulse to
penetrate, as the father does. There are cases, among both the
sexes, in which both active and passive genital impulses ensue.
All of these variations are generally accompanied by conflict and
some anxiety.

EARLY ALLOEROTIC BEHAVIOR

The forms taken by the genital impulses newly emerging
in this phase of life are various, and depend to some extent upon
the specific nature of their provenance in a given case. It has
usually been supposed that they always take the adult shape of
sexual intercourse in active or passive form, and the classic psy-

choanalytic concept of the Oedipus complex* is postulated upon this.

The terms *active* and *passive* as applied to genital impulses are not without a degree of equivocation. Clearly signified by the terms is the *visible* behavior in sexual intercourse, in which the male generally appears as active, the female as passive. When one comes to consider the less visible aspects of heterosexual behavior, the female genital functions as an active organ no less than the penis does; in certain respects, more so. Actually, the penis per se is not an active organ except at the moment of ejaculation; its apparent activity during intercourse is loaned to it, so to speak, by the body of which it is a part. The female genital may, indeed, behave passively; but it need not and often does not. By the contraction of its more external musculature in vaginismus, it can put up a strong resistance, sometimes successful, to penetration; or it may for a time imprison the penis in the vagina against the will of the penis-bearer, causing him pain when he attempts to withdraw it. Also, at the moment of orgasm, the vaginal musculature contracts in a rippling fashion upon the penis, producing distinctive sensations in the latter as if it were being "milked."

The genital impulses of this era may take quite other forms than the adult one, either in addition to or to the exclusion of the impulses toward the adult form of intercourse. In both boys and girls, the impulse may have the passive aim of having the genital organ touched by the hand of another person. It may be conjectured that this is the most common early form taken by these impulses.

In the case of the boy the impulse may include not merely touching the penis, but also squeezing it, stroking and caressing it, and in some cases mouthing and sucking it (which clearly follows the pattern of the see-touch-swallow sequence of the

* The term *Elektra complex,* sometimes found in the older psychoanalytic literature as the female counterpart of the Oedipus complex, has fallen into disuse. In this text, as in the current literature, the term *Oedipus complex* or *Oedipus situation* applies to both sexes.

late oral phase of experience and results from the child's ascription of his own sequence to the other person). When the boy's genital impulse includes the aim of having his penis mouthed and sucked, this result, if achieved, turns out to be a way-station toward oral pleasure of his own; but it must be realized that he does achieve genital pleasure in this sequence of events and that this is likely to become an integral part of the total pattern.

In the case of the girl, the impulse to be touched genitally includes stroking and caressing of her genital, with, in some cases, the addition of slight digital penetration of the vulvar cleft and manipulation (tickling) of the parts within the cleft, especially of the clitoris. It cannot be supposed that the girl of this age is aware of the existence of the clitoris as such. At most, she knows that she has a cleft in the perineal region, and that pleasant sensations are produced there upon masturbatory activity (of the nonmanual type already described) or upon digital manipulation within the cleft by herself or by another. Recent clinical observations by Phyllis Greenacre [41] indicate that the girl's genital sensations at this phase do not always arise from the clitoris exclusively: some little girls apparently experience vaginal sensations without clitoral sensations, while others may experience both. It is probable, however, that clitoral sensations alone are those most commonly experienced.

The genital impulses of this era may also take the form of wanting to see and to touch the genital organs of another person. Such impulses clearly show the continued operation of the see-touch-swallow sequence, the more clearly the younger the child. Where the object of this impulse is the male genital, mouthing is of almost automatic occurrence in the younger children of this epoch, whether boys or girls. The older the child who touches another child's penis, the more likely it is that the see-touch-swallow sequence will be inhibited at the point where mouthing would be the next step. The child who is being touched, if he is aware of wishing to have his penis mouthed, can often induce the other child to do so, but this no longer occurs automatically, as it were, and a certain amount of persuasion has become prerequisite. Such interruption of the sequence is often the result of the deepening conviction about the "dirtiness" of the genital area of the body and its products; the disgust, which was learned during the disciplinary experiences of toilet-training, has been gradually transformed from being an unwelcome opinion of the mother to a kind of eternal verity, "always" known by the child. One sees here the automatism of the superego in typical and unmistakable form: a viewpoint which, when first put forth by the mother, was of dubious validity to the child becomes, once superego-formation has been instituted, an absolute truth, which, since its origins and history are now forgotten (repressed) by the child, has all the subjective feeling of something always known, therefore "innate" and "instinctive."

Where the genital impulses take the adult form of penetration and being penetrated, it is often the case that some observation of sexual intercourse, whether between animals or human beings, has preceded this. But this is not always a necessary prerequisite. In sexual play among children, it may be that one of the children of the sexual pair has had such experience and initiates the other child, by word or act, into such behavior. Sexual seduction of children of this age by adults is of exceedingly rare occurrence, but it is not totally unknown. In such cases, the victim is usually a female child, the seducer an adolescent brother (or other adolescent boy), but sometimes a grown man. Still more unusual is the situation in which a governess or older sister places a small boy on top of her, his penis in apposition to her vulva, and has him go through the motions of sexual intercourse. Such seductions of small children by adults are so uncommon that they cannot rank high among the sources of those genital impulses of this era which involve penetration, whether active or passive.

Clinical experience sometimes suggests that the boy's genital impulses toward penetration may arise from a process of logical thought whereby observation of the female genital leads him to conclude that the existence of such an opening implies that something, namely the penis, could be put into it. Male patients occasionally produce memories of having reached such a conclusion at the age of five or six. It should be noted that such a process of thought implies awareness of the anatomical difference of the sexes and a full acceptance of what has been here observed. We shall later see that a complex psychic process is likely to have preceded such acceptance. Moreover, it would appear to me likely that patients who report such logical conclusions are not remembering the occurrence with complete accuracy: they are forgetting (repressing) the then-existing emotional element of a strong wish to penetrate, and are reporting the incident as if it had been an exercise of mere intellect. In other words, it seems likely that the child reaching so "scientific" a conclusion already has derived from some other source the impulse to penetrate genitally. In one such case, it was possible, later in the analysis, to demonstrate that this impulse derived from the witnessing of a primal scene, memory of which was repressed at the point in treatment when he reported his logical conclusion at the age of six.

THE CHOICE OF A PARTNER

Whatever the form taken by the genital impulses of this era and whatever their provenance, it seems of almost invariable occurrence in our culture that the partner vastly preferred over all others is one of the parents. For the great majority of boys this is the mother. In the case of girls, the classic concept of the Oedipus complex requires that the preferred partner shall be the father. This is said to be an instinctive choice, though in his earlier work on infantile sexuality Freud [33, pp. 2–24] was at some pains to point out that the sexual instinct per se implied no specific object and no specific manner of operation (aim). The idea of a ready-made object and aim of the sexual instinct was the old popular notion that Freud there questioned and refuted.

It might be more reasonable to assume—and clinical observation often bears out the assumption—that the girl's object in the early manifestations of impulses toward genital pleasure with a partner is the same as the boy's, namely, the mother. This is the more likely in those cases in which the form taken by these impulses involves touching and being touched, but does not yet involve penetration. The person of principal importance in the girl's life hitherto—during the oral and disciplinary phases—has been, as in the case of the boy, the mother, and this would suggest that the girl's early genital impulses would be directed toward the mother and that these impulses would continue to be so directed until something happened to produce a change. The girl's earliest wish for penetration takes the form, as already noted, of desiring to have the interior parts of her vulvar cleft caressed and tickled by a finger—usually the mother's. Failure to achieve this may lead her to perform such manipulation herself or to seek it from another child. If the other child is a boy whose own genital impulses have reached the stage of wanting to penetrate, being tickled by his penis may be regarded by the girl as an entirely adequate substitute for being tickled by a finger, especially so if this occurs before she has learned to regard the penis with misgivings (a topic later to be discussed). Failing such experience, the girl may look to the father as a substitute for the nonacquiescent mother, just as she may have looked to him in the postweaning situation. Her impulse toward being penetrated may gain greatly in strength if, as quite commonly occurs, she has interpreted her vulvar cleft in terms of a kind of mouth. Then, supposing she has in the postweaning situation thought of the father's penis (or, more vaguely, his genital bulge) as a substitute for the mother's nipple, it follows almost automatically that she will regard this as an appropriate target for what might be termed genital mouthing. It should be noted that she expects here to behave actively, to move toward the penis (as toward a target) and to mouth it genitally. Such an expectation could exist without misgivings only prior to her conceiving of the penis as an aggressive, attacking organ (as she invariably does at a later stage of this era). When these anticipations are frustrated by the father's failure to play the role she assigns to him, she may well assume, upon a basis similar to the boy's assumption, that the mother is a rival for such favors from the father, and will then be submitted to the typical Oedipal impulses of desiring exclusive genital possession of the parent of opposite sex and wishing to eliminate from the situation the rival parent (the mother).

The girl's conflicts here are likely to be sharper than those of the boy, owing to the fact that she must now feel hostility toward the parent who heretofore had been the object of her libidinal drives and who had provided her with security. However, feelings of hostility toward the mother are by no means novel to the girl, since, like the boy, she has experienced disciplining at the mother's hands and is likely to have felt resentment toward her on this account. The more unheroic her adaptation in that experiential area, the more troublesome and conflictful her Oedipal hostility toward the mother is likely to become. Under these circumstances, conflict may be sufficiently intense to tempt her to abandon the father as the object of her genital impulses and to return to desiring the mother as such an object. This tendency may become strongly reinforced after she has learned that the penis cannot be regarded as merely a target for genital impulses but is in itself an aggressively attacking organ. The girl's return to the mother and flight from the father, in these terms, may well initiate, among other possibilities, a neurotic pattern of homosexuality, later on to be discussed.

In any case, whether the mother or the father is the object of the child's blossoming genital impulses, he rarely achieves gratification of the impulses and ordinarily experiences continued frustration. But the rage and its manifestations which we have learned to anticipate as a reflex emotional response to frustration are modified by numerous factors and are rarely, if ever, seen in their crudest, most overt forms. The child's behavior in seeking genital gratification through one of the parents is not commonly open and unequivocal, but takes, rather, indirect and devious forms—hints and intimations rather than frank demands or requests. The most open form of behavior here is likely to be the boy's exhibition of his penis to the mother, with or without hints that he would like her to touch it; or the girl's frequent sitting on the lap of the father (or other male adult), whereby she brings her vulvar cleft into close apposition with his penis (or, as she may see it, his genital bulge). Direct requests for touching, both by boys and girls, do occur, but this approach is of relatively rare occurrence. Hints and devious efforts at seduction, such as those recorded in the case of Little Hans [24, pp. 162, 163, 166], are much more common. But there is no doubt that a large number of children do not even hint: they merely hope. Such indirection would suggest that in most cases a certain diffidence coexists with the impulse or becomes a regular concomitant of the impulse soon after it comes into being. The explanation of this diffidence offers little difficulty to those who in the manner of Freud believe that the impulses arise constitutionally from the naturally developing libido and encounter inherited taboos (arising from the collective unconscious) which are their "natural" concomitants.

The attempt to understand this commonly encountered diffidence by means of experiential factors alone offers certain difficulties, but enables us, at least, to account for individual differences in the degree of this diffidence, which the Freudian concepts cannot so easily explain. The experiential factors would have to be of almost universal occurrence in our culture, since some degree of diffidence is almost regularly found. The search for them leads in the direction of those factors which, in the later oral phase of experience, deter the child from the expression of frank demands for restoration of the nursing situation. While, in discussing such demands, we have stated that only those children who are traumatized in the attempt to find a substitute via the see-touch-swallow sequence are likely to become aware of a wish to have the full nursing situation re-established, we have also said that the children not so traumatized nevertheless maintain the wish unconsciously and more or less strongly and permanently repressed. Children in both categories have had to learn, during weaning, that the mother no longer wishes them to have certain of the intimate bodily contacts of the total nursing situation and would expect to experience her disapproval if they made efforts in that direction. In our culture this expected maternal disapproval is perhaps the universal, or almost universal, early experience which makes children more or less diffident about manifesting impulses toward bodily contact of the new kind under discussion. If this is true, then the specific intensity of maternal disapproval encountered by a given child will play a role in determining the precise degree of diffidence with which a child makes his bid for genital pleasure with the mother. Other and more adventitious factors of experience may contribute their share toward such results. Among these the degree of distaste learned in toilet-training for the organs of elimination and their products—how dirty they seem to the child—may be of some importance, in as much as the child would be trying to induce the mother to touch a part of his body which, in varying degrees, he regards (and knows she regards) as dirty. The child who in the initial stages of desiring genital pleasure with the mother is relatively lacking in diffidence and therefore makes more overt hints and bids for gratification, is likely, nevertheless, through the mother's sharply disapproving and threatening or punitive response to such attempts, to become a great deal more diffident.

In any case, the child who is already more or less anxious about the outcome of manifesting his genital impulses is the less likely to experience intense rage when the impulse is frustrated. His uncertainty has the tendency to make him feel that his impulse is more a wish than a need, to evaluate its expression more as something that *could* happen than as something that *must* happen. When such distinctions are made in attitudes toward one's own impulses, they are likely to affect the reaction to their frustration.

Another factor likely to influence the reaction of rage in this situation is a temporal one. No single occasion of frustration is apt to have a decisive quality for the child. If on one occasion his wiles and stratagems prove inadequate to produce the desired result, he may still hope that in the future he will be more successful. In other words, he does not ordinarily experience frustration in the sharp and definitive manner that might evoke clear-cut and intense feelings of rage and the manifestations thereof. Rather, the frustrations tend to be cumulative and it may be that no one experience of failure to seduce the parent is regarded by the child as decisively and finally cutting off all hope for the future.

Still another factor, not necessarily affecting subjective feelings of rage, but rather its manifestations, is the child's perception that expressions of anger toward a person in whom he wants to evoke affectionate, pleasure-producing behavior toward himself are apt to generate resentful, hostile feelings in this person, thus defeating his ultimate purpose. He has gained in sophistication since the days when without self-criticism he evinced rage if his thumb-sucking was prevented or his play was interrupted by demands to have a bowel-movement. Increased concern about the behavior of another person toward himself has fostered the defensive device of trying to foresee such behavior. One of his methods here is that of projection or analogy, that is, to ascribe to the other person what he himself would feel in a given interpersonal situation. ("Projection" as used in this book simply means the ascription to another of one's own feelings, but without any attempt to repudiate them as one's own; in psychiatry, projection usually signifies the denial of one's own feelings or intensions by ascribing them to another.) The child behaves, then, in accordance with what his projection teaches him and refrains from evoking resentment in the person from whom he desires something. This defensive device is an outcome of the child's heightened sensitivity to maternal disapproval in general and is related to superego formation.

In attempting to explain why the usual reflex frustration-rage is not encountered in the frustrations experienced by the child in the efforts to seduce the mother, I have not intended to imply that rage does not occur at all; rather, that it must, for the reasons given, undergo drastic modification. Rage here takes the form of subjective feelings of resentment and hostility, which may be expressed in displaced form—that is, in irrelevant or apparently irrelevant situations—or may achieve no overt expression whatsoever. The resentment here would be felt toward the parent (usually the mother) who does not accede to the child's wishes.

RIVALRY FOR A SEXUAL PARTNER:
THE OEDIPUS COMPLEX

Very early in this process of genital wish and frustration, speculation occurs of a type identical with that described in connection with the later oral phase of experience and seeks explanations and solutions of the frustration. Spurred on by the feelings of resentment toward the mother and the need to keep these at a minimum (lest they reach expression and endanger the child's hope of ultimate gratification), he discovers that he has a rival, the father, whose claims to the mother's genital favors are in sharp opposition to his own, and thus the lines of a battle are drawn. Many factors may support this explanation of rivalry. If the child has already set up a proto-Oedipus situation in his speculations about why the nursing situation was not restored, this greatly favors the recurrence of the idea of rivalry in the matter of genital frustration; in such cases, in fact, the idea of rivalry in the new situation is of almost automatic occurrence. The witnessing of a primal scene would produce in obvious fashion a conviction of rivalry, as would information from another child about parental sexuality. The observation that the parents occupy a bed or a bedroom together, from which he is excluded, particularly at night, or the observation of affectionate (not obviously sexual) exchanges between the parents—any or all the items which might have conduced toward the concept of rivalry in the late oral phase—may here be factors in generating a conviction of rivalry in the child's mind. In addition to these, the behavior of the father in response to the child's indirect overtures to the mother may well be conducive toward or supportive of this conviction.

It may, at first glance, seem absurd to suppose that a grown man would take with any degree of seriousness the rivalry of his young son for his wife's affection and favors. However, not only does direct observation show this to be by no means absurd, but theoretic considerations make it quite inevitable. Each father has once been a son of his own father and has thus experienced toward the latter the feelings engendered by rivalry—envy, hatred (sometimes murderous in its intensity and design), fear, anxiety, and the like. In the Oedipus myth, Laios takes with utmost seriousness the prediction that his son will kill him and marry Jocasta, and, by attempting to do away with the infant Oedipus, sets in motion the tragic sequence of events. Theodor Reik has concluded [59, pp. 85 ff.] that the custom of couvade has the purpose of diminishing and rendering harmless a father's hatred and enmity toward a son as a rival, such hatred being based upon the father's own experience as a son. The father of Little Hans shows clearly his objections to his son's competitive efforts to secure the mother's favors, as in his admonitions to the child and to his wife regarding her habit of taking the child into her bed in the mornings. Clinical observation of male patients whose wives were pregnant or had recently given birth to a son often shows that they are of two minds about this. Consciously they are often quite pleased at the prospect or actuality of a son, but their dreams indicate hostility toward this son and the need to intensify the wife's libidinal attachment to themselves—in general, an unconscious revival of Oedipal impulses.

The result of the establishment of the conviction of rivalry in the child, male or female, at this epoch is the Oedipus complex or situation, so highly typical and characteristic a feature of our culture. In its basic or positive form, as Freud termed it, this situation is marked by two impulsive tendencies in the boy, and *mutatis mutandis,* in the girl: an impulse toward exclusive genital possession of the mother, as we have already discussed at some length, and an impulse toward the elimination of the father, as the sole or principal rival for such exclusive possession.

The establishment of the conviction of rivalry brings nothing new to the child's genital impulses aside from the factor of *exclusive* possession. Up to this point he would have been content simply with the mother's participation in the activities implied by his impulses; now, since he conceives that his unsuccess in this is occasioned by the father's success in achieving such participation, it becomes necessary to demand (inwardly) that the mother cease her acquiescence to the father's genital claims and become complaisant to the child alone. In so far as this is his sole demand, the frustration of this produces in him resentment and hostility toward the mother, with a certain indifference, emotionally, toward the father. But this is not what it seems, and it is safe to say that such an attitude is always preceded by the usual hostile attitude (if not behavior) toward the father as a rival for exclusive possession of the mother.

In later life, the attitudes of certain men toward their love-objects would seem to demand the reconstruction that, in the Oedipus situation of childhood, hostility was felt toward the mother alone for her complaisance to the father's genital wishes, no blame or hostility accruing to the father. Some men, having to experience the infidelity or flirtatiousness of wife or other female love-object, develop intense resentment and hostility toward her, with little or no resentment toward the man with whom she flirts or is unfaithful. Their feeling appears to be that this situation has been mainly or solely engineered by the woman and that the rival has been merely acquiescent. This feeling exists even where, from the patient's own account, the rival played an obviously active and even determining role in the flirtation or infidelity. Such patients seem wilfully blind to this fact and insist upon providing the rival with so colorless and inactive a role in the events that no hostility beyond a mild envy is consciously felt toward him. When the analyst attempts to demonstrate this distortion, strong resistance is usually encountered, but it can be ultimately shown that hostility toward the rival is merely repressed. This would indicate that, where it exists, such concentration upon the mother's acquiescence to the father as the sole basis for the child's resentful feelings results from factors which deter the child from frankly hostile attitudes and behavior toward the father. As a solution of the child's Oedipal problem, such an attitude lies somewhere between the maintenance of relatively overt, hostile, competitive aggressiveness toward the father and the homosexual solution, to be later discussed.

The early stages of this rivalry are marked, as a rule, by greater frankness than is likely to be seen in the later stages.

Verbalized wishes that the father might remain away from home, temporarily or permanently, are more common than openly or deviously expressed wishes for his death, though the latter are by no means of infrequent occurrence. Frank defiance of the father, a characteristic manifestation of the child's rivalry, is seen either in displaced situations, or in situations involving more or less directly the genital wishes of the child. Being taken into the mother's bed (of which the behavior of Little Hans furnishes a classic example), being taken to the toilet and helped by the mother to perform his functions there, being dressed and undressed by her, being bathed by her, accompanying her to the toilet, or watching her take a bath, may become typical situations displaying the child's defiance. In these and similar situations the father may object more or less, voicing the opinion that it is improper or that the child is now too old for this sort of thing; or may merely frown or otherwise show irritation and nonapproval.

Competitiveness with the father, taking the direct form of verbalized comparison of bodily parts (in the child's favor) or indirect forms, such as in games of one or another sort, is another typical manifestation of rivalry at this time. Physical attack on the father (beating him with the fists, kicking him, scratching him, and the like), either without provocation, or in the course of a quarrel or of a game designed to make such violence plausible, is seen in some instances, though it is probably less common than some of the other manifestations. Similar behavior by the girl toward the mother is seen in this phase, but with great emphasis upon disobedience and defiance of her disciplinary authority in general.*

What has been described is typical of the behavior of the child whose effective aggression has not yet been forced, by in-

* The reader should understand that descriptions of behavior couched, as in many paragraphs in this book, in terms of the boy, apply, with appropriate changes, to the girl's behavior as well. It is cumbersome to repeat such descriptions, merely altering the terms, and while certain variations do occur, depending on the sex of the child, it has seemed to me wiser to abandon these occasional nuances than to risk losing the reader's attention by mechanical repetition.

timidation or other means, to find distinctly indirect and devious modes of operation. But it will be noted that even those relatively overt modes of hostile and competitive behavior toward the rival offer a considerable range of variation in overtness. Defiance of the father's objections against situations of physical intimacy with the mother is a more overt form of rivalry, perhaps, than verbalization of the wish that the father would stay away or would die, especially so since such wishes are rarely put into verbal juxtaposition with the child's genital impulses toward the mother. Physical attack on the father is a more overt expression of hostility toward him than comparison of bodily parts or defeating him in a game. Also, within these various categories of behavior, expression may be more or less direct.

Although it may be assumed that all these modes of behavior are characteristic of the child who has been least intimidated, whose fears of father and mother are much less intense than those of other children, and whose past experiences have encouraged him toward the more heroic choices in general, it will be seen that there is a wide range of adaptations within the category of the more heroic choices. Even among this group of children there are differences in degree of sensitivity to the disapproval and hostile behavior of the parents, and the precise mode of behavior will depend upon how greatly the father is feared and how great the necessity to avoid the mother's disapproval. Abstention from the most overt manifestations of hostility to the father may in some cases be occasioned by the anticipation of the mother's disapproval for such behavior as much as by the anticipation of paternal reprisals; this is apt to be a factor, even if not a weighty one, in determining the child's precise behavior in many instances.

RIVALRY AND HOSTILITY

The anxiety about arousing the father's hostility and about the consequences of this becomes a more and more cogent factor in the Oedipus situation as it advances toward its later stages. This anxiety is often based upon the father's actual behavior in response to the child's more or less overt hostile rivalry—the father's irritation or anger and the threats and actual chastisements that may emanate from this. Where such response is absent or minimal, the child reasons by projection or analogy that, since *he* would be angry and hostile if treated as he treats or wants to treat the father, such behavior can be anticipated even if it has not yet emerged. Indeed, as he conceives it, the greater his triumph over his rival, the more bitterly hostile his rival will be.

The consequences anticipated as a result of the father's hostility are reprisals and punishments taking the form of strong measures looking toward the definitive failure of the child's genital impulses toward the mother and the prevention of his success in this direction. Such measures assume, in the child's mind, the form of banishment from the parental home (thus being cut off from security as well as all possibility of intimate contact with the mother) or of castration, which is used here in its technical psychoanalytic sense to signify forcible removal of the penis. We have seen that the former of these was thought of by some children, during the oral and disciplinary phases of experience, as an outcome of extreme maternal disapproval. Its recurrence now, in such children, would be entirely predictable. The idea of castration, however, is a new one, as regards specific content, and requires some explanation.

Obviously, castration has no bearing in the case of the female child. She can—and does—fear that the strong disapproval and hostility from the mother as a resentful rival may take the form of banishment from the mother's favor and even from the parental home. But clearly the girl cannot fear the loss of a penis that she does not have, nor can she anticipate physical loss of the vulvar cleft or its interior. Freud offered a choice of two assumptions here: (1) that the threat of withdrawal of the mother's love was equivalent to the threat of castration; or (2) that, since the female child can experience no threat having the cogency of castration, she does not have the boy's incentive to repress the Oedipal impulses; thus she does not form a superego as stern and severe as that of the boy and therefore inclines toward compromise with her Oedipal impulses to a much greater extent than the boy can permit himself to do. These mutually contradictory choices seem to reflect Freud's uncertainty as to how precisely the girl normally solves her Oedipus situation: Does she repress—or renounce—the impulses, as the boy does; or does she actually retain them and behave more deceitfully and hypocritically than the boy? Something rather equivalent to the boy's castration-anxiety is, however, to be observed in the girl. Her initial attitude of genital aggression toward the penis (as a passive target), modeled upon her earlier pattern of oral aggression, suffers disintegration as experience teaches her that the actuality of the penis necessitates for her a dual rather than a unitary concept of it: she must now take into account the possibility (even the probability) that the penis will not behave for long as a passive target, but will turn on her and attack her genitally, causing pain, injury, and damage to the interior of her body. This is what she must anticipate, she thinks, if she continues to campaign for genital gratification via the father's penis. So it becomes the part of wisdom to abandon impulses which may result so catastrophically. There is, for the girl, this castration equivalent: fear of bodily damage inflicted not by the infuriated rival, as in the boy's case, but by the love-object because of the manner in which she is loved.

As has been pointed out first by Staercke [70], and later by many psychoanalytic writers, including Freud [36, p. 93], and Alexander [4, pp. 140 ff.], the thought of castration as a possibility might arise as merely one in a series of deprivations already experienced by the child—separation from the mother's body at birth, separation from the mother's breast at weaning, separation from the stool in toilet-training. It is as if these experiences prompt him to expect the total loss of all situations and objects which provide him with intense pleasure. It would seem that this would not be a particularly cogent factor unless the child had learned to associate these deprivations, or some of them, with conduct undesirable to the mother. Otherwise it seems to involve a kind of cosmic thinking quite alien to the mind of a child. There are other factors, however, which may contribute to the anticipation of castration in the Oedipal situation. The penis is an organ whose functioning has already been submitted to discipline in toilet-training: in being compelled to learn sphincter-control (of the bladder) and to give over his free reflex mode of urination, the child has already experienced some impairment of autonomy over the functioning of the penis; it may be conjectured that he makes little or no distinction between an organ and its function. Also, if he has utilized masturbation in the regressive, consolatory manner described in the previous chapter, he has learned to value highly the organ involved. Interference with the child's masturbatory activity by the mother in her disciplinary capacity will serve to reinforce the child's doubts, aroused in learning sphincter-control, about retaining autonomy over the organ.

Furthermore, castration may seem to the child a procedure well calculated to defeat and eliminate a rival for the mother's genital attentions. If the very organ by means of which he hopes for gratification from the mother is eliminated, his hopes will be eliminated with it. In so far as such an idea is a factor in the child's anxiety about castration, it may be supposed that he has entertained the notion, more or less clearly, of castrating the father. In that case, his anxiety about his own possible castration is another instance of the child's tendency to project his own motivation upon another in analogic fashion.

MODES OF RESOLUTION OF THE OEDIPUS COMPLEX

As Freud [23] has pointed out, this castration-anxiety is a potent factor in the resolution of the Oedipus situation: the child who fears castration elects to play safe and, renouncing his genital wishes toward the mother, has no longer any reason to be hostile to the father, thus averting the dangerous consequences of this hostility. Freud stated that in these circumstances the child's Oedipal impulses are actually renounced; they are not merely repressed, but collapse and vanish completely from the psychic scene. This may be gravely doubted, since such collapse and disappearance of impulses are never seen as a response to fear and anxiety in other settings, and since, clinically, such total absence of unconscious Oedipal impulses is never encountered.

It might be adduced here that the postulated total collapse of Oedipal impulses is never encountered clinically because all analysands are neurotic and have never made this allegedly normal adaptation to the rivalry situation. However, many analysts have a good deal of experience in analyzing candidates for psychoanalytic training, some of whom, surely, might be excluded from the category of neurotic analysands. In many years of experience in these training analyses, I have never encountered an analysand whose Oedipal impulses had collapsed and were totally lacking; the impulses may have been more or less successfully repressed, but they were demonstrable in every case.

It is necessary, therefore, to postulate that in the most nearly normal Oedipal situation—certainly in the most usual in our culture—the genital impulses toward the mother and the hostile impulses toward the father succumb to repression under the spur of castration-anxiety. This repression may be more successful or less so, but repression of the impulses, rather than their collapse, marks the passing of this situation.

Freud's experience with the case of Little Hans might have suggested to him another possible solution to the Oedipus complex, somewhat different from that just described. In that case, Little Hans did not repress his Oedipal impulses as a result of castration-anxiety. Indeed, the work of the entire first portion of his analysis consisted in showing Little Hans that he was *needlessly* afraid of his father. In the single interview with Freud which marked the termination of this first portion, he was given the information that his father had known, in advance of the child's birth, that Hans would be hostile to him and why, and therefore the child need have no fear of reprisals because of hostility toward his father. The alteration in the content of Hans's phobia showed that this insight was effective and that the child no longer feared castration: he no longer feared that the horse, symbolic of the father, would bite him; rather, that the horse, pulling an overloaded van, would fall to the ground. Hans had now started on a new tack, and the second portion of his analysis centered about the issue whether, granted now that he had nothing to fear from the father, the mother would be exclusively acquiescent to his wishes. This involved the question of how much she loved others (the father and little sister), how willingly she had become pregnant, and presumably, how voluntarily she engaged in sexuality with the father. Hans concluded that his actual chances for an exclusive relation with the mother were small because she did not desire it, but his terminal fantasy is of an idyllic and exclusive relationship with her; in that fantasy the father is eliminated from the scene, but in most benevolent fashion, being granted the same boon of an idyllic relation with *his* mother (Hans's grandmother).

It will be seen that here, too, the Oedipal wishes are not lost; but neither are they, for the moment, repressed. Rather they are retained, but without anxiety. By the time Freud met him again, quite by accident, Hans was a young man of nineteen and had completely forgotten his analysis and all its issues and events. We receive no hint as to how or why these things had finally succumbed to repression.

Ultimately, it appears, the Oedipal impulses become repressed, but it would seem that this repression is not necessarily the result of castration-anxiety. A consideration of the case of Little Hans suggests that a solution in which the Oedipal impulses become attenuated through some insight into the reality of the parental relationship and the mother's attitude toward it, and in which castration-anxiety is at a minimum, is the more healthy one, though doubtless not the more common one in our society.

The reader should understand that thus far we have been considering the most favorable outcomes of the Oedipus situation and that the solution made by Little Hans comes close to being the ideally favorable one, which is a solution in which the child, realizing that various factors of reality conspire to make his Oedipal wishes impossible and doom his rivalry to ultimate failure, decides to abandon so unprofitable an enterprise.

Such an ideal solution would be in consonance with the goal of "partipotence," defined and described in a paper of mine [*68*, pp. 389 ff., pp. 397 ff.]. Partipotence marks the abandonment of the ideal of omnipotence, generally maintained by all neurotics and other immature people, and involves the recognition that forces exist, external to oneself, which require discrimination: some of them may be manipulated and controlled completely, others only partially so, still others not at all. The external forces which ordinarily operate as obstacles to the Oedipal impulse fall into the last category, and the most ideally mature solution of the Oedipus complex is based upon the recognition and acceptance of this. Observation, of oneself and others, however, indicates that partipotence is a relatively unstable adaptation, and that relapses into demands for omnipotence occur, even in those who have genuinely understood and accepted partipotence as a wise and useful adaptation. It is on this account that even the healthiest, psychically speaking, of adults in our culture show at times, in their episodes of acting out and transference, evidence of the unconscious retention of the major Oedipal impulses.

We do not know whether an ideal solution of the Oedipal situation is ever made; if it is, those who have made it never reach the analytic couch, whether as patients or as candidates for psychoanalytic training; a solution such as that of Little Hans is the closest approach to it reported in the literature.

THE CULTURAL BASIS OF THE OEDIPUS COMPLEX

If, therefore, the most favorable solutions involve repression, more or less complete and definitive, this constitutes a basis for the frequently expressed conviction that in our culture everyone is more or less neurotic and that no one attains unequivocal psychic health or normality. However, this is to suppose that we know of some universal standard of psychic health and to ignore the careful work of a Kardiner in establishing the relativity of such health in terms of varying cultural settings. The universality of childhood Oedipal situations within our culture rests firmly upon the circumstances and structure of that culture: (1) the fact that the social unit of western civilization—the biologic family, in which the child's biologic helplessness forces him to remain throughout childhood—provides for the developing child a relatively tight and narrow arena in which his impulses must operate; (2) the prolonged and deeply-ingrained prohibitive attitude toward free sexual behavior, embodied mainly in the Christian tradition and in its historical matrix, the Jewish tradition; (3) the fact that parents, raised in this prohibitive tradition, may often tend, unconsciously, to rebel against it, thus, without conscious intention, behaving somewhat seductively toward their children; (4) the fact that the parents themselves, having developed in their own Oedipal situations demands for exclusiveness, tend to inculcate by example this same demand in their children; this lesson receives voluminous support in the child's later reading of love poems and love stories (novels), as well as in his experiences with the theater in its various forms.

While it is true that different historical eras have seen considerable laxity in the actual operation of the tradition prohibiting free sexual behavior—the Elizabethan age in England, the Eighteenth Century throughout most of Europe as well as in some of the American colonies, and our own epoch—and while it is equally true that certain geographic areas have been throughout the Christian era more lax in this respect than others—notably France and Italy—nevertheless there has never been a time or place in Western civilization in which children were even permitted, much less encouraged (as in Bali, for example), to engage freely in sexual play. For many centuries now our children have been trained prohibitively with regard to sex, though as adults they have sometimes revolted on a large scale against this conditioning.

It seems, then, impossible for our children to avoid confrontation with Oedipal problems, though we know of cultures and could readily imagine others in which such problems are nonexistent or at a minimum. From the viewpoint of what is culturally possible, we would have to acknowledge that in maintaining our culture as it is we produce character-structures that are relatively neurotic at best. But careful investigation might show that we gain more, from the viewpoint of the whole culture, in maintaining these conditions than we lose by making every member of the culture somewhat "ill." The "illness" here cannot be great or very handicapping since, according to most of its denizens, the culture operates with relative success—or has done so until quite recently.*

In any case, no wise person would care to have in his own hands the decision to alter our present culture in respect to the details under discussion.

SEXUAL CURIOSITY, CASTRATION-FEAR AND PENIS-ENVY

Before going on to discuss the more pathologic outcomes of the rivalry situations in this area of the child's experience, it will be well to pay some attention to the growth, during this phase,

* The intimate psychic connection between Oedipal demands for exclusive possession and the "sacredness" of the institution of private property is too obvious to require elucidation. It may be gravely doubted whether the abolition of this institution, by coercive political means, can destroy the individual's wish for it, deeply rooted as this wish is in his earliest experiences and in the cultural circumstances that contribute to bringing them about. To obviate this wish for exclusiveness—that is, to abolish devotion, even unconscious devotion, to the institution of private property—would require more far-reaching alterations in the pattern of our Western culture (and all major cultures) than have yet been undertaken or even contemplated—even in the Soviet Union. It would mean, as a first and indispensable step, abolition of the biologic family as the basic social unit and the establishment in its stead of large communal household groups for the rearing of children, groups without centralized leadership or authority, in which the individual child would have numerous, interchangeable "mothers," "fathers," and "siblings." Such communal household groups among primitive people have been described by Robert Briffault [9, vol. 1, pp. 591 ff.]. The social ideals of Communism would require this drastic alteration in cultural patterns if they are to be established in a manner totally unconflictful—unconsciously as well as consciously—for the individual. As most of human society is now constructed, the individual person cannot avoid a yearning toward private property (an unconscious one, at least) and those who destroy this institution are bound to be faced with a tendency toward re-establishing it, both in themselves and in those supposedly benefited by the change.

of the child's sexual curiosity, what he does about this, the types of experiences he is likely to encounter in his explorations, and the convictions and theories that may be an outgrowth of his experiences. We have already seen how the extension of the child's social range at the outset of this experiential area contributes toward shaping his impulses into the form in which he desires genital pleasure with a partner. We have also seen that the see-touch-swallow pattern of behavior still operates here and that having his own genital organs *seen,* and *seeing* those of others, become important preliminaries to the *touching* which occupies so significant a position in these early genital adventures. Thus sexual curiosity (the wish to see) leads to the utilization of whatever opportunity presents itself for exploration. Children at this age are as a rule eager to show their genitals to other children and to see, in return, the others' genitals. Their interest in these matters spurs them to spy on the parents in their nocturnal privacy; frequently they come upon primal scenes in these nocturnal wanderings, and much nighttime prowling and wakefulness in small children result from such attempts. It is likely, in the course of such explorations, that a child will encounter, for the first time in his life, the fact of anatomic difference in the sexes. It is usual for boys to react differently from girls to this discovery, and we shall have to consider their reactions separately.

Owing to extreme maternal vigilance or other circumstances, not every child has the opportunity to explore. Some children appear not to explore, even if they have opportunity; while others, by the time they have become adults, have repressed the memory of their exploration. I once encountered a male patient (borderline schizophrenic) who at the age of twenty thought that the female genital was a protuberant organ, like the penis, but that it was hollow, and that intercourse took place by coupling the two organs, like a hose and faucet. Whether such conscious notions parallel unconscious ones in an individual case cannot always be determined. In the case cited, dream material indicated that his unconscious knowledge about the female genital was a good deal more accurate than the conscious version mentioned. I have seen cases, however, in which I had to conclude that accurate knowledge, conscious and unconscious, of the genital structure and function of the opposite sex was a late acquisition, at puberty or during adolescence.

It is quite common that the boy initially denies the evidence of his eyes. When Little Hans, at 3½ years, saw his baby sister being bathed, he perceived a difference in her genital region but denied its real significance: she does have a penis, though it is tiny or hidden; but it will grow and become visible. This distortion of reality is likely to persist for some time. There are two classes of reasons for this "blindness," and they often serve to support each other. The child's best instrumentality for understanding another person is, as we have already seen, reasoning by projection or analogy. This is actually an assumption that the other person is very much like himself, and this assumption has often proved both accurate and helpful. He has, of course, perceived certain differences, both of quality and degree, mainly the latter. The mother, for example, has breasts, which he totally lacks, but these make her The Mother and play a significant role in making her the object of his desire rather than an object for identification. He has perceived that she and the father, as well as all adults and older siblings, are bigger and stronger than he is, but these are differences of degree rather than of quality: he is not without size or strength and he may set his hopes upon equalizing these factors by "growing up." His projective or analogic reasoning processes produce more or less consistently accurate results—everyone else does have a mouth, for instance, and eats; everyone else has hands and feet and uses them more or less as he does—and he has come to regard these processes as reliable guides to useful apperceptions of the real potentialities of others toward him for good and for ill. The child's awareness of his own penis prejudices him, through the instrumentality of analogic thought, to conclude that all other human beings (including the mother [24, p. 151]) likewise have a penis. To believe the evidence of his eyesight, that human beings exist who do not have any penis at all, is to abandon all too readily this reliable instrumentality, which has hitherto served him well in his attempts to appraise reality.

But, rather more important than this reason for ignoring or distorting the evidence of his eyesight, the conclusion he might have to reach if he fully accepted this evidence is a most unwelcome one. He is, at this stage of development, quite incapable of the concept that the penisless little girl was actually born that way and that she has, instead of a penis, genitalia which are authentic biologic organs, having potential functions different from his own in certain respects, but none the less valid, biologically speaking. Lacking this concept and still clinging to his analogic processes of thought, he would have to assume, upon the evidence of his senses, that the little girl had been born with a penis, that she had somehow lost it, and that the vulvar cleft was the hole left by its loss. Such a conclusion would inevitably lead him to the terrifying thought that what has happened to the little girl could also happen to him. Rather than accept such a possibility, he denies the actuality of what he has seen and creates hypotheses which support the denial; in effect, he says, "It is tiny, but it will grow; it is now hidden, but will one day emerge."

The conclusion about the possibility or likelihood of his own castration will be the more terrifying and the more avoided depending upon the degree of insecurity already felt by the boy concerning the retention of his penis whole and intact. This insecurity and the degree of it are dependent upon the existence and the details of certain previous experiences: actual threats of castration (upon his exhibiting his penis, for example, or as a deterrent to masturbation) ; the stringency with which sphincter-control (of urination) is demanded in toilet-training; whether masturbation has been made a disciplinary issue and to what extent; the child's manner of adaptation to previous deprivations. The more secure the child in general, the greater will be his feeling of security about retention of his penis. The relatively secure child will usually take without great seriousness castration-threats made prior to his discovery of the difference in the sexes, though after this such threats may produce anxiety, and it sometimes occurs that the threats previously made now retrospectively become a source of anxiety.

The anxiety produced in the course of these early explorations may be such that exploration ceases and is even avoided when another child suggests it; in such cases, the knowledge gained in the explorations is apt to be repressed and is overtaken by an amnesia which, in later life, may produce the conviction of never having known about the facts of sexuality until puberty or adolescence.

It is, however, uncommon for such intense anxiety to emerge thus early in this area of experience. Much more common is the initial denial or distortion of the visual evidence, with continuation and extension of exploratory activity. This leads, sooner or later, to acceptance of the fact of real difference, always on the basis of postulating that the little girl once had a penis but lost it. With this acceptance, the boy's concern about the possibility or likelihood of his own castration, either at the hands of his hostile rival, the father, or of his nonacquiescent, disapproving mother, becomes so great that his anxiety causes him to begin repressing his Oedipal impulses in order to avert this danger. As a rule the father presents the major threat of castration. Often the boy is convinced that the mother secretly favors his designs and would acquiesce if she, too, did not fear the father.

What is the nature of this danger? How does it come about that the possibility of losing his penis, quite actual to the small boy at this era, is so cogent a motivation for repressing his Oedipal impulses? Freud's answer to this question is to the effect that the essential nature of all danger is helplessness, which he defines as a condition in which one has strong impulses which it is completely impossible to put into operation. This might be further defined as a condition in which disturbance in homeostasis cannot be terminated, in which equilibrium cannot be restored. Helplessness, in other words, is a condition in which aggression is totally ineffective. The specific kind of helplessness foreseen by castration-anxiety is one in which the child will have genital impulses in full intensity but no means whatsoever for discharging them, since, in the boy, the penis is the organ essential to this. Rather than risk this danger, the boy decides that discretion is the better part of valor, and he abandons, by repression, the impulses that tend to place him in this situation of helplessness.

Freud brings the anxiety about death into the same category as castration-anxiety. He implies that death is ordinarily conceived, not as a state of nothingness, but as a state in which one perceives (receives stimuli), develops inner disturbance and impulses to do whatever would be appropriate to restore homeostasis, but, being paralyzed in a motor sense, is totally unable to effect such restoration and must exist in a perpetual state of helplessness, as defined in the preceding paragraph; in other words, a living death. Many descriptions of the Christian hell, notably some of those in Dante's *Inferno,* correspond to this concept of death.

What are the initial reactions of the little girl to the discovery of an anatomic difference between the sexes? We may suppose that she, like the boy, has hitherto assumed, by her instrumentality of analogic reasoning, that all beings are, like herself, endowed with a vulvar cleft from which urine emerges and which, upon appropriate stimulation, is the seat of certain pleasant sensations. If in the course of the speculations of the late oral phase she has discovered that the father has a penis, the significance of this appears to be solely that this protruding bodily part might serve as a good substitute for the mother's nipple: it does not at this stage seem to cast doubts upon her analogic process of reasoning any more than the mother's possession of breasts, she herself having none, tends to do.

The reasons for the emergence of genital impulses, their nature, and the curiosity and exploration which ensue, are entirely similar for the girl to what has been described in the case of the boy. When these explorations are carried on with a boy, she discovers a protruding organ where there should be, according to analogy, a cleft. Her reaction to this discovery contains certain elements of similarity to that of the boy, but also certain significant differences. She does not tend so strongly to deny the evidence of her eyesight: it is considerably more difficult for the human psyche to deny the existence of an object actually seen than to affirm the existence of an object actually nonexistent. Hallucinations tend rather to fabricate persons and objects than to do away with them.* Furthermore, the girl does not have the little boy's motivation for distorting the visual evidence in order to avoid the conclusion of the possible imminence of castration. In so far as the idea of castration is an element in her reaction, it is already accomplished, a thing of the past and not a future danger to be averted: the *consequences* of castration might arouse concern in her, but not the *act* of castration, as the boy fears it.

The discovery of the boy's possession of an organ she does not possess may be illuminating to her and may appear to explain to her certain circumstances of her existence which were hitherto puzzling and troubling to her. These circumstances are the result of cultural and specific familial outlooks which have tended to place her at some disadvantage, in her own eyes, to boys (whether siblings or playmates). She has, perhaps, had experiences of being regarded differently and of having been discouraged from or forbidden certain behavior which her male peers were privileged, even encouraged, to engage in. "Little ladies," for example, do not, in some families, climb trees or play in such a way as to tear or soil their clothes, or fight with other children; whereas "boys will be boys" and their mothers are often pleased and proud when they behave like "real boys" and climb trees, play hard enough to tear holes in their clothing and get thoroughly dirty, and engage in bodily combat with their male playmates. These and innumerable other items relate to cultural ideals and to specific familial notions involving evaluations which place males in a superior position to females. The orthodox male Jew, for instance, thanks God each morning that he was not born a woman. The little girl

* This is not to deny the existence of the scotomata (blind spots) sometimes encountered in hysterical and other patients. One patient had been coming to my office daily for six months before she noticed that it contained a grand piano which occupied fully a quarter of the floor-space. In the text, I speak of a *tendency* rather than an invariable principle of human psychology.

may have felt keenly the lower evaluation placed upon her and the underprivileged status to which she has been relegated, but without any satisfactory means of explaining to herself why these distinctions were made. She has known that the privileged beings were called "'boys" and that they were dressed differently, but this explained nothing and may have seemed an arbitrary kind of distinction: for some unfathomable reason, discipline was made harder and stricter for her than for them, and she has felt resentment toward the disciplinarian on this account, but, until the discovery of the difference in the sexes, she has not understood the reasons for all this.

Now, after this discovery, a great illumination appears; she thinks that boys are valued higher and are more privileged because they possess a *something* where she, as she supposes, has a *nothing* [51]. This would seem to have a purely narcissistic basis, since it contains in itself no inkling as to why otherwise this something is more highly to be valued than the alleged nothing. However, for the little girl whose speculations in the late oral phase have included explanations involving a *quid pro quo* in the form of a mutual nursing situation, the high value she places upon the possession of a penis would not be so exclusively narcissistic: the boy is valued more highly by the mother because the penis is seen as a *quid pro quo,* placing him in an advantageous bargaining position. This line of speculation may also account to the girl for the breaking of the promise, if she has already felt victimized in this respect. Such considerations have greater cogency for the girl who has male siblings (whether older or younger) than for the girl who is an only child or whose siblings are all female. However, in so far as she has regarded the father as the privileged rival, the illumination emanating from the discovery of the difference in the sexes may be applied to this rivalry.

The outcome of this discovery cannot, however, consist wholly in this intellectual enlightenment which enables her to explain to herself why she has hitherto been regarded and treated as an inferior kind of being. A further result, which appears inevitable in our culture, is that she *envies* the boy the possession of his penis: she wishes that she, too, had one or, at the least, that she might somehow deprive him of this advantage. Along with the emergence of the factor of envy there begins a process of speculation in which the girl attempts to find explanations for her lack of so apparently valuable an organ. Here she is likely to suppose that she once had a penis and that it has been somehow lost. She may suppose that her mother has cut it off, as a punishment for some offense, but her ideas as to the nature of this supposed crime may be vague and may relate merely to a generalized nonconformity to the mother's disciplinary demands, or they may be more specific. In the latter case, her crime is likely to have been the consolatory masturbatory activity, already discussed as a common outcome of frustration both in the oral and disciplinary areas of experience. Notions of this kind, adopted at this phase of childhood, are often encountered in the adult psyche, where they persist as unconscious convictions protected by stubborn resistance. As they gradually emerge into consciousness, these ideas are apt to appear in truncated forms. Frequently the idea is expressed by such female patients that the penis they once possessed was removed by the mother for spite, though further overcoming of resistance usually enables the patient.to elaborate that this was not really spite but was a punishment for persistent masturbation. Occasionally encountered here is the idea that the loss of the penis was the result of self-inflicted damage due likewise to persistent masturbation and conceived of as a process of erosion. The degree of conviction accruing to such ideas bears close relationship to the degree of guilt concerning consolatory masturbation, which, as we have already seen, is in its turn dependent upon the incidence and extent of such activity and the manner in which the behavior was handled by the disciplining mother.

Thus far we have dealt with the girl's discovery of the difference in the sexes, the illumination she receives as a result, the emergence of penis-envy, and her attempts to account for being without a penis, as if these various reactions were explicable on the basis of experiences derived from cultural factors alone. The implication is that there is no psychobiologic basis for penis-envy and its outcomes and that if the culture were altered in a direction tending toward elimination of prejudices favoring men over women and toward equalization of the sexes, females would not experience penis-envy. This ascription of penis-envy to cultural factors is, so far as I can gather, the position taken by several writers of the so-called "culturalist school," notably by Clara Thompson [74, 75, 76, 77] and Karen Horney [42, chap. 6]. I am not aware that Sullivan, who must be regarded as the historic founder of this school, ever expressed views along these lines.

While there can be no doubt that cultural factors play a highly significant contributory and supportive role in creating and maintaining penis-envy in female children and the women they later become, it should not be overlooked that penis-envy has also an important psychobiologic basis. In the attempt to question and refute Freud's position that penis-envy has a *solely* psychobiologic provenance, Thompson and Horney have gone to the other extreme of denying that it has *any* biologic basis. A position which acknowledges the existence and significance of both types of factor seems better able to account for the actualities of penis-envy. Few writers have taken into consideration a male counterpart for the penis-envy of the female, though Little Hans's intense wish to bear children of his own might have led Freud toward formulating such a concept. Envy of the vagina is frequently seen in male homosexuals and has generally been regarded as a feature specific to this neurosis. However, the close relationship of vagina-envy to male envy of the child-bearing function of women has not been appreciated, and the latter has not generally been given any significance in the psychology of the male. Felix Boehm [8] and Lucile Dooley [11] have written along these lines and, more recently, Frieda Fromm-Reichmann [40]. Male envy of the vagina and of the child-bearing function is a factor which needs much greater theoretic and clinical elucidation.

There is, however, at least one psychobiologic factor that requires consideration as an element in the production of penis-envy in the girl. This is the marked difference in the mode of urination of the two sexes. The boy urinates in a standing position in a relatively forceful stream which he is able to direct at a target by manipulation of the penis. The girl urinates in a relatively feeble stream, which she can direct only by standing or squatting over the target. Freud [*31; 38,* p. 50 n.] took note of this difference and used it to formulate a hypothesis to the effect that women, rather than men, are traditionally keepers of the hearth because they are unable to extinguish a fire by urination without the risk of getting burned; men, on the other hand, can stand at a safe distance from the hearth fire and still extinguish it by the urinary stream. This hypothesis requires no comment, though a Middle English meaning of the verb "to piss" is given by the *Shorter Oxford English Dictionary* as "to wet with urine; to put *out* (fire) in this way."

The boy's mode of urination gives him an advantage over the girl, since it enables him to attack her (by urinating on her) without her being able to retaliate in kind. As a method of attack, this scarcely seems effective until it is recalled that children learn in the course of toilet-training to regard urine as disgusting and dirty (as poisonous, in some cases) and that such a form of attack would be regarded as soiling and humiliating to its victim, regardless of its harmlessness in more material terms.

It happens not infrequently that the girl discovers the anatomic difference in the sexes through witnessing an act of male urination (by sibling, playmate, or adult) rather than through mutual exploration. The effects of making the discovery in this manner are the same as above described, except that the idea of the penis as an organ of attack is conceived in immediate association with the discovery. The girl's evaluation of the penis as an organ of hostile aggression is made clear to many mothers and to many teachers in play-schools and nursery-schools by the vehemence with which the child expresses her wish to urinate standing up and in a stream, as well as the seriousness and vigor of her attempts actually to urinate in this manner. Such behavior is frequently observed, though it is not of universal occurrence. Nowadays, with children being sent to play-schools and nursery-schools at two and three years of age, this behavior under the egis of penis-envy, long regarded as typical of the phallic or Oedipal stage of development, is seen a good deal earlier. This kind of behavior is obviously the result of introducing the child into more complex social situations than he would ordinarily seek of his own accord at this age. Such evidence gives strong support to the view that psychic development is a correlate of specific individual experience rather than of "natural" evolution of a libido factor, a development that would occur when its time has come, regardless of the accidents of external happenings.

Some mothers, moved by the distress and agitation of the little girl over her disadvantage (as she sees it), attempt to alleviate the child's emotional disturbance by pointing out the advantages of being female, notably the potentiality of bearing children in the future. While this is often in a measure comforting to the little girl, it never seems to her to offset the present advantage over her enjoyed by the boy, and it becomes her ambition, often verbally expressed, as well as in a rich variety of speculations and fantasies, one day to have a penis. The way in which this ambition may be realized is variously conceived, even by the same child: the penis will appear (or reappear), by natural processes, as she grows up; someone (often father or mother) will one day give her a penis; she will castrate some male and will then somehow attach this penis to her own body. The last method will be particularly favored by those children whose penis-envy takes the form of wanting to equalize matters by depriving the boy of the organ that makes him superior. All these patterns of ambition are observed in many females in later life as unconscious motivations giving distinctive coloring to their characteristic attitudes toward men and to the interpersonal behavior emanating from these motivations, which also produce many of the phenomena of acting out and transference seen in psychoanalytic situations involving female patients. The psychoanalyst is familiar with the female patient whose unconscious motive in seeking psychoanalytic treatment is thereby to acquire a penis—by "natural" growth (somehow impeded hitherto), by gift from the analyst, or by theft from the analyst (castration). He is likewise familiar with their vindictive bitterness toward him as they begin to realize that their wish to acquire a penis is doomed to disappointment in the psychoanalytic situation, as it has been elsewhere. It is often through the interpretation of this apparently irrational bitterness that these patients become aware of the deadly seriousness with which, unconsciously, they regard this wish to have a penis.

The unconscious wish to have a penis produces likewise the emotional phenomena toward men typified in general by one female patient who experienced seizures of what she called "black rage" toward men, whenever she felt at any disadvantage with respect to men in general or to one in particular. In this same category of adaptations, though markedly different from the viewpoint of emotional coloring, is the occasionally observed phenomenon of the fantasied penis, at times amounting to an almost hallucinatory paresthesia of actually having one [66, p. 388].

The observed difference in mode of urination and the inferences drawn from this by the female child constitute a psychobiologic factor of great importance in the origin of penis-envy. Other psychobiologic factors may operate to some extent at this early epoch and contribute their share toward the production of penis-envy, or they may not be taken into account until somewhat later, when they serve to reinforce and maintain penis-envy. These are the factors of body size and strength, which may or may not be of importance in any given contest between a girl and a boy, though in general the statistical differential is a valid consideration. These physical factors again result in advantages to the boy in terms of hostile attack and are thus in the same general category with mode of urination.

All the psychobiologic factors that produce and maintain penis-envy converge upon the biologic fact that anatomic and physiologic differences in the male and female genital apparatus make it possible for the female to be coerced sexually (raped) by the male, while the reverse is not possible. The male may be seduced, against what may appear to be his conscious will, by a female; but this requires stimulation of some sort (psychic, somatic, or both) to produce an erection of the penis. This will not occur if the male's unwillingness is unconscious as well as conscious—as in the case of some homosexuals, for example—whereas it is possible for the female to be raped even when her unwillingness is thoroughgoing and deepseated, unconscious as well as conscious. In this ultimate sense, the male can successfully attack the female sexually (without her acquiescence), while the female cannot succeed in her sexual attack on the male unless he acquiesces. These factors are not apperceived in this way by the female child, it may be assumed. Her concern, at this age, is not the possibility of rape; rather, it is the possibility of being submitted to the indignity and humiliation of urinary attack on her person, without being able to inflict a like indignity and humiliation upon the boy. It is perhaps because of her need to compensate for this lack that her attack upon boys so often takes the form of throwing some liquid at him —a glass of water or a bottle of ink (sometimes the container as well as its contents).

In attempting to evaluate the relative importance to be ascribed to cultural and to psychobiologic factors in the production of penis-envy, it seems to me clear that neither category is likely, alone and unaided, to generate penis-envy of the intensity so frequently observed, clinically and otherwise. In the absence of a biologic basis for penis-envy, the culturally based handicaps to which the girl is subjected might make her envy the penis as the sign or badge of a privileged caste in society, but the emphasis would be placed most strongly upon envy of the *position* of the male, not upon envy of the bodily part which is merely his ticket of admission, so to speak, to this position. In the absence of cultural factors, the advantage of urinary attack possessed by the boy would not seem so great. It is the combination of the two kinds of factors which, as it seems to me, produces penis-envy to the extent and in the degree so commonly seen in the females (children and adults) of our society.

THE PHALLIC STATE OF MIND

It was one of Freud's most astute formulations that children (both male and female) in this stage of concern over genital matters feel, think, and behave as if there were only *one* genital organ, the penis. It was this formulation that led him to name this the *phallic* stage of libido development, and he regarded this conviction concerning the one genital organ as highly characteristic of this phase of life and as determining sexual attitudes and behavior in the child at this age. We have seen how the boy ultimately supposes, after he has accepted the evidence of his senses, that the girl once had a penis but has lost it. We have also seen how the girl jumps to a similar conclusion: she had a penis at one time, but has lost it, through punishment or self-inflicted damage. She sometimes supposes that she was not given a penis at birth, through the mother's spite or negligence and unconcern. In any case, both boys and girls suppose that everyone is or should be born with a penis and that there is no other sort of genital organ. The important question, then, for both sexes centers about the presence or the absence of a penis. The possibility of two different kinds of genital apparatus, each valid in its own way, is not even considered by the child of either sex. Attempts on the part of parents or others to introduce this idea are rejected and ignored almost automatically both by male and female children. The attempt made by some mothers to console their little daughters in the throes of penis-envy by adducing their future capacity to bear children has little effect on the girl's troubled state of mind; often this capacity appears merely to confirm to the little girl her handicapped condition. When this is not the case, it is apt to appear to her an irrelevant matter: her trouble and her disadvantage are here and now; to be able in future to bear children is all very well, but her problem is how to get a penis, now or soon, and what, she is apt to ask herself, does bearing children have to do with that?

This conviction about the one genital organ, the phallus, leads to other important convictions in children of both sexes, highly determining in their attitudes, both then and in later life, toward themselves and toward others, of their own and opposite sex. The boy regards himself as intrinsically superior to the girl: he has a genital organ, she has none; he has been able somehow, despite all perils, to retain the precious organ, she has failed to do so. By the same token, the girl considers that she is inferior to the boy. Furthermore, he can utilize this intrinsic superiority to exploit the girl by attacking and humiliating her with his urinary stream. This actually occurs on occasion, as reminiscences of male and female adults attest. One female patient recalled how, at the age of six or seven, she was held from behind by one boy, while several other boys took turns in urinating on her. She recalled vividly her feeling of being soiled and humiliated, as well as the triumphant glee of her attackers.

The boy feels contempt, scorn, and on occasion pity for these inferior beings, as well as a smug complacence and self-assurance because of his superiority. His penis is to him an organ of effective aggression not only because it enables him to attack with the urinary stream, but because, in numerous cases, it has become the means (through masturbation) of compensation for failures in effective aggression: he supposes that without a penis such masturbatory consolation is impossible and that the little girl cannot, as he can, by such means turn frustration into gratification, failure into success, defeat into triumph. This gives him additional reason to feel pity and contempt for her, since he is unaware that she too can masturbate, although lacking a penis.

As soon as the boy reaches the conclusion that he can achieve pleasure for himself by inserting his penis into the vulvar cleft (the hole left, as he imagines, by the removal of the penis), his feeling of intrinsic superiority is magnified by the belief that he can exploit the girl's inferiority for his own pleasure. That the girl might enjoy this, too, does not enter his calculations here, as this seems to him not even remotely possible. Here again, he reasons by analogy and attempts to understand the sensations of a vulvar cleft by means of the only analogous organ he possesses in that general region, namely, the anus. The insertion of his penis into the vulvar cleft, in anticipation so pleasurable to him, would be felt by the girl, he imagines, exactly as he would feel the insertion of some foreign body into his anus—as, indeed, he may have already experienced with enema nozzles or rectal thermometers. He visualizes her experience as an unwelcome, painful, humiliating invasion of bodily privacy and intactness, which, nevertheless, he will force upon her for his own pleasure.

In so far as the girl contemplates the possibility of insertion of the penis into her vulvar cleft, as she is bound to do if a boy attempts or suggests it, she may imagine this in similar terms of unpleasure and humiliation, since she, too, may reason in this situation by the same analogy of the anus. Thus she sees the boy as wanting, in this act, to exploit her disability (the site and vestige of her mutilation) for his own pleasure. Nevertheless, she may be driven, particularly in the later phases of this phallic era, for reasons already discussed, to desire such insertion, notwithstanding her misgivings. In such girls, the certainty of exploitation in the sexual act may be considerably less than it is in boys, since the latter are not so subject to conflict in this respect; but many such girls resolve this conflict negatively; that is, they avoid intercourse for fear of exploitation, attack, and damage.

The girl's state of mind which regards insertion of a penis into her vulvar cleft as humiliating and exploitative is by no means of invariable occurrence; it is more apt to exist and to persist in those girls who have merely contemplated the possibility, rather than in those who have actually experienced it. One female patient, a hysteric, related that such insertions were a matter of almost daily occurrence between the ages of four and eight, with two brothers (two and four years older) and two other boys of like age. She could not remember having enjoyed this, although she remembered no great unpleasure in these experiences; she persisted, throughout a long analysis, in claiming that she had merely acquiesced in order to be allowed to participate in the other play activities of these boys. However, she could recall, at the age of eight, the sudden resolve to refuse further participation in this sexual play. Her reason for this refusal, as was revealed at long last, was the attempt on the part of her brothers to include two older boys (aged thirteen and fifteen), new to the neighborhood, and her fear that their penises, if she permitted their insertion, would be large, painful, and damaging, as compared with the small, prepubertal penises of the other boys. Another female patient recalled feeling indignant, at an early age, when a boy induced her to mouth his penis but did not reciprocate in terms of manual stimulation of her genitalia. Despite these experiences which seem to imply, if not pleasure, at least no unpleasure in this matter of invasion of the genital cleft, both these patients suffered from sexual disturbances in adult life: the first was in such genital conflict that she had excluded all sexual experience; the second was frigid. Regardless of certain exceptions, the attitude that they are exploited in the sexual act is very common in women of our culture, and many men share this attitude.

A further consideration tending to reinforce the boy's conviction that girls object to the insertion of the penis and are exploited if this occurs is his wish-fulfilling idea, arising from Oedipal rivalry, that parental intercourse is not desired by the mother, is really objected to by her, and is forced upon her by the father. Indeed, this is often enough actually the case in marriages in our culture and is conveyed to the boy (and to the girl) by what they overhear (in primal scenes or in parental quarrels), sometimes by direct statements of the mother, though such statements, when they are made, are generally made to children older than those now under consideration. One male patient could recall having had described to him, at the age of nine, the father's brutality and lack of consideration in sexual matters, and recalled having taken the implication that he was to rescue his mother from this. A female patient recalled, at the age of six, when sleeping in the parental bedroom, having heard her mother's vain pleading with the father to desist, that he was hurting her. But still other children make this assumption without such evidence. Additional clinical material is contained in my paper on homosexuality [64, p. 43].

The attitudes which in both sexes emerge from the phallic

conviction of one genital organ are of great significance in determining some of the solutions of Oedipal rivalry and, because of this, in determining or giving specific form to later character traits and symptoms. In the immediate Oedipal situation the boy's high evaluation of his penis is enormously enhanced by the considerations which emanate from this phallic state of mind: it makes him all the more unwilling to face the loss of so advantageous an organ, thus strengthening the cogency of the threat of castration and intensifying the anxiety arising in the supposed imminence of this danger. Having repressed his Oedipal impulses and having thus ensured the retention of his penis, he may now enjoy the fruits of the sacrifice of these impulses and lord it over those who are without a penis. The tendency is seen, once the Oedipal turmoil has subsided, for the boy to join forces with others who have managed to retain the precious organ, and to engage with them in games and other activities, to the contemptuous exclusion of those who lack the all-important genital. The girls, thus excluded from the boys' activities, have no other recourse than to band together themselves and, perhaps, to exclude the boys, as a retaliatory measure.

Thus is joined a battle of the sexes which, for some of its participants, continues throughout life, even though puberty and adolescence bring a certain mitigation of this mutual ostracism, and even though falling in love and marriage may appear to declare a truce to this warfare. For many, this battle rages throughout friendships with members of the opposite sex, through courtship, through love-affairs and marriage, and has but temporary surcease, if any at all. To describe its many variants would be to describe a vast number of individuals in our culture, and no exhaustive account can even be contemplated. A few typical manifestations may be described. Of frequent occurrence is a banding together in homogeneous groups which exclude the other sex— gangs, clubs, secret societies, and the like, for men or for women. Until recently, the barbershop and the saloon were taboo for women, and men's clubs often contain certain rooms (lounges and dining rooms) to which female guests are admitted, the remainder of the premises being reserved for members and their male guests. Certain unmarried men, without this paraphernalia of exclusive clubs and societies, tend to band together for all their recreational activities—card games, drinking parties, bowling games, hunting and fishing expeditions—and wander from such exclusively male groups for sexual purposes only. After marriage, men who have been members of such groups before marriage tend to return to them on frequent occasion and chafe under what they regard as the unreasonable complaints of their wives at being left alone so often: such disturbance may be settled, more or less, by an agreement between the couple that certain nights of the week are "my night with the boys."

Women tend less to such exclusive banding together, and it is more commonly seen among career-women than among housewives. After marriage, women as a rule abandon their girl-friends as a group and resent it when their husbands endeavor to continue participation in their male groups, to the exclusion of the wives.

Another typical manifestation of the battle of the sexes is seen in the excessive chivalry of some men toward women. There is always a certain condescension in such gentlemanly behavior, as if the man were making allowances for the intrinsic inferiority of the female and making magnanimous compensation for it. Some women sense this condescension and resent the assiduous opening of doors, holding of coats, and other acts that imply consideration for a weaker, inferior being. Other women, on the other hand, enjoy these attentions, taking at face value the false implication of their own intrinsic superiority, not understanding the gentlemanly pretense that lies behind such behavior. Still other women, realizing this truth, enjoy egging the man on to dance attention on them, taking an attitude that might be expressed as, "If he is going to feel so damned superior, by God, he's going to pay for it!"

Still another typical phenomenon is the notion, extremely common in our society, that "nice" women do not enjoy sexual intercourse and do not have orgasms. For men who hold such notions, women are divided into two classes: nice women—wives, mothers, sisters, and other females with familial status—who do not enjoy sex and merely submit to it as a marital (sometimes a premarital) duty; and "fast" women—prostitutes, "kept" women, many divorcees, some married women—who are abandoned enough to desire sex and to have orgasms. The phallic belief about the one genital organ is hard at work here.

The notion that the prostitute regularly enjoys her many sexual experiences is a cherished one among a large number of men in our culture, and they like to imagine that women become prostitutes because they cannot withstand the temptation of pleasure in frequent and varied sexual experiences. This illusion does not ordinarily succumb to the reality of experience in which it becomes apparent that the prostitute is actually out to fleece and "castrate" men—that this is her mode of fighting the battle of the sexes. Men who experience this often assume that the woman involved is an exception to whom her prostitution is nothing other than a commercial enterprise; they continue to cherish in their minds The Prostitute with all the glamor that the wickedness and depravity of female sexual abandon (as they see it) can lend to such a figure.

Nice women do not glory in the shame of their castrated state; they accept it as a regrettable fact and allow it to be exploited for love of the man and because of the status they achieve by being associated (through marriage) with one of the superior caste, but never in any physical sense enjoy this "mutilation." Such enjoyment is a sign of depravity in a woman, exciting and gratifying as it may be to a man. It is as if a person should glory in his mutilation and be glad of being mutilated, as if an amputee were able to achieve such erotic pleasure from the amputated stump that his misfortune becomes for him the greatest good fortune; it is as if the shame and disgrace of being castrated and the exploitation and victimization which ensue from this had become a source of sensory bliss and ecstasy. So the phallic-minded man's contempt for such a creature is unbounded, though, from another point of view, he would sacrifice much to encounter one.

Actually, few men in our society ever experience such "depravity," since frigidity is so common an attribute of American women. To a large number of American men, the woman who enjoys sex is not within their experience but remains a figment of their imagination, a somewhat legendary and mythical figure like The Prostitute, already referred to. They may have a rich fantasy-life with such figures, utilizing them frequently in dreams and in masturbation fantasies, and hoping one day to have experience of such a woman, but they rarely encounter one in actuality. When such encounters occur, they may greatly influence the man's unconscious phallic conviction, and often have a disastrous effect upon marriages, even of long standing.

Parallel to the practice, so commonly seen in American society, of the categorizing of women by men into "nice" women and "fast" women, is the highly prevalent mother-worship, described as "momism" by one author [78], which often takes the form of idealization of "American womanhood," as well as the antithetic idealization of The Prostitute. An attempt to account for this characteristically American categorizing—or the intensity with which it is insisted upon—would carry us far afield into discussions of American social history. An important basis for this might be found in the study of the detailed nature of frontier communities, for so long a period a characteristic feature of our society, and their influence upon the American ethos.

It may be remarked parenthetically that the defense of Negro slavery and its attenuated twentieth century version—Jim Crowism in its various forms—by the rationalization of protecting American (or southern) womanhood hints at the psychic linkage of oppression of the Negro and the phallic conviction of one genital, possessed by the male alone: it is as if the alleged necessity (implied by Jim Crowism) to protect women served to support and maintain the phallic belief.

Phallic-minded women are prone to take similar views of their orgastic potentialities, and such views, which arise quite spontaneously from their own phallic convictions, are supported and greatly reinforced by the man's identical opinions. Thus these women tend to suppress and inhibit their orgastic potentialities, and this becomes a contributing factor to their frigidity [77], which is likely, however, to have much deeper roots in adaptations made in the oral and disciplinary areas of their experience.

The battle of the sexes frequently manifests itself in competitiveness—individual toward individual, individual toward group, or group toward group. The little girl who feels she is at a disadvantage because she lacks a penis is likely to speculate about how to compensate for this lack. Such speculation occurs in addition to or instead of the speculation, above described, as to how she is to acquire or reacquire so valuable an organ. The more uncertain she feels about the possibility of acquiring a penis, the more likely it is that she will speculate about ways of making up for the lack. She is here in a position somewhat similar to the child who, in the late oral phase of experience, speculatively searches for a *quid pro quo* whereby the nursing situation may be restored. Outdoing the rival in what she regards as his key activities is here a favorite subject of speculation and endeavor. If she cannot win equality with or superiority over the boy by the simple means of having a penis like his or a better (presumably, bigger) one, perhaps she can outdo him in aggressiveness, in enterprise, in athletic games, in intelligence, in artistic accomplishment, and the like. The girl's striving for proficiency in athletics and in studies through school and college years has often such a basis; the boy who appears relatively apathetic to the superiority of other boys in these fields may spur himself to intense efforts in order not to be "disgraced" by being beaten by a girl. A male patient, having been bested by a girl in a prize contest at the end of his high-school years, attempted to seduce the girl sexually in order to demonstrate what ultimate superiority consists in.

In later life, a business or professional woman will often find herself in intense competition with some man similarly placed in the career situation. She may feel and behave competitively toward men in general in her particular field and may join forces with female colleagues who likewise are highly competitive toward males. She is more likely, however, to play a lone hand here and to set almost as much store by demonstrating superiority over other female competitors as over males. With regard to other females, she is apt to feel the same scorn for their "castrated" state as does the phallic-minded male; she herself will be someone special, eminent as a female who has managed in unique fashion to surmount her initial handicap. She will be the rare woman to whom competing with men in a man's world offers no difficulties.

Women whose circumstances offer them no opportunity to compete with men (and other women) in career settings may nevertheless attempt competition by minimizing the value of prestige in career endeavors and magnifying the value of housewifely activities in which they excel—cooking, sewing, running a home, rearing well-behaved children, and the like. Such women often "humor" men in subscribing to the importance of the latter's business and professional achievements, or of their hobbies —whether intellectual or otherwise—while smiling knowingly among themselves over the "fact" that the real business of life is eating well and healthfully, having a comfortable, attractive home, having clean, well-mended clothing, bearing children, and rearing them well, in the carrying on of which, men play but a tangential role, enjoying the fruits of women's labors but not otherwise participating in the domestic activities to any great extent. Still other housewives, merely resigned more or less to the inferior cultural role assigned to them, attempt to coerce their husbands into sharing this position by insisting that the spouse help clean up after a meal, do some of the marketing, pick up the baby when he cries at night; or they may insist upon some compensation for the "menial" work they do, such as being taken out often and being given frequent gifts. All such behavior may have additional sources which support or are supported by these phallic motivations.

Both men and women may greatly resent the attempts on the part of the other sex to influence them to accept and live by cultural tenets which they regard as opposed to those of their own sex. It is here as if there existed separate and different cultures, a male culture and a female culture within the same society. This distinction is quite valid in some of the so-called primitive cultures in which there exist men's customs and rituals that women are forbidden to know about, and vice versa. In some of these cultures there is actually a "women's language," used by women when talking among themselves, which often has a grammar and vocabulary quite different from the official language of the group as a whole.

The expressions "a man's world" and "a woman's world" are highly indicative. A masculine culture would be typified by some of the American frontier communities—mining towns and the like—prior to the introduction into them of "respectable" women and the institution of marriage. Here established law and order were at a minimum; if a man wanted justice, the law was his six-shooter and his trigger finger. In general, might made right; the strong, the brave, the quick-witted were free to triumph over the weak, the cowardly, and the gullible, without concern about rights abstractly possessed by the latter. A man was free to live as he pleased: he could be as dirty, as unshaven, as untidy, as irregular in his personal habits as he chose to be; his language could likewise be free, filled with grammatical incongruities and profanity. No woman was there to plead for the weak, to trouble his conscience about ruthless, overbearing, predatory behavior toward others, to insist upon a modicum of cleanliness and tidiness in his personal habits and language. Such refinements were for the effete and woman-ridden East, which the Western frontiersman had left far behind him with a "good riddance." The attitude toward women in such communities was that they existed for the entertainment and delectation of heroes in their brief intervals of rest and relaxation from important activities, and only those females who took this view of their social function were suffered gladly.

As, slowly, a few men, spurred by a certain nostalgia,

brought wives into these communities and began to raise families, the pervasively male quality of the society became diluted by female influence; the married men established governments of law and order which afforded protection to the rights of the weak; better built and furnished homes began to appear; men, however grudgingly, began to clean themselves up, became neater, shaved and ate their meals with greater regularity; and profanity became more whispered and was indulged in freely only when no ladies were present. And the men began to eye askance, as those who make distinctions, women of the type of their former female playmates.

Not that the female culture had things all its own way; often a hard struggle preceded its establishment, and its instability, once precariously established, was manifested in frequent outbursts of lawlessness, just as now alternations of periods of tolerance of conditions of vice and periods of reform governments characterize so many of our municipalities.

Many men, even today, harbor resentment against "petticoat government" and show it in a variety of ways. It is to be noted how this masculine revolt against feminine cultural influence reflects the heroic rebellious tendencies of some of the adaptations to the disciplining mother: when the cat's away, the mice will play. It is of significance that such rebelliousness is closely linked to the phallic conviction. The latter tends, as it comes into being, to undermine the authority of the mother by placing her also in the category of the handicapped. That there is a certain conflict here, that the majority of men tend, after a period of revolt, to "return to the reservation," might seem to indicate unconscious uncertainty whether to include the mother among the "castrated," a lingering unconscious possibility that she may, by way of exception, have a penis after all. She has shown strength enough to force discipline on the boy: could anyone possess this strength and not have a penis? So the so-called phallic mother remains, unconsciously, either a certainty or a possibility for many men.

PATHOLOGIC OUTCOMES OF THE OEDIPUS COMPLEX
Degrees of Repression

We have already discussed the relatively normal or healthy outcome of the situation of Oedipal rivalry in our culture; it consists, ultimately, in the successful repression of the major impulses that create the situation: exclusive genital possession of the parent of opposite sex, and hostile elimination of the rival. In the consideration of the less healthy, more neurotic forms and outcomes of the Oedipus situation a factor of great importance is the degree of success with which repression of these impulses is accomplished. The most thorough-going repression would have the result that these impulses would never spontaneously reappear in any form. Less successful repression of either or both of the major impulses leaves open the possibility that the Oedipal impulses may later tend to emerge from repression ("the return of the repressed," as Freud termed it), thus re-encountering anxiety as a forewarning of danger, and may on this account be remolded by the ego into a variety of forms which manifest themselves as neurotic character-traits or symptoms. Or it may become necessary for the ego to find additional devices, other than repression.

An obvious question here is, Why is repression complete in some instances and incomplete in others? In attempting to find an answer to this question, it seems reasonable to assume that individuals vary in the degree of willingness with which they abandon or disown an impulse. We cannot describe the intimate details of a process of repression, but we may define it descriptively as a process of defensive renunciation and adduce the empirical fact that some individuals are more wholehearted and sincere in their renunciations than others are.

Repression appears to have originally a function similar to the somatic act of flight from danger: the ego flees from the danger-provoking impulse by standing still, as it were, and thrusting the impulse away from itself. Carried out in this manner, repression is complete. However, if the ego judges the danger to be temporary and circumstantial, its flight is then not intended to be absolute and conclusive; it is, rather, a tactical maneuver, calculated to weather an immediate storm, a later "return" to the impulse—when the storm has blown over—being contemplated. The turning back of Lot's wife to gaze—regretfully, we may assume—upon Sodom and Gomorrah would represent inconclusive flight, while Lot's stern mode of departure—without even one backward glance—would represent absolute flight. This folk story would seem to point a moral: when giving up wickedness, do it thoroughly or not at all; halfway measures are disastrous.

Incomplete repression would seem to indicate incomplete renunciation and would suggest that there are individuals who take their claims to ultimate omnipotence more seriously than others do. In childhood, these quasi-omnipotent Oedipuses would be the same children who, though frustrated, do not altogether give up, as their luxuriant speculative activity demonstrates, the hope of re-establishing the total nursing situation; they are the same children who, in the disciplinary area of experience, make tacit bargains with their mothers and must suffer the broken promise; they are the children who conform outwardly to discipline, but inwardly rebel, while carefully concealing this inward rebellion—those who make the less heroic of the heroic choices. They are, in a word, those children who intensely wish what they wish but, having been confronted with sharp, persistent frustration, can neither give up wishing nor achieve fulfillment. It is as if complete repression results in a condition wherein the specific impulse no longer has enough energy to cause the slightest disturbance of homeostasis; therefore the effectiveness of the ego's aggression (and self-esteem) never becomes challenged in terms of this impulse. On the other hand, incomplete repression, depending on the degree of incompleteness, leaves the impulse with enough energy to cause some disturbance of homeostasis. Thus the ego's effective aggression (and self-esteem) are challenged, and the ego is compelled to adopt measures looking toward an increase in its effective aggression and a raising or maintaining of its self-esteem.

This incompleteness of repression may occur with reference to both the major Oedipal impulses or it may be that one of them is somewhat less completely repressed than the other. It may be, in the case of the boy, for example, that the impulse toward exclusive genital possession of the mother is more completely put aside than the hostile impulse toward the father. This might be the case in a situation in which the boy senses that the mother would be nonacquiescent (regardless of the father's attitude) and punitive in her own right. In such case, he makes obeisance to the greater danger while permitting himself the luxury of not abandoning so completely the hostility toward his rival, conceived by him as a lesser danger. However, since the latter is not altogether without risk (as he sees it), he may now encounter some anxiety (castration-fear) with respect to this. In this type of situation the ego is confronted with the task of averting danger, while simultaneously maintaining a degree of effectiveness of aggression by keeping the hostile impulses more or less intact and operative. There are, of course, other possible constellations: the situation described is presented merely as one example of unequal repression of the two Oedipal impulses.

Displacement

In such predicaments, the child's ego may make use of the device of displacement. This device is an outgrowth of the substitute-finding that originates in the early phase of oral experience, where it is relatively simple. As utilized in attempts to adapt to the Oedipus situation, displacement may become very intricate, since the displaceable factors are numerous and in themselves complex. Displacements may affect the object of the child's genital impulses and the precise nature of these; it may affect the object of the child's hostile impulses (the rival) and the manner in which they operate. A variety of patterns emerge, their precise nature depending upon the specific displacements and the circumstances which determine their necessity. In the example given, in which the child makes incomplete repression of his hostile impulses toward his rival, he may displace the object of his hostility by substituting for it another object, which functions either as a target for his hostility or as a source of retaliatory hostility (father toward child) or both. Such displacement may manifest itself as sadistic behavior (toward animals, for example) or as a phobia (of animals, policemen, or old men, for instance). In the former case the hostile behavior which the child would visit upon the rival, if he dared, is directed, without provocation, upon an animal—often a pet—or upon another child. In the latter case, the child irrationally fears being harmed by an animal or some adult figure who can represent, in the child's mind, the hated and feared rival who desires, according to the child, to punish him in retaliation for his hostility. Thus Little Hans, displacing the fear that his father would castrate him, feared that a horse would bite him. As Freud points out, unpleasant and handicapping to the child as his phobia is, it offers a better situation to him than the undisplaced, unmodified one: he still fears; but now more manageably, since he can somehow avoid encounters with the phobic object, while he cannot avoid encounters with the feared rival, being unable to prevent him from entering the house at will. The phobia resembles repression in that it achieves *distance* between the child and the feared object, which is placed out on the street (in horse, dog, or cat phobias) where it may be avoided by the relatively simple expedient of not going out of doors. Like the ego in performing repression, the child stands still, as it were, and thrusts the feared object away from him: flight, if one assumes the viewpoint of relativity—flight achieved by the creation of distance rather than by locomotion.

Displacement is not the only source of sadistic behavior. We have already seen another in the typically phallic attitude of the boy that, while penetration of her vulvar cleft is painful and humiliating to the girl, she will nevertheless be forced to submit to this for the boy's pleasure. This comes close to the classic concept of sadism, defined as a type of sexual behavior in which a person achieves erotic gratification (to orgasm) by inflicting pain upon the sexual partner. In psychoanalytic writing, the term *sadism* has become vastly extended in meaning and now frequently includes all behavior which may cause suffering of any kind to another person, whether the hurt is consciously intended or not, and whether or not it affords the perpetrator conscious pleasure, erotic or otherwise. The assumption appears to be made—often quite irresponsibly—that such behavior is always engaged in with at least unconscious purpose and that the other person's suffering, no matter what its nature, gives erotic pleasure to the perpetrator, at least unconsciously. It is then small wonder that the understanding of sadism, thus diffusely and carelessly defined, and particularly the explanation of its psychic origins have offered an insoluble problem to the psychoanalyst. Too many kinds of behavior and therefore too many types of dynamism are included under the head of sadism to permit it to be anything like a unitary concept. We should make the attempt to understand sadism in its classic, clearly erotic form before we take the liberty of extending so widely its field of application. What has been said here applies with almost equal validity to the psychoanalytic use of the term *masochism,* about which Berliner [7] has tended to clarify our clinical thinking.

Compulsiveness

Another device of the ego to maintain incomplete repression is the dynamism of obsessional or compulsive thought or behavior. When there is danger of one of the partially repressed impulses breaking through into motor expression, one thinks of something else, preferably something remote from the impulse. But the nature of the psyche is such that the "something else" proves to be uncomfortably closely associated with the precariously repressed impulse, and a second something else replaces the first one, or it may become necessary to replace *thinking* of something else with *doing* something else. The child who utilizes this device finds himself compelled to have thoughts and to perform acts which he does not choose to think and to do; it is as if those things were forced upon him by some agency external to himself, and the whole situation in which he now finds himself appears irrational to him. The original something else, both in terms of thinking and doing, cannot be, for reasons already stated, very remote from the repressed impulses, and these tend to break through into the very thoughts and activities intended to maintain repression. So the ego is launched on a process of finding a series of "somethings else," wherein it manages to keep just one step ahead of the impulse continually hammering on the gate to consciousness and motility.

The precise coloring of the obsessional thoughts and compulsive behavior will depend upon which aspects of the Oedipus situation are of major importance to the specific child; this in its turn depends upon the detailed circumstances with which the child was confronted, as well as upon the adaptations he had already made in the previous experiential areas—the personality with which he entered upon this third area of experience.

The compulsive behavior seen in children attempting thus to solve their Oedipal difficulties may be exemplified by ritual counting, which often begins as counting on the fingers—"something else" to do with the fingers rather than use them to touch the love-object, to scratch or pinch the rival or to masturbate. Another ritual which serves the same purpose involves taking off the clothes in a certain order when undressing, and placing them in a certain arrangement on a chair—something else to do and think of rather than to be aware of desiring the mother at bedtime, or of the hated rival who prevents this, or of the masturbation which could, if it were not forbidden and contrary to the precepts of the superego, give some assuagement to the implied frustrations. Such rituals are likely to undergo vast and luxuriant ramification as time goes on, and in the adult they often present baffling clinical puzzles for the analyst.

Reaction-Formation and Regression

The ego of the Oedipal child, if it is unable to achieve complete repression of the impulses, makes use of numerous auxiliary devices in addition to the devices of displacement and refocusing of attention just described. Reaction-formation and regression may make important contributions to the otherwise precarious maintenance of repression. As applied to the genital impulses, reaction-formation would result in a horror of sexuality, the belief that gratification of these impulses is specifically not desired. Such a belief gains support from the desire to maintain security by conformity to parental demands and from the need to remain on good terms with the superego, the internalized representation of the parents. Further support may be gained by the use of the device of regression, in which the dangerous genital gratification may be replaced by oral gratification or by anal gratification, as in the case of the child accustomed to being given enemas by the mother.

As applied to the hostile Oedipal impulses, reaction-formation may take the form of loving and cherishing the rival, which, in the case of the boy, may gain support from his having looked to the father, in the late oral phase, as a possible substitute for the mother in a restored nursing situation; or, in the case of the girl, reaction-formation gains obvious reinforcement from the mother's having been her chief love-object before rivalry set in. In both cases, such reaction-formation is conducive to and supportive of homosexual adaptations, which we shall presently discuss. Regression plays a part in maintaining such reaction-formations in that the type of gratification looked for in reactively loving the rival is an oral or an anal one.

Alloplastic Maneuvers

Schizoid, magical, and transference maneuvers may also play auxiliary roles here. Masturbation with fantasies is of great importance in this regard. We have seen the use made of this, presumably without fantasies, as a consolation for frustrations in the oral and disciplinary areas of experience. The assumption was made that in those areas disturbance of homeostasis could be alleviated by the relief from general somatic tension afforded by masturbation, although we cannot be certain that fantasy never plays a part in such masturbatory activity. What is certain, however, is that masturbation, as it is practiced in this area of phallic and Oedipal experience, is accompanied by rich and varied fantasies, a feature generally characteristic of masturbation at this period and of the masturbation of puberty and later life. Whereas earlier masturbation, particularly in the oral phase, is not likely to be of the manual type, Oedipal and post-Oedipal masturbation is manual, though there are exceptions to this.

The masturbation-fantasies of this period are either of

frank incest or of incest thinly disguised by symbolic or other means. They come into the category of schizoid maneuvers and may take on sadistic or masochistic coloring in certain instances. Because of the fantasies, wherein the semirepressed genital impulses come to at least schizoid expression, and because of the exigencies occasioned by the superego (now completely formed), far greater and more troublesome guilt is likely to attach to the masturbatory activity of this phase than to that of the earlier phases. The entire Oedipus conflict may become displaced to this area of masturbatory activity, and the child may attempt to handle this conflict by the same means of displacement (phobia) and compulsiveness that he may have applied to the original conflict.

In later life, many hypochondriacal fears represent the punishment anticipated from persistence in the Oedipal wishes via masturbation with fantasies and often take a form closely related to or symbolic of castration—for example, syphilophobia, cancerphobia, fear of insanity. The masturbation-conflicts of later life are more likely to derive from the activities and issues of this Oedipal period than from the masturbation of the earlier phases, though exceptions to this are occasionally seen clinically.

The fear of insanity affords an excellent example of the manner in which crime and punishment—gratification and punishment—may converge in one idea. Insanity is often consciously conceived by the layman as a state of wild uninhibitedness, as it regularly is conceived of unconsciously; that is, as a condition in which one behaves impulsively with a certain impunity (because one is sick and therefore not responsible for what one does—a viewpoint encouraged by the legal fate of some murderers). On the other hand, insanity means incarceration, thus placing insanity in a measure among those states of helplessness in which one has impulses but is impotent to carry them out.

Schizoid maneuvers may be carried out with respect to aspects of the Oedipal situation other than that of gratification of genital impulses. Much fantasy may occur having as its central theme the death or discomfiture of the rival, his defeat in competition, his acknowledgment of the child's superiority, and the like. Such fantasies may be merged and blended with the fantasies of incest, in direct or disguised form, or they may occur quite separately from them. Fantasies of this type, too, may become sources of guilt or anxiety, though this is by no means always the case, and conflict over them may replace the conflict over the more direct Oedipal impulses, requiring handling by means of the same devices as described above.

The magical maneuver, as utilized in Oedipal situations, takes the form of the child seeking aid to avert the danger of castration by the rival; rarely, if ever, does the maneuver take the direct form of hoping for aid in the achievement of genital gratification with the love-object. Often it is the father to whom is ascribed such omnipotent power that he will preserve the child from the danger of castration. Behavior in terms of this maneuver may take the form of a kind of flattery of the father, imitating him in every possible way, adopting his likes and dislikes in matters of food, dress, games, and other interests, as well as more direct expressions of admiration: if the child thus becomes the father's *protégé*, a kind of reconciliation is anticipated in which the father will protect the boy from all manner of danger, including the danger of his own (the father's) hostility. Reaction-formation against hostile impulses plays an important supportive role here. The same *démarche* can be made via the mother, though it is not so commonly seen as the former, since it comes dangerously close to an intimate, exclusive relationship with her. This whole maneuver, if circumstances favor it, may be displaced to the plane of religion where the figure of God, often in view of certain contracts and bargains, is seen as constrained to give the boy protection from danger. The thin disguise of a parental figure as God is often evidenced by irruption into consciousness of hostile, derogatory impulses and attitudes toward the figure of God. Compulsive rituals, often extending far into later life, are undertaken by the child to guard against such dangerous outbursts.

The girl, in performing this maneuver, looks to the mother

as an omnipotent helper to protect her against the consequences of hostility to the mother herself—a hostility which, as we have seen would be apt to take the form of nonconformity to discipline. She looks to the mother to make her be obedient, as the boy may similarly look to the father. On the religious plane, the many prayers which in later life take the form of petition to be granted an attitude of submission and obedience to God's will, bear witness to the existence of such psychic patterns in childhood. Furthermore, the girl may look to the mother (or to the father) as the magical helper who will save her from the damage and humiliation of the attacking penis. The strong libidinal attachment to the father and its continuation into adult life often receive support from the hope that the disastrous consequences anticipated from phallic attack will be averted, or at least mitigated, by the "fatherliness" of the father or, in transferences, of the analyst.

Magical maneuvers always include the attempt to constrain the omnipotent figure to be helpful by the expedient of a *quid pro quo,* thus indicating their linkage with the explanations and solutions of the late oral phase. The child's mode of bargaining is to offer up the kind of behavior (good conduct, pious, or ritual acts) apparently desired of him by the omnipotent figure, and the resultant pattern is thus seen to resemble closely the background of the broken promise. The promises here, however, are much less likely to be broken than those of the disciplinary area of experience: the child rarely experiences any of the graver consequences which he foresees as ensuing from hostile rivalry. Therefore the alliances made in these magical maneuvers may be lasting and may well endure well into adult life. However, their highly conditional quality becomes apparent when, if such an alliance is translated to the religious plane, prayers couched in terms of a bargain fail to be answered. The sudden and rapid shift from confident, devout belief in God to bitter skepticism or unbelief reveals the conditional and unstable quality of the original belief. In such circumstances, phenomena of behavior are seen which are identical with those which ensue from the broken promise: the self-restraints and other manifestations of piety, which had constituted the believer's part of the bargain, are at once reversed (though with certain misgivings at the outset) and the former believer becomes an infidel, often rationalizing on scientific grounds his bitter repudiation of the treacherous ally and of his former faith in him.

The transference maneuver is the alloplastic maneuver most frequently utilized in the attempt to aid repression of Oedipal impulses. This is a form of massive displacement in which the impulses are kept intact, with full hope and expectation of their fulfillment one day, but in which new situations keep being chosen—even created—as the setting for ultimate success of effective aggression. These new situations must contain certain elements which resemble, or can be made to resemble, the original Oedipal situation. Thus, a situation offering too easy a success is not an appropriate one for this maneuver; it must contain some of the difficulties of the original situation and must therefore have for the protagonist a quality of unpleasure. (The reader is referred to my paper [67] for a more thoroughgoing exposition of transference than will be attempted here.)

Analytic situations, as pointed out in a recent contribution [52], are particularly well adapted to provide some of these "difficult" features so essential to the operation of the transference maneuver, and no analysis is carried out, so far as I am aware, without the emergence of such maneuvers, in particular those of Oedipal provenance. If the maneuver were to be successfully carried out, which is never the case, the Oedipal impulses might be retained in a state of repression. Since ultimate unsuccess is the rule here, the tendency is for the impulses to emerge from repression—one reason why the analysis of transferences is so useful a procedure for the production of insight.

Transference maneuvers may be and are made on the basis of frustration or conflict in any of the experiential areas. Episodes of "acting out" and transference contain, as Freud [21] pointed out, a quality of remembering without recall, thus indicating that incompleteness of repression of the specific impulses involved which underlies the use of transference maneuvers. As the factor of incompleteness of repression is of especial significance in the phenomena and outcomes of the experiential area now under discussion, little reference has been made to the transference maneuver before this. But it should be understood that its use as a device of the ego is widespread and pervasive.

The use of the maneuver in childhood is more likely to be seen in the later portion of the Oedipal period than in its earlier phases. Its forms are so various, depending, as they obviously must, upon the child's environmental opportunities, as well as upon the specific nature of the child's constellation, that only a few of the innumerable possibilities can here be mentioned.* It is seen, for example, within the family circle itself when the child attempts to win over an older sibling of opposite sex from the rival parent or from another older sibling of the same sex. The maneuver may operate through devotion to some adult friend of the family, particularly one who is occasionally or frequently a house guest, remaining overnight for longer or shorter periods. Fantasies of ultimate marriage with such adults are frequent accompaniments to these infatuations and are often frankly verbalized. The latter is often thought to be "cute," and the child is thus encouraged, by being frequently reminded of his plans for marriage and by being asked about details, to maintain in operation this form of the maneuver.

In school, the child will frequently form a similar infatuation for a teacher and will try to win her exclusive love and attention. This applies particularly to the boy, since teachers of the lower grades in American schools are usually female. However, girls also may become infatuated with their female teachers. These infatuations may succumb to the mockery of the other children and their taunts of "teacher's pet," but are nevertheless sometimes maintained despite such discouragement, especially if

---

* Furthermore, the two major impulses—possession of the mother, and hostile elimination of the father—may become transferred as a single *Gestalt*, as it were, or either one or both may be transferred separately, each one carrying into the transference its specific, individual coloring. The examples given illustrate the first-mentioned possibility.

the child interprets such taunting as the obliquely expressed resentment of unsuccessful rivals. The transference maneuver may be observed operating in games: for example, the game of Musical Chairs in which the single chair for which two children must compete symbolizes the mother (or father). Freud [24, p. 182 n.] pointed out that sitting on something symbolized possession of it. He alluded to the etymology of the German word *besitzen* = to possess, as indicating and confirming this. Our English verb, to possess, is of similar derivation, through the Latin *possedeo* (*pos* + *sedeo* = I sit) = I possess. While it is true that games such as Musical Chairs are not invented by children and are usually introduced by adults at children's parties, nevertheless children take to them with an enthusiasm, interest, and competitiveness which indicate some understanding of their transferential nature.

The transferences of later life which derive from Oedipal situations are so numerous and so varied in subtle differences of detail that it is a hopeless task even to begin enumerating them. Besides this, they are such commonplaces of analytic experience that even exemplification would be supererogatory in a work of this kind. Nevertheless the reader can find such an example in my paper on transference [67, pp. 312 ff.].

ANOTHER PATHOLOGIC ADAPTATION: NEUROTIC HOMOSEXUALITY

An adaptation of considerable importance frequently seen in this experiential area is that of homosexuality. The obvious goal of all unmodified and uninhibited Oedipal strivings would be the separation of the parental couple, as is clearly implied by the combining of the two major impulses. We have seen how this goal may be renounced—completely, if repression is complete; more provisionally, if repression is only partial and incompletely maintained. We have discussed a number of possible outcomes in instances of the latter, all of them based on the retention, even in cases of partial repression, of the Oedipal impulses in their original forms—in the case of the boy, impulses toward exclusive genital gratification via the mother and impulses toward the elimination of the father as a rival. In the homosexual solution the objects of these impulses appear to be reversed, the boy's love-object being the father, his rival the mother. It cannot be too strongly emphasized that, like the other solutions, the homosexual adaptation ordinarily remains, during the Oedipal period itself, in the realm of speculation and fantasy. It may be that some children attempt to realize such fantasies via the actual parent concerned, as clinical evidence above described suggests, but, if so, the attempt is of extremely rare occurrence. The earliest overt behavior deserving the designation "homosexual" is regularly transferential in nature, occurring with partners who can be regarded as substitutes for parental figures.

It must be understood that the reversal of love-objects represents a shift from the original Oedipal position, which was precisely the same for the boy who later adopts a homosexual solution as it was for the boy who did not make this reversal (and herein lies the hope for "cure" of neurotic homosexuality). The implication is that something has happened to produce or encourage such a reversal. This reversal requires no alteration of the general Oedipal goal of separation of the parents; only the projected outcome of this separation may be different: it may be that the "homosexual" boy anticipates remaining with the father, once the mother is eliminated. Generally, however, he contemplates nothing so drastic; he will be satisfied if he can just put a stop to parental sexuality. His homosexuality is dependent upon the ingenious method whereby he hopes to achieve this aim.

There are two possible methods here, which will have to be considered separately. The first is postulated on the belief that the factor which keeps parental sexuality so persistently in operation is the father's insistence upon phallic gratification. Parental sexuality might cease, therefore, if the father could be induced to accept a substitute for the mother as the means of such gratification. The substitute thought of by the boy is himself, but since he has no vulvar cleft, as the mother has, he conceives such substitution in terms of those bodily orifices which he does possess: anus and mouth. The origin of homosexuality is thus seen to be a strategy in which, by drawing the father's aggressive genitality upon himself, this can be made to deviate from the mother as its target. The aim of such a strategy is apparent: if it is successful, the mother will be left "unpossessed" by the father and thus open to the boy's "possession" [*64*, pp. 42 ff.].

The arrival at such a strategy carries a number of implications. (1) It implies that the boy has fairly accurate knowledge of the way in which heterosexuality operates, and (2) that he has had experiences which give him this knowledge or allow him to divine it. (3) It implies that up to the point of conceiving this strategy, he has not repressed either of his Oedipal impulses; if he has attempted such repression, it has been highly unsuccessful. (4) This implies, in its turn, a high degree of unwillingness to renounce these impulses; at least, the one looking toward exclusive genital possession of the mother. (5) By the same token, it implies that he retains a high degree of hostility toward the father, though toned down and not given frank expression, which may now begin to assume the disguise (via reaction-formation) of love. (6) Furthermore, it implies that the child anticipates a modicum, at least, of somatic pleasure for himself in the carrying out of the strategy. This possibility of somatic pleasure derives from the solution in the late oral phase in which the father's penis is seen as an acceptable substitute for the mother's nipple.

The anticipated somatic pleasure is ordinarily oral in kind. Where the orifice to be offered the father for the latter's phallic gratification is the anus, the reason for this may be (1) that the anus has already become a zone for pleasurable stimulation, as perhaps in the case of the child receiving daily enemas, or (2) the anus is apperceived as a possible substitute for the mouth, by a displacement similar to that already mentioned in the case of the girl who comes to regard her vulvar cleft as a kind of mouth. In all such cases, however, the boy's conscious orientation toward the father is passive and submissive, and may therefore more readily pass the censorship of the superego as being less obviously hostile than the clearly aggressive oral attack upon the father's phallus. The latter may even, in some cases, include the fleeting notion of biting off the father's phallus, though the hostile impulse rarely, if ever, takes such a form in this strategy. If the boy could contemplate daring to behave in so hostile a manner toward the father, he might not find it necessary to adopt so devious a strategy as the one under consideration.*

It should be clearly understood that in the origin of the strategy in this "passive" form, the directly libidinal aspects of the anticipated homosexual experience with the father are, so far as aim goes, decidedly secondary and play only a supportive role to the more important role of the strategy as a device of the ego: they make it possible to contemplate performing the strategy, which, if it were conceived by the boy as altogether unpleasant, would be dropped as an impractical idea, impossible to carry out. Indeed, when the contemplated experience—usually when visualized as anal—is seen as potentially painful and damaging, as in Freud's case of the Wolf Man [27, pp. 519, 555, and elsewhere], the strategy is regarded without that degree of en-

* The homosexual practices of later life are more varied than is implied by the consideration of activities involving only the mouth and the anus. Masturbation, mutual or otherwise, is of frequent occurrence: where it is the sole form of homosexual activity, it may be conjectured that fear of phallic attack upon the orifices exists, somewhat similar to that experienced by the female child upon contemplating phallic penetration of her vulvar cleft. Intercrural intercourse is a common homosexual practice, having doubtless a similar basis; such intercourse may also occur heterosexually to avoid defloration or pregnancy, or if the woman is motivated by the belief, conscious or not, that penetration will be painful and damaging. Other practices, such as axillary intercourse, are of much rarer occurrence and have complex, highly individual conditionings in addition to the more common ones. Among the individual conditionings would be included the desire of a male to be urinated upon by another male. With regard to all these practices, it must be understood that the homosexual man may engage in different ones upon different occasions or within the same occasion: such differences would reflect differences in external circumstances and corresponding fluctuations of motivations and anxieties within the individual psyche. It is for this reason that a diagnosis of "homosexuality" tells us little of significance for individual psychotherapy: so many different possible types of behavior and underlying psychic patterns are included under this rubric that it is of little more specific value for the psychotherapist than it would be for the internist or surgeon to learn that his patient is "ill."

thusiasm which might, in later life, bring it to transferential fruition in overt homosexuality, and such children tend to become latent rather than overt homosexuals. Often enough, the potentialities of the strategy for pleasure and for unpleasure may be seen as so nearly equal that the matter is left undecided by the child; this indecision may cause him to vacillate between regarding the homosexual "solution" as workable and as unworkable, and it may persist unconsciously in later life. In such adults, the latency of their homosexuality is not so deep as in some others: they are likely to be aware of homosexual conflict and may be among those who become overtly homosexual relatively late in life. The person who is more or less without these somatic misgivings is likely to seek homosexual experience at the age of 8 to 10 years (during the alleged latency period) or at puberty or during early adolescence. Cases are seen in which the earliest sought homosexual experience occurs in adult life—sometimes in the thirties or forties. These persons are likely to have restrained their homosexual impulses as a result of the somatic conflict already mentioned and may, at this late date, decide to "take a chance," since they feel that time is running out and that now, if ever, they must begin to have erotic experience other than masturbatory and other than the highly tentative and generally unsatisfying heterosexual experience which they may have had hitherto.

A sharp distinction is here implied between homosexual latency which derives from this strategy *plus* libidinal impulses stemming from the late oral and/or the disciplinary areas of experience and that which derives from the latter *alone*. Without the background of this contemplated strategy, the latency contains merely the potentiality for being seduced homosexually on occasion or for accepting homosexual gratification *faute de mieux* and in preference to masturbation (in prisons, on long sea-voyages, in lumber camps, and the like). Such practice should be regarded as homosexual behavior rather than as diagnostic of neurotic homosexuality (or homosexual neurosis). Neurotic homosexuality requires the background of the contemplated strategy described or the variant of it shortly to be discussed, and is differentiated from homosexual behavior by the fact that the neurotic homosexual *seeks out* homosexual experience rather than merely acquiesces to it.

The distinction between homosexual behavior and homosexual neurosis should not be made clinically merely on the basis of the patient's descriptive statements. It happens frequently that a patient will represent himself as having been merely acquiescent in homosexual experience in order to acquit himself of the charge of having sought it out. For example, the homosexual prostitute of the type who allows himself to be fellated or consents to perform pedication generally regards and proclaims himself merely as being acquiescent (in order to make money), but it may be doubted that this self-diagnosis is accurate. To make the distinction requires clinical judgment and deeper evidence than the patient's mere statement. Many people are latently homosexual in the homosexual behavior sense, and the figure given in the Kinsey Report [49, p. 623] for "homosexual outlet" (37 per cent of American adult males) undoubtedly reaches this extraordinary height by reason of the great prevalence of the latency that derives from the late oral speculations involving the father as a substitute for the mother in a nursing situation. The true homosexual—the neurotic one, as above defined—is represented in the Kinsey Report by the more exclusively homosexual categories of Kinsey's heterosexual-homosexual series and would come close to matching Havelock Ellis's estimate [13, vol. 2, p. 64] of a probable 2 per cent (and maximum 5 per cent) of the adult male population in the early years of the century.

The second method by which the boy contemplates making a homosexual adaptation to his Oedipal difficulties seems a much more daring one than the first and can only be considered seriously by the boy whose father, so far as the boy is consciously aware, constitutes less of a threat to him than is the case with the boy who tends to adopt the first method or, indeed, with the great majority of boys in the Oedipus situation. This method also envisages the break-up of the parental sexual couple, not by

means of gratifying the father's phallic impulse via an orifice of
the boy's own body, but rather by means of using the father's
orifices for the phallic gratification of the boy. The father is to
be converted into the equivalent of a female, and it is assumed
by the boy that the father will be so gratified by this that he
will no longer seek gratification by means of his own phallus.

Whereas the first type of homosexual solution is based upon
the boy's conviction that parental sexuality is kept in operation
by the father's phallic drive, which he understands and postulates by the analogy of his own phallic drive, the second type
would appear, at bottom, to be based upon the opposite conviction: parental sexuality is kept going by the mother's drive for
vulvar (or vaginal) pleasure. This would signify that boys making this solution have tended to identify themselves with the
mother in primal scenes or their equivalents, not as a suffering
victim, but as the more intensely gratified participant. In its
turn, this would imply that such boys anticipate more intense
pleasure from stimulation of their orifices than from stimulation
of the penis, and, reasoning by analogy with themselves, make
this identification with the female in a primal scene. They ascribe
to the father this same preference for orificial pleasure over
phallic pleasure and hope therefore to prevent parental sexuality
by offering orificial pleasure to the father.

This formulation, however, raises the question of why a
boy so constituted would engage in a strategy ultimately looking
toward exclusive *genital* possession of the mother. Such boys may
be presumed to be in a state of indecision as to which type of
pleasure is the one more greatly to be desired, and their bisexual-
ity in later life mirrors this uncertainty. Furthermore, analysis of
such adults often shows that they have, as a result of castration-
anxiety, regressed from genital to oral pleasure as the favored
experience, and that, while the pleasurable potentialities of the
phallus are not ignored, its chief importance to them is as a
quid pro quo whereby the nursing situation may be restored, and
the latter is what, unconsciously, they chiefly desire. In later
life, a homosexual pattern of this type is sometimes seen in com-

bination with alcoholism. This combined pattern represents a complex transference deriving from all three of the experiential areas: the intense unconscious impulses toward restoring the nursing situation manifest themselves in the drinking of alcohol, which represents for them the milk imbibed with such ecstatic effect in the nursing situation; their drinking in unrestrained and lawless manner—often to spite someone (a wife, for example) who objects—is an acting out of rebellious impulses toward the mother as a disciplinarian; their homosexuality expresses the Oedipal hostility toward the father. The behavior as a whole marks them as among those whose late oral speculations have included a prevalent tendency to set up a proto-Oedipus situation of rivalry, in which a supposed mutual nursing situation was the central factor.

The active type of homosexual solution carries most of the implications enumerated in the discussion of the first type and has certain additional ones. (1) One of these has already been mentioned: the boy does not consider the father to be seriously threatening in terms of castration; but possibly, since this strategy exists only as a fantasy, this is more wish-fulfilling than reality-based. (2) It implies, as described, that the boy can conceive of the female deriving *greater* pleasure from an act of sexual intercourse than the male does; otherwise, what he contemplates offering the father as an inducement to abandon phallic gratification would appear to have little value. (3) This in its turn implies, as already indicated, that the libidinal potentialities of mouth and anus are particularly cogent with such a boy, since it would be by a process of analogy that he would ascribe them such cogency in the father's mind.

These implications raise important questions concerning this second form of the homosexual strategy, as adopted in the speculations of the period of Oedipal difficulties. If the boy has such disdain for the father as a threatening figure, why does he not merely ignore him and proceed to try to win exclusive genital possession of the mother? Moreover, if he is convinced of the superior value of oral (or anal) over genital pleasure, why does

he not simply renounce the latter and make the same adaptation
as the first boy, with even greater enthusiasm?

The reader will see that these two questions point in opposite directions, the first toward an unimpeded drive for genital
gratification with the mother, the second toward an intensified
drive for oral (or anal) gratification via the father. This hints
at the fact that the boy who contemplates the second type of
solution is in a state of great vacillation and conflict. He is not
actually so contemptuous of the father as a dangerous figure as
his daring fantasy might imply. This bold fantasy may indicate a
more exigent need to ignore the father's reality than is felt by the
child who less boldly fantasies being outwardly submissive and
passive toward the father, while secretly scheming to hoodwink
and outwit him under the guise of love. In other words, the
second boy's fantasy implies a more drastic and schizoid distortion of reality and its significance than that of the first boy.

Furthermore, the second boy may be even more uncertain
of the mother's acquiescence, should his homosexual strategy be
successful, than the first boy is. It is a striking fact that in the
transferences whereby, in adult life, these two schemes reach
overt expression, the objective for whose sake the entire strategy
was created—genital gratification with the mother (in the transference, a woman who substitutes for her)—is lost sight of. This
objective is, in actuality, more completely ignored by the first
boy than by the second, for the latter often becomes "bisexual"
and is much more likely than the former to undertake marriage.
But one gains the impression clinically that the latter boy, in
adult life, is even more chary of emotional involvement with
women than is the former. While the "passive" homosexual
avoids women sexually, he is more apt to accept and seek them
out as companions than his "active" counterpart does. The latter
is likely to be a more thorough-going "woman hater" than the
former.

"Passive" is used for want of a better term. These people
are so aggressive in seeking out and seducing sexual partners and
are so active in their oral behavior with these partners that

"passive" seems a misnomer, being highly misleading as to the motivations, conscious and unconscious, that produce their sexual behavior. The "active" homosexual is, as a rule, not so aggressive in seeking out homosexual partners. He tends to let himself be seduced, although by means of direct or devious exhibitionism toward a prospective partner he sometimes seduces seduction, as it were. His behavior is often passive, as in fellatio, which, in many instances is the experience exclusively desired by the "active" homosexual. Moreover, both the "passive" and "active" homosexual are concepts rather than actualities, since the practicing homosexual may be both "passive" and "active," whether in different experiences or within the framework of a single experience. As these terms are used, "passive" designates the male whose chief interest in a homosexual experience is concentrated upon the phallic gratification of his partner, his own phallic pleasure being, at the moment, a matter of relative unconcern to him; while "active" describes the male whose principal concern in a homosexual experience is with his own phallic gratification, that of his partner being a matter of indifference to him. Although in both instances the actual behavior is just about opposite to what the adjectives signify, and although no individual homosexual falls exclusively into either category, it is useful to make the distinction if it is understood that what is referred to is a predominance of tendencies toward certain attitudes and behavior.

While the passive homosexual's relations with women do not often include sexual intercourse with them, the understanding of such relationships is not exhausted by the explanation that he enjoys being "a girl among girls," for his attitudes and behavior toward women are not altogether epicene. Nor is this understanding completed by the explanation that he uses companionship with women as a means of deceiving the world, of concealing his homosexuality from the hostile, punitive eyes of society. Passive homosexuals often use this as a rationalization for such friendships with women, particularly to allay the envy or jealousy of their homosexual confrères and partners. Their female companions, when ultimately frustrated in whatever hopes they may have entertained for sexuality or marriage with such men, often manifest their rage and resentment by statements that they were merely being used as a blind to conceal the deceiver's homosexuality. However, while these are unquestionably factors in the passive homosexual's relations with women, detailed observation shows that these relations often contain genuine heterosexual qualities, though well concealed within a welter of inconsistent motivations and rationalizations. The women involved are often mother-figures with whom the passive homosexual is engaged in a transference maneuver. However, the transference role of the female companion is sometimes not so obvious or exclusive, and it may happen that attempts are made—usually not very successfully—to initiate genital experience with the female friend.

The passive homosexual, while more afraid of women sexually than his active counterpart, is in general less contemptuous of them as persons than is the active homosexual, whose contempt for them aids him in a sexual approach: they are good for nothing except phallic targets.

It would seem that, underlying the passive homosexual's fear of and repulsion toward women as genital objects and the active one's hatred and contempt for them, is the old phallic belief that women are castrated men. In both there appears to exist the deep-seated conviction that the vulvar cleft (or vagina) is the site of a castrated penis. The passive homosexual cannot, as a rule, tolerate the perception of this site, since it tends to revive his castration-anxiety. Furthermore, he often has the unconscious belief that the woman, out of resentment for her "castrated" state and envy of his intactness, may castrate him by means of her vagina: like the mouth, it may have teeth concealed within its hidden depths; or he may simply fear that castration is contagious, as it were. To him, apparently, his measures for the retention of his phallus seem less certainly efficacious than is the case with his active counterpart, who is, as a rule, much more convinced that his phallus will emerge from the vulvar cleft whole and intact. While this might seem to indicate that the active homosexual is better adjusted to reality than his passive counterpart, the reverse is actually the case: the active homosexual supports his phallic state of mind by denying that the female has any power at all; thus she can be exploited without fear of danger to his phallus. The passive homosexual, while he distorts her power by exaggeration and maintains his phallus whole by never entrusting it to the dubious mercies of her vulvar cleft, is yet nearer to the truth, in that he ascribes *some* power to the female, which assuredly she has.

The general tendency on the part of both types of homosexual men to fail to capitalize on their transferential strategies— to possess the mother genitally now that the father is placed out of competition—is seen to rest upon a basis which originates in the phallic state of mind. Even if the rival for exclusive genital possession of the mother can be set aside by these ingenious strategies, the mother, as a "castrate," is a dangerous person to whom to entrust the phallus. This belief remains consistently cogent for the passive homosexual; for the "active" homosexual its cogency is intermittent: at times she appears dangerous, while at other times her dangerousness is discounted by phallic contempt.

The factors which, in the childhood experience of the boy and in the fantasy-life and speculations to which they lead, constitute homosexual solutions of Oedipal difficulties may be summed up: (1) Basic to such solutions is the solution of the late oral phase wherein the father's penis is hopefully regarded as a substitute for the mother's nipple. Kinsey's figure on "homosexual outlet," mentioned above, would indicate that at least 37 per cent of boys in the late oral phase contemplate this as an important possibility.* This factor alone cannot produce neurotic homosexuality in later life; nor can it produce an ardent seeking out of homosexual experience; rather, it produces only that form of latency which may lead to acquiescence constituting mere

---

* It is probable that the percentage of boys having this fantasy is a good deal higher, since it seems safe to assume that not all boys who engage in this fantasy actually participate in acting it out in adult life.

homosexual behavior on infrequent occasion. (2) Essential to
the formation of a later neurotic homosexuality is the boy's arrival
at the conclusion, in the Oedipal phase of childhood experience,
that the most effective way of eliminating the father as a rival
for exclusive genital possession of the mother is to break up
parental sexuality by offering the father erotic pleasure via the
boy's own body; either by giving him phallic pleasure by means
of one of the boy's bodily orifices or by giving him pleasure at an
orifice by means of the boy's phallus. (3) Further essential to a
later neurotic homosexuality is a fear, at this Oedipal stage, of
the mother's vulvar cleft, a fear based upon the phallic conviction that, like all females, she is a castrated male. This fear may
be one which is in constant readiness to emerge into consciousness, or its tendency to emerge may be intermittent. The variants
noted under the second and third headings permit some understanding of the variations and inconsistencies in the attitudes and
behavior of all neurotic homosexuals in later life. (4) Whatever
the forms taken by the preceding factors in the Oedipal situation
itself, they cannot operate to produce the seeking-out (neurotic)
type of homosexual behavior in later life without the mediation
of transference maneuvers.

The girl in the Oedipal area of experience may also adopt
homosexual "solutions" in her fantasies, speculations, and schemes.
As in the case of the boy, the girl who favors this solution regards
it as essential to break up parental sexuality, thus achieving a
separation of the parents which, presumably, will open the way
for her toward the father as a genital object.

The terms "active" and "passive" as applied to female
homosexuality are more accurately descriptive than they are in
the case of male homosexuality. The active female homosexual is
the one who is aggressive in seducing her partner and who, in a
homosexual experience, plays an active role: she engages in
stimulation of the partner's vulvar cleft (clitoris or vagina) with
finger or artificial phallus or by active coital movements against
the partner's vulva (so-called *tribady*). The passive female homosexual is truly passive in that she permits and enjoys having these

things done to her. However, with respect to play with the breasts, which is an important factor in female homosexual practices, a reversal in meaning of these two terms applies: the partner who is active in the genital sense is generally the one who is passive in allowing her breasts to be sucked, while the genitally passive partner does the sucking. But, as in the case of male homosexuality, exclusively active or passive behavior is rarely seen in any individual Lesbian, and the distinction is valid only in terms of predominant attitudes and behavior.

The active type of female homosexual solution is based upon the idea that parental sexuality is mainly initiated and maintained by the mother's desire for genital stimulation by the father's penis. Therefore if she can devise a method for affording, via her own body, such genital stimulation to the mother, she will be able to accomplish separation of the parents, and the father will be left isolated for her own genital gratification. The finger is the only bodily part she possesses that seems appropriate for this purpose; she feels keenly the need for a penis, and girls contemplating this solution of their Oedipal difficulties generally experience penis-envy in an intense form. The derivation of this type of solution from the *quid pro quo* explanations and solutions of the late oral phase of experience is so obvious as to require mere mention. The analysis, in later life, of female homosexuals of this type generally reveals intense oral impulses underlying their homosexual impulses. While they tend generally to "baby" their homosexual partners and to grant them the boon of taking the "baby's" role in play with the breasts, the roles of "baby" and "mother" are often interchangeable in this nursing behavior, and often an intense dependency upon the passive partner is found to underlie the apparent self-sufficiency and assured self-reliance of the active Lesbian.

The girl who, in the Oedipal phase, adopts a homosexual solution of a passive type has the same strategic aim, common to all homosexual solutions, of breaking up parental sexuality by means of offering genital gratification to the rival parent. Here, however, the premises postulated are a great deal more complex

than in the case of any other homosexual solution, male or
female. She makes the opposite assumption to that of her female
counterpart: parental sexuality, in her view, remains operative by
reason of the father's phallic impulses. Such a view would seem
well calculated to make her tend toward "solving" rivalry with
her mother by the simple (supposedly normal) expedient of offering her own vulvar cleft for the father's genital gratification:
she might then encounter the same anxieties concerning pain and
damage through penetration of her vulvar cleft as those already
described, might experience the same conflict, and might attempt
to resolve it by repression, more or less complete, of her Oedipal
impulses, just as her more normal sister does.

However, what complicates her psychic situation and makes
this relatively simple solution impossible for her is her belief,
gained from the witnessing of a primal scene or its equivalent,
that the supreme—perhaps the only—pleasure in genital intercourse is experienced by the male, similar to the phallic belief of
the boy. Her strategy then takes the form of offering her body to
the mother so that the latter will be enabled to enjoy this active
type of gratification. She postulates here that the mother has a
phallus as well as a vulvar cleft, the implication being that the
girl believes that she alone is "castrated" without remedy: the
mother may have been "castrated"—perhaps in the same manner
as she supposes she herself was, or perhaps through bearing children—but a "new" penis has been somehow acquired. It may be
that in some cases she supposes that the mother lacks a penis, as
she herself does, but regards penetration of a vulvar cleft, even
with the finger, as the supreme interpersonal pleasure of genital
type. If such cases exist, I have not encountered them, though
theoretically such a concept might be linked with the desire to
touch noted previously in this chapter as one of the early forms
of genital impulse in this experiential area.

As in the case of the "active" homosexual boy, the girl
making these assumptions would be subject to vacillation with
regard to where, in the experience of genital intercourse, the
greater pleasure lies—in penetrating or in being penetrated. In

so far as she contemplates offering her own body to be penetrated by the mother, in whatever terms, her purpose is to place her rival out of competition and to leave the father in isolation as the object of her own genital impulses. But if the latter is her objective, then it would seem that after all she regards genital stimulation by the phallus as *her* supreme pleasure. This is somewhat less inconsistent than it at first appears to be if it is recalled that she regards her own "castrated" state as exceptional, the mother's "castration" having been remedied. Her own pleasure is a second-best one, with which, in her "maimed" condition, she has to be satisfied: to penetrate may be preferable, but for this one needs a phallus.

This complex concatenation of thought and feeling is rare, and the passive Lesbian generally becomes so on a quite different basis: she has the usual female impulse to achieve pleasure from the phallus by dealing with it as a target for vaginally displaced oral impulses, but has a more than ordinarily intense fear of the phallus as an attacking organ, as well as a more than ordinarily intense fear of open rivalry with the mother. The phallus is also apt to be seen by her as a symbol of disciplinary demands, like the upraised finger of warning, admonition, and command. Her tendency to avoid the phallus may thus also be derived from her aversion to the disciplinary aspects of the mother: she insists that the mother be only the indulgent, nursing mother who gives her sensory gratification and the security of her approval. In the transferential situations of later life in which such motivations are acted out, the passive Lesbian's homosexual partner is generally required to play the role of an indulgent mother, giving the "baby" the breast both actually and in displaced fashion by digital stimulation of the vulvar cleft. Though the active Lesbian may behave, in the nonsexual aspects of such relationships, in "masculine" fashion, appearing to be the leader and the one who commands and is obeyed, the relationship behind the scenes, as it were, is frequently one in which the passive Lesbian tyrannizes cruelly over her partner. The passive Lesbian is ordinarily not so thoroughly and neurotically tied to the homosexual relationship as her active partner is: she may have occasional relationships with carefully selected men—selected on the basis of their unaggressive manageability—which may be sexual or not (the passive Lesbian is often a married, though heterosexually frigid, woman), and tends often to use her greater mobility as a weapon to bring to heel her more neurotically immobilized active partner.

Passive Lesbians, in the sense of those who seek out passive homosexual experience, are less commonly seen clinically than any of the other homosexual types. This fact may or may not indicate that they are less commonly to be found in the general population. It would suggest, however, that passive female homosexuals are for the most part merely acquiescent and that their neurotic quality relates much more significantly to their fear of the male phallus and their resentment of phallic "superiority" than it does to separation strategies. The extreme intricacies underlying the latter in the few cases of passive Lesbians in which, in my experience, a homosexual separation strategy could be demonstrated, would suggest that not many girls adopt passive homosexuality as a solution to Oedipal rivalry.

It must be realized that the entire Oedipal situation is much complicated for the girl, particularly so in the matter of homosexual solutions, by the fact that her rival, toward whom she must now entertain hostile impulses, is the mother who until now has been the object of her love, no matter how much this love may have become attenuated through the experiences of the disciplinary period. The boy's rival is the father, a comparative stranger, who until now has been loved in much more tentative fashion—as a potential substitute for the nursing mother or as one who may aid him in escaping some consequences of the mother's disapproval in disciplinary matters. The girl's new Oedipal attachment to the father is therefore likely to be more unstable and tentative than that of the boy to the mother, which has been lifelong. She may on this account find it more difficult to sustain hostile motivations toward her Oedipal rival than the boy does toward his. Since all homosexual fantasies are in essence an expression of hostility toward a rival, the girl who attempts such a solution tends to be much less wholeheartedly committed to her homosexuality than the boy who adopts the homosexual solution. She vacillates a great deal more; just when she thinks she has found *the* solution to her Oedipal difficulties, she may be assailed by doubts to the effect that this is her beloved mother against whom she is scheming. This tendency to vacillate may be greatly lessened when penis-envy is intense, since the blame ascribed to the mother for the child's "castration" may give strong support to hostile attitudes toward the mother. Such is often the case with the girl who attempts the active homosexual solution. But in the case of the passive homosexual girl such vacillation remains an important factor and determines the instability of this solution, except in those rare children with the complicated motivational background above outlined. In general, it seems true that the girl's stable and enduring Oedipal attachment to the father is dependent upon her coming to regard him as a glorified mother-figure, a matter for discussion in the following chapter. Only under these circumstances is she able more or less to ignore her former devotion to the mother and to regard her as an interloper and comparative stranger, much as the Oedipal boy is able, without these complications, to regard the father.

Many adult homosexuals like to regard their homosexuality as having an exclusive basis in constitutional factors; this seems to exonerate them from all responsibility for their tendencies and behavior and frees them from the obligation to attempt to change these. Unfortunately, some psychiatrists have similar views, though their number steadily decreases. One cannot deny the possibility of some such predisposing organic factor, though endeavors to discover this—in cerebral pathology and in endocrinopathies—have so far conspicuously failed.

Freud's concept of biologically latent homosexual tendencies in all human beings was based upon two factors: (1) the high incidence of latent homosexuality in the general population; (2) the embryologic fact that sexual differentiation proceeds from an identical anlage in the developing fetus, the essential genital organs having homologues in each sex: penis and clitoris, developing from the same embryonic structure; likewise the uterus and the *uterus masculinus,* a tiny cul-de-sac in the male urethra. This concept has been utilized by some who hold with the constitutional theory of homosexual origins.

But we have already seen the danger of attempting to make too precise parallels between psychology and biology. Such attempts are indeed seductive, since they have often a certain validity, but they frequently lead our thinking astray, and tend to make us ignore those experiential factors which may have a determining significance—at the least, a contributory one—and which are the ones whose effects may, we hope, be altered by an adequate psychotherapy.

Particularly in this problem of the sources of latent homosexuality it would seem that insistence upon the great importance of experiential factors, as compared with biologic parallels or other constitutional factors, justifies itself. These factors of individual experience, more than once referred to in this volume, are: (1) in the case of the male, the frequent occurrence of hopeful speculation, in the late oral phase, concerning the possibility of finding in the father a substitute for the mother in a restored nursing situation; (2) in the case of the female, the universal fact that the mother is the child's first source of sensory gratification and of security. This would imply that there may be a sexual differentiation in terms of latent homosexuality; that it could be demonstrated as universal among females, less so among males—unless the line of speculation above referred to is of universal occurrence among male children in the late oral phase of experience. A reliable psychologic test for latent homosexuality might show whether such a prediction could be verified.

VI

PSYCHOTHERAPEUTIC AIMS

PRIOR TO 1900, before he had begun to evolve the libido theory, Freud held that neurosis (hysteria) had its origin in a traumatic experience during childhood; specifically, in an experience of sexual seduction by an adult or by an older child [18]. This hypothesis had evolved out of his work with Breuer in seeking to use catharsis as a cure for hysterical symptoms. Catharsis consisted of evoking, under hypnosis, the memory of a traumatic event which bore a causal relationship to the symptom, though memory of the event had been lost to consciousness. Some of the traumas thus remembered seemed to Freud, after a time, both ineffective for and inappropriate to the production of the specific symptom in question. Such memories he termed "screen-memories" [30] and regarded them as merely representative of memories of genuinely traumatic events that had occurred at an earlier period in the patient's life. In the pursuit of the recollection of earlier and genuinely traumatic events, he was led into the realm of memories of childhood experience, and specifically of childhood sexual experience. With remarkable regularity his patients of both sexes recalled having been sexually seduced at the age of three, four, or five by an adult (parent, relative, governess, maid, or manservant) or by an older child. On this clinical basis Freud stated categorically that such experiences furnished the specific etiology of all cases of hysteria and argued vehemently in support of this hypothesis.

At some time and in some manner he became aware that this was an untenable hypothesis; he described [*19*, p. 244] his disillusionment but gave no clue as to just when or just how this occurred. He refers to these traumas as "fictitious" and says that this etiology "broke down under its own improbability and under contradiction in definitely ascertainable circumstances." Though tempted to abandon the work of psychoanalysis at this point, he nevertheless persevered; he saw that the "fictitious traumas" could be regarded as fantasies of childhood, fantasies of sexual seduction by adults, and, equating fantasies with dreams, concluded that they must have been wish-fulfilling. If these patients as children *wished* to be seduced sexually by parents or other adults, the strict conclusion might have been drawn that all children destined for later neurosis have such fantasies, which he soon saw as evidence of an Oedipus complex. However, transcending strict logic, he divined that *all* children have such fantasies and that *all* children pass through a developmental phase describable as the Oedipus complex.

According to notions then current, the sexual impulse made its first appearance at puberty, with the somatic maturation of the genital parts. Freud's hypothesis of an Oedipus complex in early childhood was in contradiction of this notion and demanded a revision of it to the effect that the sexual impulse of puberty is merely the final stage of a psychosexual evolution that has its forerunners in childhood and even in infancy. Freud's findings in matters of infantile sexuality offered good evidence for an emergence of sexual impulses at a period much earlier than the age of puberty. He hit upon the concept of libido—somewhat analogous to the energy concept then current in physics—and thought of it as a sexual energy of definite quantity undergoing development from birth into adult life, development which might be either normal or pathologic.

Thus, out of the ruin of Freud's theory of a specific traumatic etiology of neurosis, evolved the libido theory of person-

ality-development and its accompanying theory of neurosis,
whereby the latter results from "fixations" or arrests in the evolution of individual libido. It should be carefully noted that the
direction taken by Freud's thinking after the breakdown of his
experiential theory was not the only possible one, though it seems
a highly predictable one, in view of his previous work on dream-
interpretation and infantile sexuality. He might, however, have
concluded that, while his original intuition that neurosis is based
upon specific traumatic experience was correct, he had been for
a time satisfied with too narrow a definition of such experience.
There are many varieties of traumatic experience other than that
of sexual seduction by an adult, of which the three preceding
chapters of the present work have offered many an example.

Here it is necessary to ask what is the position occupied by
the factor of experience in the libido theory of neurosis. Does
the libido, according to Freud, develop in a predestined manner
(already laid down in the germ plasm) regardless of the accidents of individual experience? Despite certain passages in
Freud's writings which would seem to support an affirmative
answer to this question, the body of Freud's work demands a
negative answer: Freud's position in psychology does not parallel
that of Calvin in theology. Individual experience is the factor
which may so interfere with the development of the libido that
the latter may become arrested or "fixated" at a given point or
may retrogress to such a point. It must be stated, however, that
in this theory of neurosis the details of individual experience are
regarded as having little specific bearing upon later happenings.
The main interest in any given individual experience is in its
effect, not in its nature, and lies in the answer to the question:
Does it interfere with the evolution of the libido? The concern,
for instance, is not with whether the child has been intimidated,
by whom, in what circumstances, with what background; rather
it is with whether libido has been arrested in its development
and thus rendered less manageable by the ego.

The libido theory visualizes neurosis as a state in which
there exists a constant threat of being overwhelmed by the

demonic in one's nature and in which are contained the measures taken against this threat. An experiential theory visualizes the individual as having become conditioned, defensively and offensively, by certain traumatic interpersonal experiences, so that the ego is relatively weak and disorganized and is thus unable to achieve much beyond its own, often precarious, safety. The difference between the two is more a difference in emphasis than in kind: the latter theory stresses the importance of details in early traumatic situations and their effect in molding specific defenses in the form of later symptoms and character-traits; the former theory accents the fact that libido has been interfered with at a specific point in its evolution, and, while recognizing that this interference occurs as the result of a specific experience, pays little attention to the details as constituting in themselves formative factors.

The theoretic viewpoint of the present work might justly be termed paleo-Freudian, for it represents a return to the crossroads at which Freud found himself when faced with the collapse of his traumatic theory of the etiology of neurosis; a return and an affirmation that Freud was right in his first intuition that neurosis emerges from traumatic experience and its specific details. The therapeutic task which emerges from such a viewpoint is in essence that of reconditioning the ailing ego and may be divided into two main categories which, in terms of technical procedure, are overlapping: (1) the exploration and elucidation of the current structure of the character; (2) the discovery of original and later historical deviations from a supposed norm of personality-development.

The former task involves the detection and description of the various devices, originally adopted in response to specific stresses, which have now become characteristic of the given ego, and the interrelationships of these devices—how some are supportive of others, and how some involve counteraction toward and contradiction of others. Structure of the character may be likened to structure of an architectural edifice, provided that the analogy is not pressed beyond its usefulness. Though the neurotic character-structure holds together and bears up after a fashion under some stress, it is like an ill-made building with serious faults of construction: some parts of it are solidly built, with good, workable arrangement of thrust and counterthrust, pressure and counterpressure; while other parts are rickety and are flimsily built, the result of hasty, makeshift construction, in which excessive weight rests upon too fragile a support, in which counterthrust and counterpressure are inadequate to meet anticipated thrusts and pressures. Such faulty sections of the structure may collapse under stress of additional thrusts and pressures and may be so placed in the whole fabric of the personality that their collapse will bring the entire structure to ruin.

The work of therapy, to continue this analogy, is to detect and to demonstrate these weak spots in the structure and to take remedies to repair and strengthen them. At this point the analogy breaks down, for in psychotherapy we deal with a living organism having self-awareness, and not with an impassive and unaware contraption of wood, stone, and metal. In our efforts at reconstruction of the latter, we deal with it as a passive, lifeless object, completely subject to our remedial manipulations. We cannot deal so with the human personality. If its faults of structure are to be remedied, it must itself become aware of the faults and must itself apply the remedies. Furthermore, the historic reasons for structural faults in a building need not be known and if known are of mainly academic interest to the new architect; the faults can be repaired without such knowledge. In the case of the human being, a knowledge of the historic reasons for the adoption of those devices which have resulted in the weakening of the character-structure are of peculiar importance in the taking of remedial measures. Such devices are always adopted in the attempt to avert a danger or to overleap an obstacle, and it is typical of the neurotic human being that he continues to operate as if the original danger or the original obstacle were still present— at the least, potentially so.

If this belief in the continued presence of the original danger or obstacle is to be put to the test of actuality and to be at long last set aside, it is essential that the person become aware not only of his belief—for such beliefs are regularly unconscious— but also of the circumstances in which the belief arose. The belief may originally have corresponded with the facts of his then circumstances; or it may have been in part justified by the actual circumstances, though not *in toto;* or it may, as in the case of the "broken promise," have resulted from a complete misapprehension of actualities. Since such beliefs remain current unconsciously, it is necessary to bring them to awareness and to put them to the test of comparison with actuality—actuality as it was when the belief originally arose and actuality as it is currently. Concepts of actuality and reality may become the object of much philosophic speculation. They are concepts constantly in use by the psychiatrist, who does not ordinarily concern himself with metaphysical refinements. What he means by them is what the layman usually understands—what Sullivan termed "consensual validation," that which is taken as valid by two or more than two persons. In the psychiatric sense, actuality or reality is merely what most people would agree is fact, however rightly or wrongly to the metaphysician.

The procedures of structural exploration and investigation of origins are the essential groundwork for a process of reconditioning to be engaged in by the neurotic patient. If he is to succeed in accomplishing such a reconditioning, he must be an active participant—not merely passively acquiescent—in the exploration of his own character and the investigation of pathologic origins. He is, ultimately, the only person capable of bringing about alterations in his personality, supposing that it can be done at all.

Behind this brief account of the psychotherapeutic task lies the notion that we know what is a normal or healthy personality, since we imply a rather detailed knowledge of what personality deviation consists in. This concept of a healthy personality has been an insoluble psychiatric problem. Many solutions have been attempted, but psychiatrists in general have been unable to agree upon any one of them. The lay public, with some justification, has regarded this difficulty of defining the normal or healthy personality as casting doubt upon the validity of all psychiatric work, whether theoretic or therapeutic. If the psychiatrist cannot define the norm, deviation from which constitutes illness, and the norm which encompasses the result he is striving to achieve with his patients—thus reasons the layman—how can he know what he is doing and how can he know whether his efforts have failed or succeeded, even in a relative sense?

The efforts of the internist or the surgeon are not subject to such doubts in the lay mind. The layman believes that somatic health is easy to define. He thinks: if a man has intense pain in his right lower abdomen, is feverish and prostrated, he is obviously ill; if the surgeon proceeds skillfully, presently the man will no longer have pain, his temperature will hover about 98.6° Fahrenheit, his health will have been restored, and he will be able to go about his ordinary affairs. Somatic health in this instance would be defined as freedom from pain, freedom from wide bodily temperature deviations from a mathematical norm, and the ability to function as usual.

In some cases, similar standards could be applied to the psychiatric patient. If he has a belief that his hands become contaminated if he touches certain objects and that his hands can transmit contamination to other persons and objects, and he therefore feels compelled to wash his hands fifty or a hundred times a day, he is, again obviously, ill. If, after a period of therapy, he no longer entertains such a belief and washes his hands only when they look dirty, he is obviously now healthy. Since illness involves symptoms, whether somatic or psychic, the implication is that one factor of health is freedom from symptoms —which is a highly tautologic statement, since a symptom is merely a sign of disease.

In psychiatry, we have no mathematical measures comparable to those, such as temperature, in somatic medicine, unless one wishes so to consider the intelligence quotient arrived at by various tests. The intelligence quotient is a relatively minor indication in psychiatric work, even if it could always be relied upon as a reliable measure and even if we were quite certain, in all

instances, what is measured by it. It is possible in time that we
shall have psychologic or other tests whose numerical results will
give us valuable and indicative data about a person. Psychiatric
research is now being done along such lines, but its results have
not thus far proved fruitful.

The criterion, useful in somatic medicine, of the patient
being able to function "as usual" is useless in psychiatry, except in
certain acute episodic illnesses closely connected with somatic occurrences, such as toxic deliriums incidental to systemic infections
or the various types of delirium associated with alcoholism. In
the latter case, functioning "as usual" after the termination of an
episode of delirium tremens may well consist of diligently imbib-
ing whiskey preparatory to a new episode. Indeed, even in somatic medicine, the ability to function "as usual" after an appen-
dectomy may mean, in psychiatric terms, neurotic or even psychotic functioning.

In considering the psychic status of an individual, we are
constrained to recognize that we are dealing with an enormous
number and range of variable factors. The person with the
hand-washing compulsion, above referred to, is obviously ill. But
what is healthy with regard to the issues there concerned? Is it
healthy to wash the hands once a day, or five times a day, or
every fourth day, or once a week? What is to be regarded as dirty?
What is to be regarded as contamination? Is it healthy to regard
all contacts of the hands as sufficiently contaminating to warrant
a habit of always washing the hands before eating? Or to warrant
a habit, in physicians and dentists, of always washing the hands
before and after handling a patient? Are all the rituals of surgical asepsis warranted by bacteriologic actualities or do some of
them spring from an unhealthy state of mind with regard to contamination? Is it psychically healthy or unhealthy for a person
to be unconcerned if his hands are theoretically dirty, actually
slightly dirty, dirty, or very dirty?

We see here that concepts of mental health might vary
considerably in detail, depending upon cultural postulates or

upon class postulates or upon other special postulates within a culture.

It is obvious, then, that a concept of mental health cannot be defined in universal terms, but only in terms relative to a given culture and often to specific classes and groups within the culture. It would seem to follow from this that the psychiatrist, in his effort to define what is mentally normal or healthy, is bedeviled by the existence of a number of norms within his patient-population or, to put it otherwise, by the existence of so wide a range of variation of so large a number of different factors that he cannot give a simple definition of "normal" or "healthy."

It might seem that mental health could be simply defined, in terms of the preceding chapters of this volume, as the outcome of the passage without traumatic experience through the various experiential areas laid down by the culture for each child. This would seem to mean that such a child would have been free of the necessity of adopting pathologic ego-devices and would be perfectly adapted to this culture, or, at the least, to his specific group—class, caste, or otherwise—within the culture. Let us examine this notion more carefully.

This mentally healthy person would presumably as an infant have been given an ideal nursing situation by his loving, nonrejecting mother; he would have been breast- or bottle-fed with plenty of bodily contact with the mother, and would in the early weeks have been given breast or bottle frequently (whenever he was hungry); in the later months he would have been allowed to be frustrated by gradually increasing delays between hunger and feeding and would have been weaned gradually (not abruptly), at nine months or a year. While being weaned, he would have been given sucking substitutes and would have received a good deal of bodily contact with the mother, being frequently picked up and embraced, rocked, kissed, sung to, talked to, cooed at, and the like.

Toilet-training would not have been begun the instant he was weaned. It would have been started several weeks or months later, and then conditioning would have been by approval only, not by disapproval or by "regularization" methods. When he began to crawl about the floor, the behavior attendant upon his see-touch-swallow sequence would have been interfered with only when absolutely essential for somatic health and survival. In all matters, disciplinary action by the mother would be at a minimum and her "do's" and "don't's" would concern only those things known by her to be essential to his adaptations in later childhood and life.

Thus far the alert reader will have noted many questionable statements in the description. When the child enters the realm of genital experience with others and rivalry for genital favors, we encounter difficulties in attempting to describe experience relatively free of frustration which, at the same time, makes for later mental health. If the mother accedes to the boy's seductions, touching and fondling his penis, allowing him to enter her bed and take genital liberties with her, the boy is indeed not frustrated, but does such experience make for later mental health in our culture? Clinical observation of older children and adults who have had experience approximating this description indicates that it leads in our culture to maladaptations of the gravest kinds. Shall the boy's father accede to the boy's wishes for his elimination from the scene and become as a stranger to the home or obligingly fall ill and die? Again, clinical observation shows that a father's desertion or death during the Oedipal period may have grave outcomes for the boy's later mental health. In this experiential area, then, it becomes clear that the factor of nonfrustration does not per se make for mental health in our culture. The corollary to this conclusion is that frustration in this experiential area is essential to later mental health, the only question being the degree and manner of it. Understanding parents will be prepared for the child's impulses, anticipating their high probability, if not inevitability, and will handle the frustration of them firmly but with sympathy and commiserating gentleness. But such handling calls for an objectivity and absence of personal involvement which, considering the likelihood of unresolved unconscious Oedipal vestiges from the parents' own childhood, are not often encountered among parents in our culture. The chances are that the majority of children will not only be frustrated in this experiential area, but more or less traumatically so.

Even if it were possible to describe with utmost accuracy of detail and with all its range of variation the pathway of personality-development leading toward mental health in adult life, we should still not have defined criteria for that state. To describe the manner in which a result is achieved is not to define that result. In the quest for such criteria it is therefore necessary to search elsewhere than in the genetic processes whereby personality is formed.

If mental health depends on relative freedom from traumatic frustration in the experiences of childhood, it can be seen that few adults, if any, in our culture could be cited as examples of the mentally healthy. Such a conclusion would be entirely in keeping with Freud's assertion [38] that civilized man is doomed to be psychically ill. But the standard of mental health here is that of the biologically free animal, untrammeled by self-criticism and self-restraint, opposing his wholehearted utmost in strength and shrewdness against all things which threaten to frustrate his drives for satisfaction and survival. Man, even civilized man, strives thus for his survival, with certain notable exceptions; but for his satisfactions much more deviously and less singleheartedly.

While philosophically we may conclude that civilized man is a sick animal, we cannot be satisfied with the corollary that there is no such thing as mental health among civilized human beings. Civilized man has, in general, shown himself too competent an animal to admit of such a conclusion. This statement holds good, I believe, despite the current dire prophecies concerning the imminent collapse of civilization by mutual destruction which amounts to self-destruction. The present crisis is not the first of its kind in the history of human affairs, and the race has always somehow muddled through, mainly by reason of its great competence as a species.

Furthermore, the current wide prevalence of psychotherapeutic efforts presupposes, as our layman would insist, that there is a distinction, if only a relative one, between mental illness and mental health. Other criteria than that of a putative biologic freedom might be sought and applied. Using the "average" human being as the criterion has been thought of as one solution to this problem of definition: if we could describe the "usual" human being, enumerating his traits and the items of his behavior as he approaches various common problems and issues, perhaps we should be justified in regarding his usualness as normative and in that manner arrive at a definition of mental health. The task, if it were undertaken, would be a vast one and its outcomes uncertain. It seems probable that it would be found that the average man conforms to the tenets of his culture. Are we to regard such conformity per se as one essential factor of mental health? Such a conclusion would lead to the statement that nonconformity is an indicator of lack of mental health, therefore of mental illness. We should thus be forced to take the position that desire for change and action toward it in a culture, whether social, economic, political, or merely technologic, can occur only in mentally unhealthy individuals; we would be thereby compelled to classify our greatest men and women as mentally ill: Washington, Madison, and Jefferson; Susan B. Anthony and Lucretia Mott; Morse, Bell, and Edison would all become candidates for the label of mental illness by reason of their nonconformity, shown in their activity toward changes in the culture.

Moreover, how conforming is the average man, despite appearances? It is a tenet of our culture that a husband should be sexually faithful to his wife, and the average man would doubtless give at least lip service to this dictum. Yet the Kinsey Report indicated a high percentage of American husbands whose actual behavior did not conform to this tenet, and general observation, in urban settings at least, would amply support this finding. Again, it is a tenet embedded in our Constitution that all citizens of our country are endowed with equal political and legal rights. Yet, while most of us conform ideologically to this principle, how many of us conform to it in our actual feeling and behavior toward Negroes? Gunnar Myrdal [54] concludes that we have a national bad conscience because of the discrepancy. It seems likely that similar difficulties would arise in connection with other traits of the average man.

Wilhelm Reich [58] has taken the position that mental health is synonymous with orgastic potency, thus linking a psychic state with a psychosomatic and psychophysiologic process. If orgastic potency is defined in purely physiologic terms as, for the male, the capacity of the penis to erect and to ejaculate with pleasurable sensations upon appropriate stimulation, then one would have to conclude that the man having those capacities is mentally healthy, regardless of whether his orgasm occurs in masturbation, in a homosexual situation, or in a heterosexual one. Such a conclusion is obviously absurd, for the mental hospital psychiatrist commonly observes in the open ward the psychotic patient masturbating to ejaculation with apparent pleasure. When, through a third party, I raised this question with Reich, he sent back the answer that orgasm occurring in settings other than heterosexual is so impeded by feelings of guilt and anxiety as to be incomplete. How Reich would know what precise sensations the individual feels in all such instances is beyond comprehension, and one is left to wonder how it may be determined whether in a given instance orgasm is complete or incomplete. The value of orgastic potency as an objective criterion of mental health is thus vitiated by the introduction of the subjective element of how the orgasm feels to the person experiencing it. The sensations of orgasm are in any case exceedingly difficult, if not impossible, to describe in words; the best that most people can do descriptively is in the comparative terms of more intense or less intense than a previous experience. The attempt to determine completeness or incompleteness of orgasm, dependent as it would be on the individual's subjective sensations and his description of these, would seem necessarily indecisive and of dubious validity.

Furthermore, in his answer to my objection, Reich introduced the psychic factors of feelings of guilt and anxiety into what originally purported to be a purely physiologic criterion of mental health, thus implying the addition of new criteria to his concept: the mentally healthy person must not only be physiologically potent, he must also feel guiltless and secure in the sexual situation. These terms would require careful definition. Furthermore, does Reich refer merely to conscious feelings or to unconscious ones as well? The psychopath in a homosexual situation might feel consciously guiltless and secure and might be orgastically potent, having those orgastic sensations he habitually experiences. Is he mentally healthy? A man in a heterosexual situation is orgastically potent, having his usual sensations. Can we be sure he is mentally healthy until we have investigated his unconscious feelings and have determined that on the occasion he had neither unconscious guilt nor unconscious anxiety? We are forced to conclude that as a criterion of mental health orgastic potency is a will-o-the-wisp.

It seems to me, nevertheless, that we are justified in saying that, in the male, mental health does not exist without orgastic potency, though the existence of the latter does not necessarily guarantee mental health. Instances could be cited and multiplied of individuals who are, empirically at least, orgastically potent (in a purely physiologic sense), but who are mentally ill in one way or another. Another consideration enters here. In evaluating the existence of orgastic potency in the individual man, how are we to regard those men who may be physiologically potent but who are never participants in any situation that would demonstrate this? I refer here to those men who, for doctrinary reasons, have taken vows of celibacy and live up to them. I would not presume to assert that in all such cases the reasons and the vows amount to rationalizations of unconscious and neurotic inhibitions. Does the definition of orgastic potency necessarily include the actual demonstration of it? If we define it as a potentiality that does not require demonstration, how are we to determine the existence of this potentiality? In such cases we would be constrained to disregard this factor and to base our judgment of mental health upon other factors.

In the case of the female, orgastic potency appears to be uncommon in our culture, and it is difficult to know whether to regard the capacity as a *sine qua non* of mental health in women. The difficulty arises through the lack of data from wide observation. If the psychoanalyst were to base his conclusions upon what he observes clinically, he would be compelled to conclude that habitual vaginal orgasm is of rare occurrence in women, clitoral orgasm being considerably more common. However, he is reluctant to make generalizations which are based almost wholly upon instances which, by their nature, must be considered psychopathologic. Indeed, Kinsey [*49*, p. 576] has suggested that vaginal as distinguished from clitoral orgasm does not exist, owing to an apparent lack of nerve-endings in the vaginal mucosa. But under psychoanalysis, some females who had previously experienced clitoral orgasm describe new and different orgastic sensations, which they locate deep inside the body instead of close to the surface and which they describe as having a slower beginning, longer duration at the acme, and slower subsidence than in clitoral orgasm (which, like the male orgasm, is more sudden and of shorter duration at the peak of intensity). These novel orgastic sensations I have hitherto taken to signify that vaginal orgasm had occurred, but I would concede that the difference may be based upon some factor other than a difference in site. However, husbands of such women have sometimes told them, as they reported in analytic sessions, that on such occasions they can feel the vagina contract rhythmically upon the penis, in a gentle, rippling motion—something that did not formerly occur. My conclusion here was that in vaginal orgasm, the vaginal musculature goes into rhythmical contraction and relaxation, like a wide tremor, thus distinguishing it sharply from clitoral orgasm, in which there may be one sharp, convulsively maintained contraction of the vaginal musculature or no contraction at all, the musculature remaining impassive.

This rippling, tremor-like activity of the vaginal musculature in vaginal orgasm has seemed to me analogous to the sucking action of the infant's mouth in a nursing situation and has led me to conclude that if the vaginal musculature behaves in this fashion (with the accompanying subjective sensations of vaginal orgasm), a certain psychic process of development is to be presupposed. This would be a process whereby a displacement occurs from the mouth to the vagina, so that the vagina in its acme of sexual excitement behaves toward the penis very much as the mouth in infancy behaves toward the mother's nipple [cf. *69*].

This displacement, apparently indispensable for the emergence of vaginal orgasm, can be prevented from occurring and interfered with by a variety of deterring factors. If oral activity of the nursing type becomes an unconscious source of anxiety and the impulse toward it thus repressed and inhibited, the analogous displaced "sucking" impulse of the vagina will likewise be repressed and inhibited. Attitudes of hostility and fear toward the depriving and disciplining mother, having operated to inhibit the oral impulse toward her, will obviously contribute toward the suppression of the vaginal sucking impulse. Envy of the penis and fear of the penis as an attacking organ, both having their beginnings in the phallic era of childhood, will serve as deterrents to the vaginal sucking impulse, as both of these will so color the girl's attitude toward the penis that its value as a substitute for the nipple becomes impaired, if not nonexistent. Envious, hostile, or fearful and anxious attitudes toward the sexual partner, who in the optimum genital situation as I am defining it, would always be viewed unconsciously as the indulgent, breast-bearing, milk-giving mother, might so contradict this unconscious optimum that the vaginal sucking impulse, which unconsciously seeks such an object, would be prevented from being set in operation. These deterrent attitudes toward the man as a potential mother may have their source in the woman's unconscious attitude toward her own mother, or they may be based upon the man's behavior toward her, which in actuality may be anything but kindly, indulgent, and benevolent. A man's selfish, contemptuous, and unmotherly behavior may validate and reinforce the woman's already negative attitude toward her own mother. All these factors which may serve to deter a woman's vaginal suck-

ing impulse may be abiding ones, so that she never experiences
vaginal orgasm, or they may function only upon occasion, so that
she fails to experience vaginal orgasm in certain specific circumstances, though capable of such orgasm in other, more favorable
ones.

Overemphasis of the value of the clitoris, another factor
making for the suppression of vaginal orgasm, arises from the
phallic era of experience and owes its origin to excessively bitter
penis-envy and intense competition with phallus-bearers. Such
girls need greatly to emphasize their claims that the clitoris is a
kind of phallus, and in so doing they not only ignore the vagina's
validity as an organ but also attempt to overlook its existence or,
at the least, minimize its significance, since to them its chief significance is that of a handicap, an obstacle in their path toward
masculinity. Thus they value the clitoris, its significance, and its
potentialities (for producing pleasant sensations) over the vagina
and never feel inclined to ascribe much value to the latter. Its
possible value as an analogue to the mouth is overlooked—indeed, in their unconscious view, mouth-people are categorically
inferior to nipple-people—and the displacement from mouth to
vagina is not made. This displacement is avoided even though,
in those terms, the vagina would thus achieve potentialities of
aggression, which per se could become highly valued by those
girls who subjectively suffer from the relative frustration of their
aggressive impulses.

The girl's genital drive toward the father in the Oedipal
area of experience would seem, from what has thus far been said,
to depend upon a displacement from mouth to vagina, made at
least tentatively. If this is so, then the father's penis would be
regarded unconsciously as a substitute for the nipple, and the
father as a person would tend to be regarded as a new mother,
a new kind of mother. He would thus tend to inherit whatever
feelings of tenderness and love had in the past been lavished upon
the mother as the benevolent giver of all good things. In the
girl's mind, the milk which she once received from the mother's
breast and which unconsciously she has never ceased to desire

has its counterpart in a substance which she does not clearly define (unless by some means she is aware of the existence of semen), but which she assumes to exist and to be at least analogous to the mother's milk. This substance she regards as lifegiving both as nourishment and as capable of assimilation by her body in such a way that a new life will be created there and will come forth as a new being, a baby. The latter conviction depends upon the extent to which the processes of reproduction have become a part of the girl's knowledge—by actual information or by hints here and there and intuitions based upon such hints.

The attitude toward the father as a new kind of mother is carried over in later life toward other men, so that attitudes toward lover or husband may be basically those toward a mother and will greatly determine the woman's capacity to love a man, both sexually and nonsexually. The enormous range of variation of this capacity to love finds its explanation in the great possible variation in girls' attitudes toward their mothers and their fathers and results from the girls' experiences with their parents, as well as the great variation of their psychic positions with respect to oral impulses, to the evaluation of the penis, and to their evaluation of themselves as females.

In the most favorable instances, vaginal orgasm will have become possible for the girl (1) because of her relative freedom from oral inhibition toward a generous and affectionate mother; (2) because the father is kind toward her; (3) because both parents accord her value and respect as a person; (4) because her self-esteem has not been seriously threatened by the phallic arrogance of father, brothers, and other boys; and (5) because, in later life, she will have found a sexually potent man who respects her as a person and cherishes her sufficiently to make her feel that, like her mother, he is basically giving and generous.

It is perhaps not difficult to understand that if vaginal orgasm is dependent upon the concurrence of so many different psychic factors, both inward (evolved from childhood experience) and outward (resulting from current actualities), it may be indeed a comparatively rare phenomenon. The capacity for vaginal orgasm is thus a delicate adjustment, readily rendered ineffective or nonoperative by the absence of any one of the factors above enumerated. In a culture having as many phallic features as our own it would seem likely that the men who are the sexual partners of women would not commonly be in a position, psychically speaking, to furnish to them those outward factors upon which the capacity for vaginal orgasm depends.

To clarify this statement, I shall have to outline the sexual evolution of the male, as I have already done in the case of the female. If we consider that the capacity for genital orgasm in both sexes evolves out of the nursing situation, conceived as a pattern and as a prototype, so to speak, of somatic intimacy in general, we are bound to conclude that, other things being equal —which they rarely if ever are, as I have indicated in enumerating the factors upon which the female's capacity for vaginal orgasm depends—the female's evolution is simpler and should be more easily accomplished than that of the male: her role of taker-in does not change from the nursing to the genital situation; only the intaking organ changes. She can remain, in displaced terms, the sucking infant. The male, on the other hand, in the course of his evolution, must function in a new role—that of giver-out rather than that of taker-in—and must also, like the female, learn to center his pleasure-seeking interest upon a new organ; his pleasure is no longer an oral one, nor even one of an oral type, but rather emanates from the penis. The former of these two changes is by far the more difficult and complex; the latter has been foreshadowed even in the oral phase of experience by accidental and random acts of genital self-stimulation and by the later integration of such originally random touching and pressure into acts of masturbation, often utilized in consolatory manner for the frustrations of weaning. Boys as well as girls experience in the later oral phase strong impulses toward restoration of the nursing situation and retain such impulses unconsciously throughout life.

One of the fantasies common to the late oral phase is that of the *quid pro quo,* whereby the child hopes to offer to the mother a bodily something in return for which she will consent to grant him a similar boon. We have already seen that acts of genital exhibitionism on the part of boys in the early phases of the phallic era of experience have as their psychic background the notion of a mutual or reciprocal sucking such as is implied in some of the *quid pro quo* fantasies of the late oral phase. It seems that the boy here ascribes his own oral impulse to the mother and supposes that she would enjoy sucking on a penis (hopefully, his own) as much as he would enjoy sucking on her nipple.

The chief difficulty encountered here in his speculations centers about the matter of substance. He is convinced, as we have seen (page 99), that the mother's breast lactates perpetually and that if he is permitted to suck at it, he can extract milk and drink it. But he has no substance to offer her in return except urine, which in the course of toilet-training he has learned to regard as a disgustingly dirty and, at the best, worthless substance, and it may even possess connotations of danger as a possibly poisonous substance. It is upon the basis of this difficulty with regard to substance that his hopes of re-establishing somatic intimacy with the mother by means of a bodily *quid pro quo* are apt to collapse. If he is aware of the existence of semen as a male adult substance, he may merely shelve these hopes and await a happier day when he will be "grown-up." As in the case of the girl, he also may suppose (on the basis of his oral fantasy of the father's penis as a substitute for the mother's nipple) that the male adult, like the mother, perpetually lactates—in that case, from the penis—and may base his hopes for a happier future, when "grown-up," upon this assumption, even in the absence of any hint of information about semen. Whenever he becomes aware of the existence of semen—and this may, in some instances, be not earlier than the occurrence of the nocturnal emissions or masturbatory ejaculations of puberty—this new knowledge may unconsciously attach to and revive his hopes of a *quid pro quo*. In this manner he may come to regard semen as something desirable to a woman and to accept as a role desirable to himself that of the giver-out of desired substance.

But by this time the oral impulses for the gratification of which the possession of such substance was essential, in terms of a *quid pro quo,* have become in all likelihood deeply repressed and their central place in the focus of conscious attention has been taken over by other impulses. These are genital impulses arising in the phallic era, as have already been described. They are closely associated with the phallic state of mind—the prideful possession of the one genital organ, the scornful and pitying contempt for nonpossessors of this, and the determination to exploit their weak and handicapped condition for his own genital pleasure. These impulses, with their sadistic coloring, are in themselves quite sufficient to serve as the psychic background and support for orgastic potency in the male; they are, however, obviously inadequate to create and maintain attitudes in the male of affection and tenderness or even respect toward a woman; nor will they impel him to seek to give her sexual enjoyment. Indeed, they are based on the unconscious assumption, as we have heretofore seen, that a female *cannot* enjoy a sexual experience, since only *one* organ, the penis, is capable of affording sexual pleasure, and she has none.

Many men in our culture go through life and carry on sex-including relationships with women, even marriage (sometimes two or more), with no psychic basis and equipment for such relationships other than this phallic one. This should teach us how idle is the concept which accepts orgastic potency as the sole essential criterion of mental well-being. In such men we may often observe perfect orgastic potency in combination with a very feeble capacity, if any, to relate to a woman with love (beyond sexual desire for her) or with the sense of her as a person to be respected and valued for any quality; he regards her "mutilated" state, which he can exploit for his own benefit, with mingled feelings of scorn and pleasurable anticipation. These impulses toward phallic exploitation of a woman for his genital pleasure seem, however, to form a necessary partial psychic basis of the male capacity for orgastic potency. They may, as has been said, constitute the entire basis for this in certain males whom we are constrained to judge immature as persons. Other males, however, while in part actuated by such impulses in the direction of orgastic potency, are also actuated by those giving-out impulses whose derivation has been outlined above. The latter impulses have become largely detached, as above stated, from their original oral setting, and the boon for which the giving-out of semen is the price, so to speak, is no longer an oral pleasure but a genital one. In this respect the male has exchanged his original role of sucking infant to that of lactating mother: his penis is the milk-giving nipple, the woman's vagina the infant's mouth. He is able to take pleasure in this new role, enjoying not only his obvious phallic gratification but also the woman's pleasure in receiving what he can give her. The purely phallic man can likewise enjoy the woman's pleasure: he has learned, in the course of his life, that some "fast" women can enjoy sex experience and feels that his self-esteem as possessor of a remarkable phallus is validated if he can compel—and the correct word is *compel*—his sexual partner to undergo an orgasm. His assumption here is that the major part in this phenomenon is played by his penis, and he underestimates and mistakes, if he considers it at all, the significance of the woman's psychosexual make-up. The man whose phallic state of mind, having been modified by the accession of other factors, is no longer paramount is likely to know better than this and to feel that his role toward the woman is to give her the opportunity of desiring and receiving his semen; whether she avails herself of the opportunity depends upon her.

The male's in-and-out movements in sexual intercourse have a psychic meaning, in addition to their obvious role of somatic stimulation. They represent a repetitious alternation of offering and threat to take away calculated to have the effect of causing the woman to "grab," as it were, for the offered penis and its desired semen before the threat of its being taken away becomes a reality. The vaginal orgasm might then be regarded as the final "grab."

Orgastic potency in the male, while requiring an exchange both of roles and of organs in terms of the nursing situation (viewed as a paradigm for all later somatic pleasure-seeking intimacy), is, despite these complexities, a less delicate and uncertain adaptation than that which vaginal orgasm demands of the female. The male's potency may be based upon either or both of the two psychic motivations that have been described and does not require that concurrence of numerous factors which gives to vaginal orgasm its uncertain and precarious character. Naturally there are both inward (developmental) and outward (current) factors which may operate as deterrents of male orgastic potency. Among the former would be the historical emergence of vengeful impulses (refusal to give, in a supposed situation of *quid pro quo*) or of feelings of excessive discouragement about the possession, even in future, of an adequate *quid pro quo.* Another historical factor would be the administering, by either parent, of severe penalties or threats of penalties for the tentative sexual aggressions of the phallic period of development, whether directed toward one of the parents or toward other children. Though such penalties may take a variety of forms, they can all be categorized as more or less drastic threats of castration, whether somatic or psychic—the latter being threats of destruction to self-esteem in the form of ridicule or other kinds of humiliation.

The various types of psychosexual impotency observed clinically in male patients carry intimations of the kind of traumatic experience which underlies them, and of the period in which this occurred. The inability to erect the penis and to maintain erection in sexual situations other than masturbatory hints at an etiology in threats of castration (or danger to self-esteem) in the phallic era. Premature ejaculation, on the other hand, would seem to relate to vengeful and fearful attitudes toward the mother, derived from experiences and adaptations of the oral area of experience; these attitudes may or may not receive support and confirmation in the current attitudes and behavior of the sexual partner. The prematurity of the ejaculation is often unconsciously intended to deprive the woman of sexual pleasure, and its effect, in any case, is to render impossible her vaginal orgasm. Or it may be the result of an excessively hasty compliance with her supposed demand for semen, a *reductio ad absurdum,* especially in cases where ejaculation is so premature as to occur before intromission. In other cases, premature ejaculation may serve, in a compulsive manner, to counteract an unconscious impulse to withhold the semen altogether. The latter impulse, in the absence of a compulsive forestalling of it by premature ejaculation, produces another form of impotency—either retarded ejaculation or none at all. These latter two forms of impotency would hint at a derivation from historical vengeful tendencies similar to those suggested as basic to premature ejaculation. The choice of retardation or complete absence of ejaculation rather than premature ejaculation would depend upon the extent to which the man dares to frustrate the mother-surrogate in her desire to be given semen; this attitude toward the sexual partner is, in its turn, perhaps dependent upon the extent to which the man as a child dared to defy and disappoint the mother in matters of discipline. The tendency to retarded ejaculation or the failure to ejaculate at all is sometimes supported by the production of lack of sensation (anesthesia) in the penis during coital movements, a psychosomatic process.

In the absence of such deterrent factors, male orgastic potency is a physiologic function easily established and maintained, as compared with its female counterpart of vaginal orgasm. The latter is based on a much more complex psychic foundation. The importance of orgastic potency in both sexes in terms of mental health is as one of many physiologic processes and functions in which psychic factors play to some extent a determining role in inhibiting or in promoting the function. It is singled out for special attention because it is the somatic function most commonly disturbed by psychic factors in our culture. In men, it may be regarded as significant of psychic difficulties if the function is impaired, but its nonimpairment carries no guarantee of mental health. In women, owing to the extreme complication of the psychic background of the function and owing to the ramification of this into numerous important phases of the personality, the achievement of orgastic potency (vaginal orgasm) may be regarded as an indicator (highly probable, at least) of mental health; lack of it must be considered indeterminate as to mental health.

Two factors other than psychophysiologic ones seem to me of importance in the attempt to delineate the nature of mental health. One of these centers about the individual's problems with anxiety; the other relates to the position he takes with regard to the matter of omnipotence.

In endeavoring in a given case to evaluate the relative degree of mental health, there are, as it seems to me, two essential questions concerning anxiety. Does the person commonly experience anxiety with respect to dangers which are not, by consensual validation, actual? In what manner does he commonly handle his anxiety, whether the danger involved is actual or nonactual? It is not possible to regard as mentally healthy a person who commonly perceives danger where, by consensual validation, no actual danger exists. If a man implies by his feelings of intense anxiety that there is a danger in walking on the street unaccompanied, we must, by the above criterion, regard him as mentally ill. Granted, as all would grant, that there is conceivable danger in walking on a city street—danger of being run over, danger from objects falling from houses, danger of being held up and robbed and injured in the process, and so on —these dangers are so remote in a statistical sense, or so easily avoided, that a mentally healthy person tends to ignore them. Very few of these statistically possible dangers would be obviated by having a companion along. Furthermore, the man who senses danger when walking alone on the street will correctly affirm that he is not concerned about any of the dangers just enumerated; and consensual validation establishes that this man is in no situation of particular danger by reason merely of walking alone on the street.

There are certain anxieties that relate to dangers concerning which consensual validation would not be quite so unanimous as in the example just given. If a man experiences anxiety when in close quarters with a dog, it would have to be granted that some dogs are vicious and ill-tempered and, unprovoked, snap and bite at people. Still, this actual danger is uncommon, and the consensus would be that the statistical actualities do not require altering one's course to avoid passing close to a dog. Similarly, if a man is anxious and panicky during a storm of thunder and lightning, people in general would agree that a danger of being struck by lightning exists, but they would also agree that the danger to a particular individual is statistically so remote that his anxiety is not justified, since there is small likelihood of the danger actually occurring. Often the person with such a phobia fears the thunder as much as, if not more than, the lightning. Everyone knows that though a sudden loud noise may be momentarily startling, it cannot do bodily harm.

It would be possible to draw up a list of conceivable dangers concerning which the degree of unanimity of consensual validation as to their nonactuality would be constantly diminishing. Unanimity of consensual validation of no actual danger would be greater in the matter of agoraphobia, for example, than in that of dog-phobias or thunderstorm-phobias. Unanimity would be still lower in evaluating the matter of stage-fright, though most people would find it difficult to define the danger involved, beyond the possibility of performing badly and being ridiculed or otherwise humiliated by the audience. What this signifies is that many of those whose votes would be included in such consensuses share these anxious feelings to some extent and would therefore be somewhat inclined to attribute actual danger to the situations involved. In the Middle Ages, we are told, it was generally agreed that the world was flat, and the danger in sailing continuously westward on the Atlantic Ocean was obvious and great: one's ship would fall off the edge of the world. We know now that the world is not flat, and our judgment as to this danger would be in complete contradiction of that of our medieval forbears. The judgment of actual danger bears a direct relationship to our knowledge of actualities, and incorrect judgments which involve one in anxiety are unhealthy in so far as one has adequate opportunity to appraise the actualities of the situation. The majority of people in the Middle Ages did not have the knowledge that the world is spherical; on the contrary, they thought they had the knowledge that it is flat. In medieval times a person who felt anxiety at the prospect of sailing for a long distance westward on the ocean would, by consensual validation, have been adjudged sensible and by no means mentally unhealthy. The person suffering from a phobia usually can assert his recognition that the situation in which his anxiety arises contains little or no actual danger and is well aware that his anxiety or the intensity of it is out of all proportion to the actualities of the situation.

Frequently the sufferer from anxiety is quite unable to say what precisely he is anxious about: he cannot define the danger implied by his anxiety. Such anxiety without precise content is practically always indicative of the fact that the person so afflicted is concerned with danger that is nonactual. In such circumstances the patient will attempt to make his anxiety seem more rational by finding something he can say he is anxious about. This something can usually be demonstrated as spurious by a little probing, but many sufferers from so-called "free-floating" or contentless anxiety will from the start acknowledge the lack of content. In such cases, not only is the danger indicated by the anxiety nonactual, but its nature and the convictions upon which the judgment of danger is based are repressed and unconscious.

In an ideal sense, the mentally healthy person would feel no anxiety except in situations involving actual danger. But the actuality of danger is not always easy to determine. This determination is easily made in the situations already mentioned, though somewhat less so as we proceed down the scale. Sometimes, however, we deal with dangers which are possibilities in situations which are, however, essentially unpredictable. Many people nowadays, for instance, experience anxiety in contemplating the world-situation; young married men and women wonder whether it is "right" or "fair" to bring children into so uncertain and precarious a world. Only the event can demonstrate whether they concern themselves with actual, predictable dangers or with dangers that are nonactual, being based on inaccurate judgments of current actualities and mistaken predictions founded thereon.

As a criterion of mental health, freedom from anxiety except in situations of actual danger would seem to be a reliable one, but it has to be acknowledged that its usefulness would be impaired by reason of the difficulty in some circumstances of defining actual danger. It is fortunate that in the vast majority of cases with which the psychiatrist is confronted this difficulty does not arise.

The matter of how a person handles anxiety seems, from empirical observation, to be closely related to the question of whether the danger implied by his anxiety is actual or not. In general it may be said that the more obviously actual the danger, the better a person handles his anxiety concerning it. By "handling" anxiety, I refer to the extent to which, in the danger situation, effectiveness of aggression is impaired. If anxiety is well handled, activity (aggression) in the situation is as effective or almost as effective as it would be if anxiety and danger were not perceived factors in the situation: the mentally healthy person functions well despite his anxiety. For example, the soldier in combat is well aware of the danger of being killed or wounded and feels anxious in proportion to the danger; but nevertheless, if he is mentally healthy, he functions well as a soldier: he advances, despite the risk; he uses his weapons as they are designed to be used, whether rifle, machine gun, hand grenade or bayonet; he cooperates effectively with his group. He is anxious, but his anxiety does not paralyze his activity, and he is able to function in terms of the actualities of the situation. Or a person in a burning building, faced with death or injury from the flames, will nevertheless, if mentally healthy, function well in attempting to devise and carry out means of escape for himself and for others. Some neurotics who quail before nonactual danger are able to function well, despite some anxiety, in emergency situations involving actual danger. Where this is true, it is more apt to be so in situations of short duration, such as that in a burning building, than in those of longer duration, such as that of prolonged combat in war. These considerations vitiate to some extent the usefulness of good handling of anxiety as an absolute criterion of mental health. But the search for such absolute, invariable criteria is, in any case, vain. All our criteria require qualification in one manner or another; and in the case of the neurotic who handles his anxiety well in situations of brief, actual danger, we generally find that he is incapable of the same in those situations involving danger that is nonactual. We are, however, justified in regarding the neurotic who functions well in actual emergencies as more nearly healthy, mentally, than the neurotic who handles no anxiety well, and therefore we have some reason to be more optimistic in prognosticating the outcome of psychotherapy in the former case.

Proneness to neurotic anxiety—anxiety evoked by nonactual danger—and impairment of effective aggression by such anxiety are factors which seriously limit the freedom of a person to utilize his potentialities and to grow in new enterprise and new achievement. The neurotically anxious person whose functioning is relatively paralyzed by anxiety is as one imprisoned: his ambit is a narrow one, and he is constrained to remain within it. In this sense his behavior is relatively rigid and inflexible. On the other hand, we must regard it as indicative of mental health if a person, by reason of his relative freedom from neurotic anxiety and from being paralyzed in his functioning thereby, is thus free to utilize his potential resources (whatever these may in detail be) and to grow continually in personality, in the sense that, being neither too rigid nor too inflexible, he is able to engage in enterprise and experience that for him are new and unfamiliar. What he may achieve in such new enterprise and experience is altogether beside the point: "the readiness is all."

The other factor, besides anxiety and its handling, which I regard as significant in the determination of mental health is the position taken with regard to the ideal of omnipotence. I have attempted to show elsewhere [68] that this factor represents the essential core of neurosis. I shall not here repeat that line of argument. The sense of omnipotence is never currently felt. Rather, it is regarded by the individual as something he enjoyed in a vague and distant past and as something that he should somehow be able to achieve again. In the latter sense, omnipotence is an ideal. As pointed out by Roth [61], the ideal is held in superego fashion, and the ego is threatened with displeasure and contempt from its superego in so far as it fails to live up to this ideal. Such an ego is indeed unhealthy, for the conditions on the basis of which its self-esteem may be effectively maintained are obviously impossible of attainment. I do not use the word *omnipotence* either in its metaphysical or theologic sense of all-power over literally all things, but rather in the psychologic sense of all-power over those forces, external and internal, which are significant to the individual in his relations with objects and persons. Even thus narrowly defined, omnipotence is obviously impossible to achieve. Yet the individual often maintains this as a condition for self-esteem, though he is usually unaware of doing this. He often pays lip-service to something less than omnipotence as an ideal, readily acknowledging that he cannot expect to control everything and everybody, but unconsciously he entertains the conviction that if he is not omnipotent, then he is utterly helpless: all or none.

Neither alternative is mentally healthy, since neither corresponds to the actualities of human existence. The fact is that we are able to control some external forces; others we can control to some extent (under favorable circumstances); while still others we cannot control at all. Such recognition of having both powers and limitations I term *partipotence* (partial power) and contrast it sharply both with omnipotence and utter helplessness.

A partipotent attitude, since it corresponds to the actualities with which life surrounds us, seems to me an essential ingredient of maturity and therefore one of the principal criteria of mental health. No neurotic person possesses partipotence as a genuine working hypothesis and approach to life, though many use the language of partipotence. It does not require much probing to discover that the typical neurotic dichotomy of all-or-none lies just behind such pious, but spurious, acceptance of partipotence.

We must not, however, be too rigorous in our expectations of partipotence in the mentally healthy. Observation, clinical and otherwise, has shown that the partipotent attitude, achieved often with the bitter struggle of self-conquest, is not a stable one and that relapse into the dichotomous attitude of all-or-none occurs frequently and easily. But the person who has once experienced the feel of partipotence, as he progresses in maturer ways and senses the realistic advantages of the partipotent approach, finds that it becomes easier for him to avoid such relapses or to extricate himself from them when they occur.

In sum, criteria of mental health, as I have suggested them, may be defined in terms of three factors: (1) freedom of operation of those somatic functions, especially the genital ones, which may be affected by psychic factors (with the reservations made above with respect to the significance of orgastic potency in the male and in the female); (2) relative freedom from anxiety based on nonactual danger and the ability to function with a minimum of impairment of effectiveness in the presence of anxiety; (3) the achievement of a genuine and relatively stable attitude of partipotence toward forces both within and external to the individual.

Many will feel that the capacity to love another (as distinguished from the capacity to desire another sexually) should be included here. I have said something on the subject in the discussion of orgastic potency. The word *love* is used by people in so many different senses that its inclusion here, in summing up criteria of mental health, would, I fear, be confusing rather than clarifying: the infant *loves* his mother; she *loves* him; she also *loves* his father; she may also *love* her own father or mother, or both; she may *love* her neighbors; she may *love* her country; she may *love* ice cream. All of these *loves* are different, though all carry the connotation of positive, friendly (rather than negative and hostile) feelings toward the various objects. Until we can agree upon a definition of love, and until we can be certain that what we attempt to define is not merely an ideal but rather a capacity actually demonstrable in a large number of persons, I feel we do well to omit the capacity for this difficult-to-define something from the list of criteria of mental health, though possibly something of the kind belongs there.

What we find in summing up these criteria is that our concept of mental health embraces these qualities: competence in dealing with familiar situations; courage and resourcefulness in meeting new ones; the wisdom and humility to know one's powers and their limitations. Mental health seems to equate with qualities of maturity: reliable competence as distinguished from occasional flashes of cleverness and brilliance; persevering courage as distinguished from rashness and bravado; and humble wisdom as distinguished from arrogant ambition and intellectual conceit. Poets and philosophers throughout the ages have told us much the same thing.

Bibliography

1. ABEL, KARL: Ueber den Gegensinn der Urworte. Reviewed by S. Freud in Jahrb. f. Psychoanalytische Forschungen 4:349–352, 1910.

2. ABRAHAM, KARL: Contributions to the Theory of the Anal Character (1921). In Selected Papers of Karl Abraham, M.D. London, The Hogarth Press, 1927.

3. ——: A Short Study of the Development of the Libido, Viewed in the Light of Mental Disorders (1924). In Selected Papers of Karl Abraham, M.D. London, The Hogarth Press, 1927.

4. ALEXANDER, FRANZ: Psychoanalyse der Gesamtpersönlichkeit. Vienna, Internationaler Psychoanalytischer Verlag, 1927.

5. ——: Emotional factors in essential hypertension. Psychosom. Med. 1:173–179, 1939.

6. BENDER, LORETTA:
——: An observation nursery; a study of 250 pre-school children on the psychiatric division of Bellevue Hospital. Am. J. Psychiat. 97: 1158–1172, 1941.
——: Infants reared in institutions permanently handicapped. Child Welfare League of America Bulletin 24: 1–4, 1945.
——: There is no substitute for family life. Child Study (April) 1946.
——: Psychopathic Behavior Disorders in Children. In Lindner and Seliger: Handbook of Correctional Psychology. New York, Philosophical Library, 1947.
——: Anixety in Disturbed Children. In Hoch, P. H., and Zubin, J.: Anxiety. New York, Grune & Stratton, 1950.

7. BERLINER, BERNHARD: On some psychodynamics of masochism. Psychoanalyt. Quart. 16:459–471, 1947.

8. BOEHM, FELIX: The femininity-complex in men. Internat. J. Psycho-Analysis 11:449–469, 1930.

9. BRIFFAULT, ROBERT: The Mothers. 3 vols. New York, The Macmillan Company, 1927.

10. BURROW, TRIGANT: Cited in MacCurdy, J. T.: Problems of Dynamic Psychology. New York, The Macmillan Company, 1923, pp. 188 ff.

11. DOOLEY, LUCILE: The genesis of psychological sex differences. Psychiatry 1:181–195, 1938.

12. DUNBAR, FLANDERS: Psychosomatic Diagnosis. New York & London, Paul B. Hoeber, Inc., 1943.

13. ELLIS, HAVELOCK: Studies in the Psychology of Sex. 6 vols. Philadelphia, F. A. Davis Company, 1926, ed. 3. (First published 1898–1910.)

14. FERENCZI, SANDOR: Entwicklungsstufen des Wirklichkeitssinnes (1913). In Bausteine zur Psychoanalyse. Vienna, Internationaler Psychoanalytischer Verlag, 1927, vol. 1.

15. ———: Zur Ontogenie des Geldinteresses (1914). Ibid.

16. FRAZER, SIR JAMES GEORGE: The Golden Bough. New York, The Macmillan Company, 1951, abridged ed.

17. FREUD, SIGMUND: Collected Papers. 5 vols. London, The Hogarth Press, 1924–1950.
    VOLUME 1 (1924)

18. ———: The Etiology of Hysteria (1896).

19. ———: The History of the Psychoanalytic Movement (1914).
    VOLUME 2 (1924)

20. ———: Character and Anal-Erotism (1908).

21. ———: Further Recommendations in the Technique of Psychoanalysis: Recollection, Repetition and Working Through (1914).

22. ———: On the Transformation of Instincts with Special Reference to Anal-Erotism (1916).

23. ———: The Passing of the Oedipus Complex (1924).
    VOLUME 3 (1925)

24. ———: Analysis of a Phobia in a Five-year-old Boy (1909).

25. ———: Notes upon a Case of Obsessional Neurosis (1909).

26. ———: Notes upon an Autobiographical Account of a Case of Paranoia (Dementia Paranoides) (1911).

27. ———: From the History of an Infantile Neurosis (1918).
    VOLUME 4 (1925)

28. ———: Formulations Regarding the Two Principles of Mental Functioning (1911).

29. ———: On Narcissism: an Introduction (1914).
    VOLUME 5 (1950)
30. ———: Screen-Memories (1899).
31. ———: The Acquisition of Power over Fire (1932).
32. ———: Review of Ueber den Gegensinn der Urworte by Karl Abel.
    In Jahrb. f. Psychoanalytische Forschungen 4: 349–352, 1910.
33. ———: Three Contributions to the Theory of Sexuality. Transl. by
    A. A. Brill. New York, The Nervous & Mental Disease Publishing
    Company, 1930.
34. ———: Beyond the Pleasure Principle. Transl. by C. J. M. Hub-
    back. New York, Boni & Liveright, 1922.
35. ———: The Ego and the Id. Transl. by J. Riviere. London, The
    Hogarth Press, 1927.
36. ———: Inhibitions, Symptoms and Anxiety. Transl. by A. Strachey.
    London, The Hogarth Press, 1936. (Also in an American edition,
    The Problem of Anxiety. Transl. by Henry Alden Bunker. New
    York, The Psychoanalytic Quarterly Press and W. W. Norton &
    Company, Inc., 1936.)
37. ———: Die Zukunft einer Illusion (1927). In Ges. Schr. vol. xi.
38. ———: Civilization and Its Discontents. Transl. by J. Riviere.
    London, The Hogarth Press: 1946.
39. FROMM-REICHMANN, FRIEDA: Contribution to the psychogenesis
    of migraine. Psychoanalyt. Rev. 24:26–33, 1937.
40. ———: Discussion of Thompson's paper. In Symposium on Fem-
    inine Psychology. New York, Department of Psychiatry, New
    York Medical College, 1950, p. 59.
41. GREENACRE, PHYLLIS: Special Problems of Early Female Sexual
    Development. In The Psychoanalytic Study of the Child. New
    York, International Universities Press, 1950, vol. 5.
42. HORNEY, KAREN: New Ways in Psychoanalysis. New York, W. W.
    Norton & Company, Inc., 1939.
43. JONES, ERNEST: The Symbolic Significance of Salt in Folklore
    and Superstition (1912). In Essays on Applied Psychoanalysis.
    London, The Hogarth Press, 1951, vol. 2.
44. ———: Hate and Anal Erotism in the Obsessional Neurosis (1913).
    In Papers on Psychoanalysis. New York, William Wood & Com-
    pany, 1918, ed. 2.
45. ———: The Anal-Erotic Character Traits (1918). In Papers on
    Psychoanalysis. New York, William Wood & Company, 1918, ed. 2.
46. JUNG, C. G.: The Psychology of the Unconscious. Transl. by

Beatrice Hinkle. London, Kegan Paul, Trench, Trubner & Company, Ltd., 1922.

47. KARDINER, A: The Individual and His Society. New York, Columbia University Press, 1939.

48. ——: with the collaboration of Ralph Linton, Cora Du Bois, and James West: The Psychological Frontiers of Society. New York, Columbia University Press, 1945.

49. KINSEY, ALFRED C., POMEROY, W. B., AND MARTIN, C. E.: Sexual Behavior in the Human Male. Philadelphia & London, W. B. Saunders Company, 1948.

50. KLEIN, MELANIE: The Psychoanalysis of Children. The International Psycho-Analytic Library, no. 22, 1932.

51. LEWIN, BERTRAM D.: The nature of reality, the meaning of nothing, with an addendum on concentration. Psychoanalyt. Quart. 17:524–526, 1948.

52. MACALPINE, IDA: The development of transference. Psychoanalyt. Quart. 19:501–539, 1950.

53. MOLONEY, JAMES CLARK: Psychiatric observations in Okinawa Shima. Psychiatry 8:391–399, 1945.

54. MYRDAL, GUNNAR: An American Dilemma. New York & London, Harper & Brothers, 1944.

55. RADO, SANDOR: The psychical effects of intoxication: an attempt at a psycho-analytical theory of drug-addiction. Internat. J. Psycho-Analysis 9:301–317, 1928.

56. ——: The psychoanalysis of pharmacothymia (drug addiction). Psychoanalyt. Quart. 2: 1–23, 1933.

57. RANK, OTTO: Der Mythus von der Geburt des Helden. Leipzig & Vienna, Franz Deuticke, 1922.

58. REICH, WILHELM: The Function of the Orgasm. Transl. by Theodore P. Wolfe. New York, The Orgone Institute Press, 1942.

59. REIK, THEODOR: Couvade and the Psychogenesis of the Fear of Retaliation (1914). In Ritual. New York, Farrar, Straus & Company, Inc., 1946.

60. ROBBINS BERNARD S.: Escape into reality. Psychoanalyt. Quart. 6:353–364, 1937.

61. ROTH, NATHAN: The acting out of transferences. Psychoanalyt. Rev. 39:69–78, 1952.

62. SAMUEL, MAURICE: The Great Hatred. New York, Alfred A. Knopf, 1940.

63. SELYE, HANS: Stress. Montreal, Acta, Inc., 1950.

64. SILVERBERG, WILLIAM V.: The personal basis and social significance of passive male homosexuality. Psychiatry 1:41–53, 1938.

65. ──: On the origin of neurosis. Psychiatry 7:111–120, 1944.

66. ──: The schizoid maneuver. Psychiatry 10:383–393, 1947.

67. ──: The concept of transference. Psychoanalyt. Quart. 17:303–321, 1948.

68. ──: The factor of omnipotence in neurosis. Psychiatry 12:387–398, 1949.

69. ──: Discussion of Romm's paper. In Symposium on Feminine Psychology. New York, Department of Psychiatry, New York Medical College, 1950, p. 68.

70. STAERCKE, AUGUST: Der Kastrationskomplex. Internat. Zeitschr. f. aerztl. Psychoanalyse 7:9–32, 1920.

71. STERBA, EDITH: An important factor in eating disturbances of childhood. Psychoanalyt. Quart. 10:365–372, 1941.

72. SULLIVAN, HARRY STACK: Conceptions of Modern Psychiatry. Washington, The William Alanson White Psychiatric Foundation, 1947. First published in Psychiatry 3:1–117, 1940.

73. THOMPSON, CLARA: "Dutiful child" resistance. Psychoanalyt. Rev. 18:426–434, 1931.

74. ──: The role of women in this culture. Psychiatry 4:1–8, 1941.

75. ──: Cultural pressures in the psychology of women. Psychiatry 5:331–339, 1942.

76. ──: "Penis-envy" in women. Psychiatry 6:123–125, 1943.

77. ──: Cultural Complications in the Sexual Life of Woman: Some Effects of the Deprecatory Attitude towards Female Sexuality. In Symposium on Feminine Psychology. New York, Department of Psychiatry, New York Medical College, 1950, p. 55. Also in Psychiatry 13:349–354, 1950.

78. WYLIE, PHILIP: Generation of Vipers. New York, Farrar & Rinehart, 1942.

Index

A

Abandonment, fear of, 48–49
Abraham, Karl, 128
Activity, sexual, 135–136, 161
Actuality, concept of, 244
Adaptation
  neurotic homosexuality as, 221–238
  in toilet-training, 120–126
  to unpleasant stimulus, 137
  See also Solutions
Aggression
  effective, 6, 18
    in danger situation, 266
    and ego, 23–24
    and id-ego, 20
    and impulse-gratification, 46–49
    and incomplete repression, 209
    maternal, 63
    in neurotic anxiety, 267
    and parental approval, 46–49
    penis as organ of, 197
    quantitative aspects of, 26
    and see-touch-swallow sequence, 76
    and self-esteem, 26–30
  and enemas, 134
Agoraphobia, 263
Alcoholism, 126, 227
Alexander, Franz, 176
Alloerotism
  choice of partner, 164–167
  diffidence in, 167–168
  early, 154–164
  rage in, 168

Alloplastic ego-devices, 33–34
Alor, 39
Analogy, reasoning by, 184
Anesthesia, penile, 262
Animal
  housebreaking of, 110
  trapping of, 99
Anus, in adaptation of neurotic homo-
    sexuality, 222
  See also Sphincter
Anxiety, 30
  due to castration fears, 177–178,
    185–187
  due to enemas, 137
  due to fear of death, 187
  in fetus, 11–13
  free-floating, 265
  Freud's concept of, 12–13, 30
  handling of, as measure of mental
    health, 263-267
  neurotic, 267
  due to primal scene, 157–158
  due to threats to self-esteem, 47
Approval
  in experiential areas, 46
  maternal, in toilet-training, 112–113
    116
  parental, 29–30
    and effective aggression, 46–49
Area of experience. *See* Experiential
    area
Attack, urinary, 192, 195, 197
Attention, maternal, and effective ag-
    gression in infant, 51–52

4   R/E37WCC

L SILVERBERG